# Italian Cinema Audiences

Topics and Issues in National Cinema
*Volume 8*

*Series Editor*
*Armida de la Garza, University College Cork, Ireland*

*Editorial Board*
*Mette Hjort, Chair Professor and Head, Visual Studies Lingnan University, Hong Kong*
*Lúcia Nagib, Professor of Film, University of Reading, UK*
*Chris Berry, Professor of Film Studies, Kings College London, UK, and Co-Director of the Goldsmiths Leverhulme Media Research Centre, UK*
*Sarah Street, Professor of Film and Foundation Chair of Drama, University of Bristol, UK*
*Jeanette Hoorn, Professor of Visual Cultures, University of Melbourne, Australia*
*Shohini Chaudhuri, Senior Lecturer and MA Director in Film Studies, University of Essex, UK*

# Italian Cinema Audiences

*Histories and Memories of Cinemagoing in Post-War Italy*

Daniela Treveri Gennari, Catherine O'Rawe,
Danielle Hipkins, Silvia Dibeltulo and Sarah Culhane

BLOOMSBURY ACADEMIC
NEW YORK • LONDON • OXFORD • NEW DELHI • SYDNEY

BLOOMSBURY ACADEMIC
Bloomsbury Publishing Inc
1385 Broadway, New York, NY 10018, USA
29 Earlsfort Terrace, Dublin 2, Ireland

BLOOMSBURY, BLOOMSBURY ACADEMIC and the Diana logo are trademarks of
Bloomsbury Publishing Plc

First published in the United States of America 2021
This paperback edition published in 2022

Copyright © Daniela Treveri Gennari, Catherine O'Rawe, Danielle Hipkins,
Silvia Dibeltulo, Sarah Culhane, 2021

For legal purposes the Acknowledgements on p. xvi constitute an extension
of this copyright page.

Photograph © Thomas Hoepker/Magnum Photos

All rights reserved. No part of this publication may be reproduced or
transmitted in any form or by any means, electronic or mechanical,
including photocopying, recording, or any information storage or
retrieval system, without prior permission in writing from the publishers.

Bloomsbury Publishing Inc does not have any control over, or responsibility for, any
third-party websites referred to or in this book. All internet addresses given in this
book were correct at the time of going to press. The author and publisher regret any
inconvenience caused if addresses have changed or sites have ceased to exist, but can
accept no responsibility for any such changes.

ISBN: HB: 978-1-5013-4768-9
PB: 978-1-5013-6933-9
ePDF: 978-1-5013-4770-2
eBook: 978-1-5013-4769-6

Series: Topics and Issues in National Cinema

Typeset by Newgen KnowledgeWorks Pvt. Ltd., Chennai, India

To find out more about our authors and books visit www.bloomsbury.com
and sign up for our newsletters.

*This book is dedicated to our questionnaire respondents and video interviewees, the young spectators of post-war Italy. Their generation has borne the brunt of the pandemic in Italy in 2020, making their memories more precious than ever.*

'Tutto quello che finisce mette tristezza. Chiude un'epoca, una parentesi..'/ 'Everything that ends brings sadness. An epoch ends, an interlude..' .. Ninetta, born 1936.

'Quando entravo in una sala provavo un'emozione profonda... il cinema per me era vita..'/ 'When I entered a cinema I felt powerful emotions... Cinema, for me, was life'. Antonio, born 1933.

# Contents

| | |
|---|---|
| List of Figures | viii |
| List of Tables | ix |
| List of Authors | x |
| Foreword by Professor Martin Barker | xii |
| Acknowledgements | xvi |
| 1  Introduction | 1 |
| Part 1  The activity of cinemagoing | 25 |
| 2  Cinemas, exhibition practices and topographical memories | 27 |
| 3  Only entertainment?: Memories inside and outside the cinema | 51 |
| Part 2  Films: Genre, taste and popular memory | 69 |
| 4  Audiences and film genre | 71 |
| 5  'Back then I believed in the nation – I don't anymore': Revisiting the national film canon through audience memories of neorealism | 91 |
| Part 3  Gender and cinemagoing | 111 |
| 6  A girl's-eye view of post-war Italian cinema | 113 |
| 7  Beyond 'belle e brave': Female stars and Italian cinema audiences | 135 |
| 8  Narrative imaginings of masculinity through cinema | 155 |
| Conclusions | 175 |
| Appendix 1 Questionnaire | 183 |
| Appendix 2 Video interview questions | 189 |
| Appendix 3 List of thematic areas | 192 |
| Bibliography | 193 |
| Index | 211 |

# Figures

| | | |
|---|---|---|
| 1.1 | TV inside a cinema for the screening of *Lascia o raddoppia?* (*Double or Quits?*) | 3 |
| 2.1 | Turnover of films in cinemas in Rome | 41 |
| 2.2 | Mapping Franca's journeys to the cinema | 44 |
| 3.1 | How to behave inside the cinema | 59 |
| 5.1 | Anna Magnani as Pina in *Roma città aperta* (*Rome Open City*, Roberto Rossellini, Italy, 1945) | 99 |
| 5.2 | Michele conveys the heaviness of neorealist cinema with a hand gesture | 107 |
| 5.3 | Sonia describes holding *Roma città aperta* in her heart | 110 |
| 6.1 | Rita describes parental control in her childhood | 121 |
| 6.2 | Princess Sissi enjoys the outdoors and romance in *Sissi* (*Sissi*, Ernst Marischka, Austria, 1955) | 126 |
| 7.1 | An English language version of Anna Magnani's infamous quote | 143 |
| 8.1 | Edoardo remembers the impact of Marlon Brando | 157 |
| 8.2 | James Dean in *East of Eden* (Elia Kazan, United States, 1955) | 160 |
| 8.3 | Giorgio imitates James Dean in *East of Eden* | 160 |

# Tables

| | | |
|---|---|---|
| 1.1 | Socio-demographic characteristics of questionnaire respondents | 14 |
| 1.2 | Cinemagoing habits and preferences of questionnaire respondents | 20 |
| 2.1 | Cinemas in the years 1938–60 | 28 |
| 2.2 | Cinemagoing statistics for Italy's major provincial cities in 1954 | 35 |
| 2.3 | The intensity of film circulation in seven Italian cities in January 1954 | 36 |
| 2.4 | Top five films in circulation in January 1954 | 38 |
| 4.1 | Factors determining film choice | 73 |
| 4.2 | Favourite film genres | 74 |
| 4.3 | Genre preference by geographical location | 84 |
| 4.4 | Genre preference by urban/provincial location | 84 |
| 4.5 | Genre preference by gender (male/female) | 85 |

# Authors

**Daniela Treveri Gennari** is Professor of Cinema Studies at Oxford Brookes University with a research interest in audiences, popular cinema, film exhibition and programming. Daniela has been leading the AHRC-funded project *Italian Cinema Audiences* and is currently leading the AHRC-funded project *European Cinema Audiences: Entangled Histories and Shared Memories*. Among her recent publications are the edited volume *Rural Cinema Exhibition and Audiences in a Global Context* (2018, with Catherine O'Rawe and Danielle Hipkins), the articles '"It Existed Indeed … It Was All over the Papers": Memories of Film Censorship in 1950s Italy', *Participations* (volume 14, issue 1, May 2017, with Silvia Dibeltulo) and 'Mapping Cinema Memories: Emotional Geographies of Cinema-Going in Rome in the 1950s', *Memories Studies* (January 2017, with Catherine O'Rawe and Pierluigi Ercole).

**Catherine O'Rawe** is Professor of Italian Film and Culture at the University of Bristol. She is the author of *Stars and Masculinities in Contemporary Italian Cinema* (2014), co-author (with Jacqueline Reich) of *Divi: la mascolinità nel cinema italiano* (Donzelli, 2015) and has published widely on gender and stardom in Italian post-war and contemporary cinema.

**Danielle Hipkins** is Professor of Italian Studies and Film at the University of Exeter. She has published widely on gender representation in post-war Italian cinema, including *Italy's Other Women: Gender and Prostitution in Postwar Italian Cinema, 1940–1965* (2016), and co-edited *Prostitution and Sex Work in Global Cinema: New Takes on Fallen Women* (2017). She is currently working on girlhood and contemporary Italian cinema, and was a co- investigator on the AHRC-funded 'Italian Cinema Audiences' project, a study of memories of cinemagoing in Italy of the 1950s with the Universities of Bristol and Oxford Brookes (2013–16).

**Silvia Dibeltulo** is Senior Lecturer in Communication, Media and Culture at Oxford Brookes University, where she previously worked on the AHRC-funded Italian Cinema Audiences project and the BA/Leverhulme-funded European Cinema Audiences project. Her research mainly focuses on the representation of identity on screen, specifically in terms of ethnicity, nationality, gender and culture. Her work also centres on film genre theory and history, audience and reception studies, cinema heritage and digital humanities. Her publications include the book chapter '"A World I Thought Was Impossible": Provincial

Cinema-Going in Italy of the 1950s' (with D. Hipkins, S. Culhane, Treveri Gennari and C. O'Rawe, in *Rural Cinema Exhibition and Audiences in a Global Context*, 2018), the article '"It Existed Indeed … It Was All over the Papers": Memories of Film Censorship in 1950s Italy' (*Participations: Journal of Audience & Reception Studies*, 2017, with D. Treveri Gennari) and the edited volume *Rethinking Genre in Contemporary Global Cinema* (2018, with Ciara Barrett).

**Sarah Culhane** is Assistant Professor in Italian at University College Dublin. From 2018 to 2021 she was a CAROLINE Marie Sklodowska-Curie Fellow in Media Studies at Maynooth University where she led the Irish Cinema Audiences project.

She holds a PhD in Italian studies from the University of Bristol. Her PhD research was conducted as part of the Italian Cinema Audiences project (AHRC 2013–16). From 2017 to 2018, she worked as a Research Fellow on the Italian Cinema Audiences follow-on project, CineRicordi (2017–18). Her recent publications include 'Bridging the Digital Divide: Older Adults' Engagement with Online Cinema Heritage' (*Digital Scholarship in the Humanities* with S. Dibeltulo and D. Treveri Gennari, 2019) and 'Crowdsourcing Memories and Artefacts to Reconstruct Italian Cinema History: Micro-Histories of Small-Town Exhibition in the 1950s' (*Participations: Journal of Audience and Reception Studies* with D. Treveri Gennari, 2019).

# Foreword

*Martin Barker*

Some years ago, I published an essay about the state and prospects for audience research. Possibly the best thing about the essay was its title: 'I Have Seen the Future and It Is Not Here, Yet …: Or, on Being Ambitious for Audience Research' (*Communication Review*, 9, 2006). But it did try to encapsulate my feeling that audience research then had gone stale, and was not building on its achievements. I want to say clearly now that I believe that this book, and the project on which it reports, is one such major achievement.

In many respects, the Italian Cinema Audiences project was absurdly ambitious. It professed and promised to root itself deeply in a combination of two major developments in our ways of thinking about film and cinema. There is the cultural studies or 'culturalist' approach, which arose from the 1970s not only to challenge then still dominant linear communication models but also to question the claims of 'textual' analyses of films, and of 'apparatus' accounts of the cinema's workings. In culturalist approaches, audiences are always multiple and complexly located, and responses to films are always intersections of personal and cultural influences and identities. Late to arrive in film studies, and encountering a deal of resistance there, the culturalist approach put at its centre the many ways we can gather audience *talk*, and then and thus listen to the ways people tell their stories of cinemagoing – including (most importantly) how these are embroidered within people's *memories* and evolving senses of self and world. Indeed, it was not long before memory effectively became its own research field, with memory studies' conferences, journals, concepts and academic association.

Alongside this, and complexly interwoven with it, came an engagement with the New Cinema History, a development which dates in particular from the 1990s, and according to which cinema needs to be studied in terms of the interwoven workings of production, distribution and exhibition, using multiple evidential resources, with the ambition of fleshing out the place of films and cinemas within the lives of different urban, rural and mobile communities, all cut through by gender, class, ethnicity, age, period and generation. New

Cinema History dramatically shifted the focus of attention from the *films* being watched to the *places and circumstances* of watching – and indeed often found that, when asked, people remembered more about the latter than the former. Methodologically, this new approach produced a focused attention to the potential value of all kinds of data archives, and researchers have gone looking for more wherever they could locate them.

Alongside these came borrowings from slightly older traditions, notably oral history which has deep roots, but came back into prominence in the 1960–70s, as part of the rise of new Social History movements. Capturing the words and lives of the otherwise unheard, the marginal, ignored or silenced people became a driving issue for a generation of historians, notably (but not only) women.

So, what has the ICA project done? At its heart are a large number of interviews with elderly Italian men and women, all video-recorded, talking about their memories of cinemagoing in the 1950s and early 1960s in different parts of Italy (north/south; city/small town/rural). Developing from the example of Annette Kuhn's earlier work (*An Everyday Magic* (2002)) on British women and men going to the cinema in the 1930s, which developed the ground for a new way of exploring the meanings and operations of memory, the project's use of video recordings allows them to consider gestures, expressions and other aspects of bodily inhabitation of responses (and with the bonus of adding to a major Italian online resource of recorded memories of older people, Memoro). Alongside this, they draw on press and trade paper reviews, data on the numbers of cinemas in different parts (cities, small towns, rural) of Italy, evidence surviving from exhibitors, official statistics of various kinds, information from and about censors (including local informal Catholic Church influences), evidence on availability and popularity of different film genres and sources (e.g. Italian or American films) and much more. And then, bravely, they have a go at triangulating their findings from these multiple sources and kinds of evidence. What's not to admire?

As an audience researcher myself, but also as joint editor of the journal *Participations*, I have become more and more interested over recent years in questions and problems of methodology: crudely, what our concepts and methods presume about the nature of the things we are trying to research and how our claims to find and learn things can be made trustworthy. One of the core virtues of New Cinema History has been its careful and thorough mining of many different kinds of data resource, often but not always quantitative (e.g.

records of attendance) or at least quantifiable (e.g. density of distribution of cinemas by area across cities and towns). At the same time, a core value of new culturalist explorations of audiences, their experiences, their memories and the place of cinemagoing and films in people's life courses has been the subtle examination of how people *talk*. The marriage of these modes of research is not easy, and has rarely been attempted, to my knowledge.

The concept of 'triangulation' has a somewhat muddy history. Originally mainly conceived as a way of giving qualitative methods in the social sciences something equivalent to the guarantees promised by statistical methods in experimental/quantitative research modes, in the 1970–80s in the hands of its foremost advocate, Norman Denzin, it had four modes: triangulation of *evidence* (though the word 'data' was used by Denzin, it did not always mean numerical/statistical); triangulation by *researchers* (e.g. more than one person conducting codings of materials); triangulation by *theories* (looking at a phenomenon through the lens of several kinds of conceptual frame); and triangulation by *method* (say, mixing ethnographic observation and focus groups as parts of the same investigation).

More recently, the concept has become much looser, becoming for some a virtual synonym for mixed methods, and largely bypassing the critical issue which had worried early researchers, of how one can use incompatibly shaped kinds of evidence to test and confirm each other.

Intriguingly to me, it seems that the authors are using 'triangulation' to mean something – or some things – rather different than the standard 'mutual (dis)confirmation via independent resources'. Instead, they are interested in pursuing the emergent contingent *relations between* several independently operating forces. So, when for instance they consider the star images in press reviews, but then find different emphases among their interviewees, the lack of fit does not imply that either is mistaken. Rather, it indicates that they are to some degree at least *operating independently* of each other. Seeing the interrelations this way allows them to ask questions about the extent to which one body of materials may have helped structure another. These can then help build into the broader meanings of 'popular taste' and 'popular culture'. Do remembered favourite genres among audiences correspond with the top grossing films, and with their industry categorizations? One is not right, the other wrong, if they don't. Rather, they are showing the signs of being semi-separate discursive spheres. This seems to me a very productive way of rethinking the very idea of 'triangulation'.

The pleasure of reading this for me was also in the fine detail of findings, which reminded me (if I still needed it) of the fluidity and nuanced nature of those necessary major categories, like gender. For example, cinema for girls could be a place for 'dreaming' (and they catch the nuances involved in that notion, along with the ways their women interviewees would move their bodies as they recalled this). But it was also a place of some risks that had to be managed. Their careful analysis allows them to distinguish the different languages accorded to the phenomenon of 'wandering hands', depicted as irritating molestation by many of the women, and as a legitimate and pleasurable try-on by the men. But it also allows them to separate nostalgic feelings among young girls for 'girlhood' as an innocent period of their lives, which they lost too soon. This includes, interestingly, the pleasures associated with going with their fathers (something I remember encountering in the very different circumstances of *The Lord of the Rings* project, where young women told us of the pleasures of re-bonding with their fathers over their shared enjoyment of the Peter Jackson trilogy).

'Cinema offered a powerful source of escapism for a country still emerging from the horrors and hardships of Fascism and World War Two. It also taught Italians about the world, about how to behave and how to love, especially those who, like many of our respondents, were very young in the post-war period' (Chapter 9). This is a central element of the authors' overall assessment of the role of cinema in their research period. It leaves me with an important, unanswerable question. To what extent was the Italian experience of these things distinctive, or in what ways might people's experiences simply be a local version of a common set of processes in this period? Clearly, some circumstances were particularly exaggerated in Italy – the role of the Catholic Church, for instance, and the memories of conflicts between followers of Mussolini and the Resistance (and the American money and glamour that flooded into Rome, in particular, after the Italians' surrender). The sharp north/south divide also is not precisely replicated in other nations. Plus, there are plenty of national specialities – stars special to Italy (for instance, Antonio De Curtis, or Totò), narrative preferences (for instance, particular kinds of comedy) and the like. But other features – like the slow loosening of rigid gender roles and the rising role of imported American cultural forms and types – would surely be more common, however much they may have been experienced as and in local contexts. It is no weakness of this project that it cannot directly answer these kinds of question, but they are definitely ones that this wonderful study provokes.

# Acknowledgements

Writing the *Italian Cinema Audiences* monograph was not only harder than expected but also more rewarding than we could have ever imagined. None of this would have been possible without the help of many we would like to thank here.

This project bears the imprint of several people and organizations. However, nothing could have happened without the financial support from the Arts and Humanities Research Council, to which we owe sincere thanks. We also acknowledge the financial support of Oxford Brookes University and the Faculty of Arts, University of Bristol.

We are eternally grateful to our advisors, Martin Barker and Mariagrazia Fanchi. They have supported us in developing the methodology and the analytical procedures to carry out our research. It was a great privilege and honour to follow their guidance.

A very special thanks to Annette Kuhn, whose work inspired us and motivated us. We are truly indebted to her research, which showed us the way into cinema memory studies. We are grateful to Jackie Stacey's generosity for giving us permission to use her questionnaire as our starting point.

We would like to express our deep and sincere gratitude to John Sedgwick, our 'economist in residence', for the valuable guidance and advice. He inspired us greatly to take the project in different directions, enlightening us on aspects of cinema culture we would not have otherwise considered.

Some organizations have been crucial to the success of this project: we would like to thank BluMedia, Memoro and UNITRE, not only for succeeding in a timely data collection, which would have otherwise been an impossible task for us, but also for going out of their way, and sharing their resources and expertise to support our project. In particular, we are grateful to Lorenzo Fenoglio, Luca Novarino, Valentina Vaio, Franco Nicola, Valentina Violi, Gustavo Cuccini, Liliana Riccardi and Laura Rabitti for their continuous presence throughout the course of the project. Special thanks to our interviewer, Maurizio Cartolano. And a very special thank you to Irma Maria Re, who wholeheartedly embraced our project from its very outset.

During our archival research, some organizations and individuals have supported us in sharing their material and ideas. We would like to thank SIAE, ACEC, Biblioteca Chiarini, AGIS, Archivio Centrale dello Stato and Centro Sperimentale di Cinematografia. Particular thanks go to Deborah Demontis, Marina Cipriani, Viridiana Rotondi, Marcello Foti, Lucilla Garofalo, Pierluigi Raffaelli, Mauro Bianchi, Cristiano Sette, Maurizio Riccardi, Roberto Parisi and Ciro Giorgini. We thank Taylor and Francis for permission to reproduce some material that appears in Chapter 8. We also thank Magnum for giving permission to reproduce the cover image.

Our project could not have taken a digital humanities focus without the generous support from a number of colleagues and organizations: first of all thanks to Robert C. Allen and Jeff Klenotic, for providing inspiration through their innovative projects and their use of digital mapping in the context of cinema studies. Thanks also to Daniel Wilkes, our web developer; Alex Friend, our Nvivo and ArcGIS expert; IT support from Mick Mullins at Exeter; Mike Pidd at the Digital Humanities Institute; Sebastien Caquard for helping us create geovisualizations of our data on AtlasCine; and Marten During for guiding us through network analysis and digital mapping on Palladio.

Other colleagues have played a very important part in the success of this project: Paul Whitty and Sarah Taylor at Oxford Brookes University for their constant encouragement during the funding application phase; the HoMER research network for providing invaluable feedback to our findings; the Jackalope research team for their support; Karel Dibbets for his ability to anticipate future developments in historical cinema research and providing inspiration in this field; and Jo Labanyi, Pierluigi Ercole, and all film colleagues at Oxford Brookes University.

All of the interns who worked on the project: Martina Lovascio, Debora Sciaciero, Marco Ammendola and Terezia Porubkanska.

A special thank you goes to Andrea Dellimauri, who kindly provided vital support in the editing process of the monograph.

The Museo del cinema in Turin, the Bill Douglas Cinema Museum and Watershed in Bristol have provided the perfect environment to disseminate our research to the wider public and to engage different audiences both in Italy and in the United Kingdom. We want to acknowledge all who participated in public engagement events in Rome, Turin, Picerno, Cagliari, Messina, Pecetto Torinese, Saronno, Manduria, Amelia and Castellazzo Bormida. A special thanks to Vincenzo Stranieri, Mara Quadraccia and Nino Rinaldi.

Thank you also to all of those who participated in our social media platforms by sharing their memories and commenting on our findings, especially Elena Corradi.

A number of people have enriched our project in different ways and we would like to mention them here: Daniele Sambo, Katherine Ford, Carla Mereu Keating, Katia Pizzi, Giovanna Tega, Clara Giannini, Antonella Veccia and Daniela Palumbo.

Special thanks go to all the people who have supported us to complete the research directly or indirectly: those who attended conference and seminar presentations of our research, all those who participated in our end-of-project conference, especially keynote speakers, and the anonymous referees for their useful suggestions.

Finally, our warmest thanks to all the participants who took the time to complete our questionnaire and who contributed so thoroughly through their further comments at the public engagement events. We would particularly like to thank those who agreed to be video interviewed, for expressing their thoughts and memories on cinemagoing so unapologetically and so passionately.

1

# Introduction

In 1988 Giuseppe Tornatore's film *Nuovo Cinema Paradiso* (*Cinema Paradiso*, Italy) achieved global success with a story that placed Italian cinema audiences at the centre of its narrative. In it, spectators are portrayed attending cinemas, bonding with the stories they saw on the screen and interacting loudly with films such as Visconti's neorealist classic *La terra trema* (*The Earth Tremble*s, Italy, 1948), Raffaello Matarazzo's enormously popular melodrama *Catene* (*Chains*, Italy, 1949) and Mario Mattoli's comedy *I pompieri di Viggiù* (*The Firemen of Viggiù*, Italy, 1949). This representation of post-war film culture demonstrates vividly both the affective charge of Italian cinema, at its peak of popularity, and its role in the social fabric of daily life.

*Nuovo Cinema Paradiso* shows the space of the cinema as both a refuge from poverty and the hardship of life, as well as a space of interaction, sociality and romance. Its nostalgic appeal to a time before television, when cinemagoing was Italians' most popular leisure activity, resonates strongly with our research project, 'Italian Cinema Audiences'.[1] Our intention was to excavate and recover memories of cinemagoing in the 1950s, by interviewing and surveying people who lived through that period. Although Italians were among the most assiduous cinemagoers in Europe (Gyory and Glas 1992), we were struck by the fact that the spectators themselves, their tastes and preferences and their emotional investment in the medium are often missing from scholarly literature.

This monograph is the final output of the ICA project, funded by the UK Arts and Humanities Research Council (2013–16). ICA expanded on the findings of two pilot projects, one undertaken in 2007 which tested our methodology (Treveri Gennari et al. 2011) and one in 2009 on cinemagoing culture in Rome (see Treveri Gennari 2015). The project focused particularly on the importance of cinema in everyday life by interviewing audience members, analysing their

[1] Hereafter ICA.

responses using qualitative data analysis software and contextualizing these responses through further archival research. With this project, oral and written accounts of film-going during this period were augmented by press reception, box-office figures and film industry data in order to uncover the hidden side of Italian film history: its audiences. Our research was guided by a series of questions: How did cinemagoing figure in the daily lives of people throughout Italy at that time? What was the relationship between audiences and film genres and stars, and how did this vary according to gender and location? How did Italian cinemagoers select and watch films? How did cinemagoing preferences relate to wider social trends and changes in Italy in the 1950s? And finally, how might our project help us to better understand the nature of memory work?

In 1997, the esteemed Italian film historian Gian Piero Brunetta asked,

> Why is the experience of the historian and the critic so rarely congruent with that of the audience? Why has nobody ever wanted to study in all its specificity the lived experience of the audience, the emotional fluctuations and the changes to social patterns that are produced by the ritual of film-viewing? ... How can systematic research be organized 'from the point of view of the spectator'? (1997: xx)[2]

Throughout the project, and the writing of this book, we have sought to address the cinemagoing experience of Italians in the post-war period, paying close attention to the lived experiences of audience members, as recounted to us. We have tried to capture, via the thoughts and words of Italians who grew up in that era, the films that had meaning for spectators, and also, as Roland Barthes (1986: 349) puts it, 'the texture of the sound, the hall, the darkness, the obscure mass of other bodies, the rays of light, entering the theater, leaving the hall'.

## The Italian audience: Myths and realities

The growth in the Italian cinema audience in the 1950s was striking: in 1955, based on SIAE – *Società Italiana degli Autori e degli Editori* (Italian Society of Authors and Publishers) – data, there was one cinema seat per nine Italians, as compared to one per sixteen in France and the United States, and one per twelve

---

[2] English translations of original material in Italian are ours, unless otherwise indicated; this includes questionnaires and video interviews, quotes from articles, trade journals, press, magazines as well as academic books and journals.

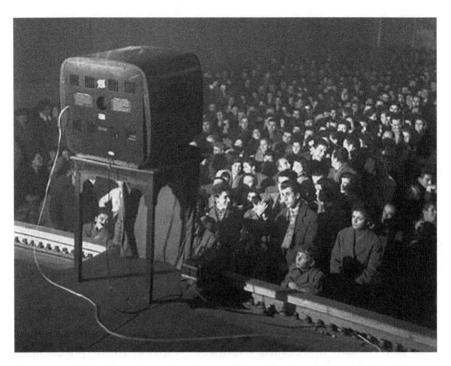

**Figure 1.1** TV inside a cinema for the screening of *Lascia o raddoppia?* (*Double or Quits?*).

in the UK (see Mosconi 1995: 332; Villa 2002: 191). By 1959, there were 10,503 commercial cinemas operating in Italy, as well as over 5,000 parish cinemas (Villa 2002: 191). Commercial cinemas were divided into different runs, according to their distribution function. First-run cinemas screened newly released films, which would then move to second- and third-run venues, with a lower admission price and a less luxurious setting.

Ticket sales peaked in Italy in 1955, with over 819 million tickets sold (Gremigni 2009: 24), before beginning to decline in the late 1950s, partly due to the arrival of television; in some cinemas, in order to avert the damage of television to ticket sales, the hugely popular game show *Lascia o raddoppia?* (*Double or Quits?*) (Figure 1.1), which premiered on Italian TV in 1955, would be shown on the big screen between films (Mosconi 1995: 332).[3]

---

[3] *Lascia o raddoppia?* was mentioned frequently by our interviewees as something they watched in the cinema.

What were these audiences watching? The boom in audiences coincided with a boom in Italian cinema production and popularity: between 1949 and 1953 Italy's film industry moved from the fourth- to the second-biggest in the world, the number of films produced grew by 100 per cent, and box-office takings of Italian films increased by 120 per cent (Corsi 2001: 64). While Rome became known as 'Hollywood on the Tiber' in the 1950s for its popularity as a filmmaking destination of runaway productions, Italian films held their own at the box office, and by 1954 they were bringing in 36 per cent of the box office for that year, against Hollywood films' 55 per cent, a 20 per cent increase from 1949.

Italians were watching many genres at the box office, but looking at the top-performing films between 1949 and 1959 one can see that, in terms of Italian productions, between 1949 and 1953 they were watching in large numbers either comedies starring the Neapolitan comic Totò or the *film strappalacrime* (weepies or tear-jerking melodramas) directed by Raffaello Matarazzo (Villa 2002). After 1954 the upbeat *neorealismo rosa* (pink neorealism) films such as *Pane, amore e gelosia* (*Bread, Love, and Jealousy*, Luigi Comencini, Italy, 1954) became more popular and paved the way for comedy Italian-style in the later 1950s, regional melodramas (with the Neapolitan kind being pre-eminent) and the epic and historical films that were widely consumed after the success of Mario Camerini's *Ulisse* (Ulysses, Italy, 1954), starring Kirk Douglas and Italian star Silvana Mangano.[4] We address genre preferences specifically in Chapter 4, but it is clear that it is genre productions of all kinds, rather than the critically celebrated and exported Italian neorealism (which had, anyway, petered out by 1953 or so), that dominated the box office, and also our interlocutors' memories.[5]

Cinema remained the principal target of Italians' leisure spending until 1964, and until 1960 Italians were still among the highest spenders on cinemagoing in Europe, even compared to countries with a higher average income (Casetti and Fanchi 2002: 140–1). However, by the late 1950s, most scholars and studies agree that the cinemagoing public had changed: it tended to be younger, wealthier and more concentrated in cities and in the north of the country. If in 1953, a survey sponsored by the Lux production company showed that 68 per cent of Italians went to the cinema at least once a month (see Luzzatto Fegiz 1956: 988), by 1960 58 per cent of Italians told a survey carried out by the Gallup-inspired DOXA

---

[4] See also Lietti (1995).
[5] For a detailed exploration of Italian genre production in the 1950s, see Noto (2011).

statistical institute that they went to the cinema rarely, or less than once a month (Luzzatto Fegiz 1966: 240).

One much-debated issue regarding the changing make-up of the Italian cinema audience is its gender composition: there is an agreement that the audience becomes progressively more male during the 1950s: by 1960, one DOXA survey has 67 per cent of female respondents saying that they rarely go to the cinema, as opposed to 58 per cent of male respondents, while 25 per cent of men questioned said they went at least once a week, as opposed to only 10 per cent of women (ibid.: 240–1). As one of the aims of our project has been to analyse the audience in this period from a gender perspective (thinking about how cinema formed part of their everyday existence as men or women, looking at how tastes and cinemagoing practices might be gendered), these findings are important. Nevertheless, as we will see, these studies may not tell the full story: while scholars assert that women, especially in the south, deserted the cinemas, and stayed at home to watch TV (see Casetti and Fanchi 2002: 147; Fanchi 2010), we should consider some of the limitations of these surveys (often sampling in larger towns and cities, not capturing the full range of attendance at, e.g. parish cinemas). In addition, a careful look at the data reveals a generational breakdown: in 1960, for example, it is older women who are much more likely to go the cinema rarely (86 per cent of women over the age of 54 as opposed to fifty-three per cent of under-35s). This desertion of the cinema by older women is consistent with what we have learned from our interviews and questionnaires: that women often stopped going to the cinema when they married and had children, and that in some (but not all) parts of Italy it was not socially acceptable for a woman to attend the cinema alone. This complex picture of female attendance is something we address particularly in Chapter 6, but it is a topic that we have kept in sight throughout.

The 1950s in Italy were characterized by, as Paolo Noto (2018: 32) puts it, a 'true obsession with the audience, shown by journals and magazines of the period, which, whatever their ideological leanings, are filled with first-person accounts, investigations, reportage, all united by the desire to identify this audience, to describe their behaviour, to outline – and often elevate – their tastes'. This frenzy of surveys and studies on the audience of different types is evidence of a genuine desire to understand the tastes and behaviour of the Italian audience, even if it often came from a place of paternalistic distrust of popular taste, and distress at the commercial success of films like the Matarazzo weepies. As Catherine O'Rawe (2008) has discussed, in relation to the debate that ran in the pages of the Communist newspaper *L'Unità* between December 1955 and May 1956, the public is often assumed to be childlike and feminized, incapable of a deeper understanding of film, and in need of education.[6] Pio Baldelli (1963: 28) confirmed this, noting that while the question of the audience lay at the heart of the post-war film industry, they had rarely been treated with respect, and were often conceived of as 'a herd of children to be guided prudently towards adulthood'.

There are countless other examples of this type of rhetoric which express a frustrated desire to get to know 'the audience, this undiscovered continent' (Morreale 2011: 89).[7] Yet, beyond the despair and paternalism, there were also many genuine attempts to map out the tastes and viewing habits of the cinemagoing public (see Casetti and Fanchi 2002). Many of these contemporary surveys were ad hoc and methodologically unsound; others were carried out by sociologists with a more systematic approach as the examples by DOXA and others above show. Some of the ad hoc studies are nevertheless extremely interesting: the study published in the magazine *Rassegna del film* in 1953, called 'Gli spettatori si confessano' ('The Confessions of Spectators'), interviews a cross-section of society, from a tram driver to a prostitute, about their cinemagoing preferences and tastes (see Peiretti 1953), showing how the often-maligned popular cinema was speaking directly to a segment of the population that did not have a cultural voice. Other small-scale ad hoc surveys investigated audiences on the outskirts of cities who frequented second-run cinemas (Redi and Rinaudo 1954), high school students (Turroni 1954), cinema owners ('Italiani ma distensivi' 1954) or audiences in small provincial towns and villages throughout Italy (Gerosa 1954).

More systematic studies include the ones carried out by sociologists Luca Pinna, Margherita Guidacci and Malcolm MacLean (1958) in Tuscany and Sardinia: their investigation, while still guided by a paternalistic conception of the audience as possessing a limited critical capacity, is extremely insightful in its desire to situate cinemagoing in its social and cultural context, and to understand how local economic and labour conditions, transport and geography as well as cultural mores influence cinemagoing habits and practices. Their approach thus in some ways anticipates that of the New Cinema History (NCH) of recent years, which draws upon history, geography, economics, cultural studies, sociology and

---

[6] We can find other despairing references to audience taste as pathological in Ottaviano (1952) and the editorial in *Cinema* by 'B' (1952).
[7] See also Casetti and Fanchi (2002: 138–9) and Renzi (1956).

anthropology, and is attentive to place-specific and particularized experiences of cinemagoing, and patterns of distribution and exhibition (see Maltby 2011). As the next section makes clear, NCH has deeply influenced our own project.

A different type of audience analysis carried out in 1961 tried to ascertain the effect of advertising on cinema audiences (CoDIS 1961). A national sample of three thousand patrons was interviewed about their cinemagoing habits: the survey also tried to establish how individual spectators reacted to the cinematic image, in order to help refine advertisements shown at the movies. The results showed that spectators are not passive, but are conditioned by the behaviour of those surrounding them: this is also in tune with more recent discussions of audiences as active participants in the film-viewing experience, including ours.

The increasing urgency to record memories as the Italian cinemagoing public, as it reaches old age, has led to only one significant study (Forgacs and Gundle 2007).[8] Forgacs and Gundle interviewed 117 people in 1991–2 from various parts of Italy about their leisure practices: however, the age of their sample means they were referring to an earlier period than ours (from the late 1930s to the late 1950s), and the scope of their investigation, which considered cinema alongside many other leisure pursuits such as reading, sport, going out and so on, means that they do not focus in detail on the national experience of cinemagoing.[9] Nevertheless, their book shows the value of situating cinemagoing as a social practice and showing its importance to everyday life, an importance which goes far beyond the films themselves. Another valuable, if smaller-scale, study is Mariagrazia Fanchi's (1995) use of the 'life story' method in the 1990s to interview eighty Italians about their memories of the *kolossal* films (mythological films, peplums, etc.) of the 1950s. Although her method differs from ours somewhat, her findings speak to a similarity in the ways that films and cinemagoing were embedded for Italians in the social and cultural context of their lives.[10]

In addition to the attention to audience reception in this period, there were parallel investigations into the success of films at the box office. While these normally bracketed out audience responses beyond the simple fact of commercial

---

[8] See also Sprio (2013) on emigrants' memories of Italian cinema.
[9] The four thousand pages of interview transcripts that were carried out for the project are deposited with the UK Data Service at Essex University, where they can be downloaded, and are a valuable resource for scholars of Italy's post-war leisure culture.
[10] See also recent work on spectators' diaries (Vitella 2015), scrapbooks (Comand and Mariani 2018) and letters to magazines (Zilioli 2019).

success, they were valuable attempts to break down the reasons for the performance of particular films, often considering region and gender preference: Vittorio Spinazzola's influential column 'Il termometro degli incassi' ('The Box-Office Thermometer') began in *Cinema Nuovo* in 1957, and attempted to use box-office data in order to offer a more rational and less prejudiced explanation of audience tastes. He was not always successful in this: for example, his explanation for the greater success of Totò films in Naples than Milan (something that might be explained by the simple fact of Totò being a Neapolitan comic) comes down to the assumption that southern audiences love sentimentalism, comedy and have more traditional tastes than northern ones (see Spinazzola (1957) and more recent interpretations of these figures in Treveri Gennari (2009b) and Sedgwick, Miskell and Nicoli (2019)).

Nonetheless, analysts such as Spinazzola, Enrico Rossetti (1957), whose articles honed in on regional programming and exhibition, and Calisto Cosulich (1957), who defended Italian popular film as the mainstay of the industry, laid the ground for serious consideration of both the popular audience and popular Italian films. Spinazzola's book *Cinema e pubblico* (1975), along with the groundbreaking reconsideration by Adriano Aprà and Claudio Carabba (1976) of the hugely popular Matarazzo weepies, much mentioned by our interviewees, are important works which try to assess popular taste, even if the 'people' remain somewhat opaque for them.

## Approaching the Italian audience of the 1950s today

In order to engage as fully as possible with the everyday experience of Italian audiences of the 1950s, the ICA project draws on a wide range of disciplinary backgrounds. In doing so, we are aligned with and inspired by NCH. Building in strength since the beginning of the new millennium, NCH was initially an attempt to redress what was perceived as a one-sided concentration by scholars of film history on the film text. Such a text-oriented approach is also found in traditional post-war Italian film scholarship predominantly focused on neorealism, auteurs like Fellini and stars like Sophia Loren, to the exclusion of contextual phenomena (distribution, exhibition and reception). This shift in 'focus away from the content of films to consider their circulation and consumption, and to examine the cinema as a site of social and cultural exchange' (Maltby 2011: 3), was nonetheless one that drew upon years of social enquiry into cinema, of precisely the kind described above in the context of Italian cinema audiences.

NCH's approaches to the commercial aspects of cinema and the sociocultural history of its audiences have inspired the methodology of our project, as we have aimed for a method of 'triangulation' of data between records of exhibition and box-office takings, press material, questionnaires and oral history interviews (Barker and Mathijs 2008; Biltereyst, Lotze and Meers 2012). Our decision to analyse quantitative and qualitative data, as discussed in more depth below, was driven by a desire to put the individual experience in the context of the ebbs and flows taking place at a national level. In the case of Italy, in particular, the tensions between different individuals and collectives are potentially quite dramatic, in the context of the north/south divide and what Fanchi (2019: 387) describes as the 'fragmented and uneven spread of moviegoing in 1950s Italy'. We have already used our questionnaire and video-interview data to examine the urban/rural divide of the time (Hipkins et al. 2018), revealing the palimpsestic, 'lost' quality of the rural cinemas of the past, in the context of an Italian landscape that has changed significantly in the intervening period of economic and industrial growth. Inevitably, in managing this quantity of data an important aspect of our approach has been offered by the recent exponential growth of the digital humanities, with 'their ethos of collaboration and the sharing of data', along with the potential they offer for new modes of data collection and analysis (Biltereyst et al. 2019: 3). One method that has proved particularly fruitful in our analysis, for example, has been the possibility offered by geovisualization techniques, which have permitted a deeper interrogation of the geographical and spatial dimensions of cinema. Elsewhere (Ercole et al. 2017) they have allowed us to plot journeys and use deep mapping to illustrate the affective and emotional dimensions of cartographic practices related to memory. This new combination of data and memory leads to a fresh vision of cinemas and their related spaces as 'emotionally heightened spaces', discussed here in Chapter 2.

The 'triangulation' approach, then, embraces so much more than different data sources. It is 'also a triangulation of methods, concepts and theories', since 'only a multiscopic perspective will provide the means to comprehend audiences' intrinsically multi-layered experiences' (Biltereyst et al. 2019: 5). One particularly rich intersection of method, concept and theory lies in the nexus oral history-memory-cinema memory that lies at the very heart of our project. We initially began with some urgency, in the very practical awareness that the subtlest account of the experience we wished to recover lay in the oral histories that the ageing Italian population could share with us. In this field the work of Annette Kuhn was of particular importance since her ethnohistory of British audiences in the 1930s gave rise to a new understanding of how cinema memory functions (Kuhn 2002).[11] If Lynn Abrams (2010: 90) notes that 'the vulnerability of memory is not a problem for the oral historian; it is an opportunity', then Kuhn (2002: 9) made the most of this by showing how it was less a question of *what* her respondents remembered than *how* they remembered. Kuhn's groundbreaking attention to 'memory-work', to how patterns or lapses in memory might reveal more than the content, is important to our project and the processes of coding discussed in the next section. Categorizing the different modes of memory, Kuhn found, with some initial surprise, that respondents tended to remember the social activity of cinemagoing and the space of the cinema, rather than the films themselves. This finding was to inform our approach to the interviewing process, which not only asked participants for memories of films and cinemas but also sought to understand the role cinemagoing played in the broader social context of their daily lives. However, like Kuhn (ibid.: 9), we were acutely aware that this inquiry was also 'as much about memory as it is about cinema. It is about the interweaving of the two as cinema memory'.

A significant difference between Kuhn's method and ours is that we were keen to make video recordings of our interviews, since we believed that this would allow us to access further dimensions of both memory, as embodied, and oral history, as performance (Treveri Gennari et al. 2019). Although there have been reservations about the use of video technology among some oral historians who raise concerns about the potential adverse effects of placing a camera in front of an interviewee, the advantages of the medium cannot be understated. Video interviews allow the oral historian to capture what Alessandro Portelli (1991: 47) terms the 'orality' of the testimony: the interviewee's accent, delivery and non-verbal expression. Not only this, as Brien R. Williams notes, video interviews can even 'expand on the meaning of the spoken word' (Williams 2012: 268). In particular, the access that the video interview provides to situating memory and discourse in the context of body language and affect constitutes an important aspect of our analysis. The 'elemental' role that performance plays for older

---

[11] It is worth noting that her project has recently found a new lease of life through an Arts and Humanities Research Council-funded engagement with the digital humanities which will involve digitization of the many resources (letters, stories and recordings) she originally collected for the CCINTB (Cinema Culture in 1930s Britain) project, now held in Special Collections at Lancaster University Library. See https://gtr.ukri.org/projects?ref=AH%2FS004742%2F1.

people in the oral history encounter, because it is 'a means by which they can become visible' (Abrams 2010: 142), became increasingly clear to us over the course of the project, as we shall discuss in our conclusion.

Two further aspects that have particularly influenced our engagement with our audience memories still have much in common with Kuhn's approach: those of gender and generation. Each generation experiences media as a collective experience, although in diverse ways. The experience of going to the cinema, often the 'only pastime' as our respondents recall, was the defining cultural experience for the two generations who fall into our interview group. The majority of our interviewees fall into either the pre-war/wartime generation (b. 1928–40) or what was defined as the post-war (b. 1940–52), by the 'Media and Generations in Italian Society' project (Colombo et al. 2012). We pay careful attention to the way in which generational identity might shape respondents' memory of the 1950s, not only regarding values and experience (of war, for example) but also in terms of whether they experienced cinema as adults or as children.

Gender has had an important role to play in structuring our project from the start, not least of all in our attention to give equal space to male and female voices, regardless of a likely predominance of men in the audience of the time. Like Kuhn, we were particularly aware of 'the silencing of "ordinary" women's voices' (Kuhn 2010a: 60), or, indeed, any women's voices in Italian cinema history. Perhaps because of the exclusion of women from film history, feminist theoretical approaches have played a very significant role in recovering women's engagement with cinema, particularly since in many cultures (if not post-war Italy), it has been associated with women as a 'low' art form of ephemeral consumption. Alongside Kuhn, Jackie Stacey's (1994) study of women's memories of engaging with film stars in the 1940s and 1950s suggested new ways of understanding cinema memory, as one that might be written on the body in creative ways in relation to fashion choices or making clothing, for example. This is an aspect that we bring to bear on the Italian situation, finding parallels and different nuances there in terms of the dual experience of Italian and foreign stars. We also stretch towards less well-researched dimensions of gender, attempting to 'recover' girlhood experiences of cinema (which form the core of our women's memories), and bringing the growing field of masculinity studies to bear on cinema memory, as we think about both star and genre preferences in relation to gender. Learning to become a man or a woman emerges as one of the lessons that audiences of the period attended to with pleasure, or at the very least curiosity, while performing gender is a key structural element of the oral history interview.

## Methodology: Oral history

In gathering memories of post-war cinemagoing, the ICA project applied a mixed-methods approach to data collection, using both questionnaires and video interviews.[12] In the first stage of this process, Italians aged over 65 – recruited through both random and snowball sampling – were asked to respond to a structured questionnaire including both multiple-choice and open-ended questions. Loosely modelled on the questionnaire devised by Jackie Stacey (1994) for her study of British female audiences of the 1940s and 1950s, our questionnaire was designed to gather both quantitative and qualitative data.[13] The administration and completion of 1,043 questionnaires by respondents spread across eight different regions was made possible thanks to the assistance of two cultural entities: BluMedia[14] and UNITRE *L'Università delle Tre Età* (University of the Third Age).[15] The cities of Bari, Rome, Turin, Milan, Palermo, Naples, Cagliari and Florence were selected from the sixteen urban centres used by AGIS (the Italian National Entertainment Association) to monitor box-office intake in the chosen period.

Urban locations were complemented by provincial locations in the same regions: Puglia, Lazio, Piedmont, Lombardy, Sicily, Campania, Sardinia and Tuscany.[16] Our responses were divided almost equally between men (448) and

---

[12] The names of questionnaire respondents are not cited in the book as this information was anonymized. However, we cite video interviewees' first names as they were not anonymous.
[13] See Appendix 1.
[14] Based in Rome, BluMedia is a non-profit cultural organization that brings together professionals with expertise in the fields of education, communication, socio-economics and cultural events.
[15] *L'Università delle Tre Età* (University of the Third Age) is a national body with a network of local entities throughout Italy that offers education courses and training to older learners and retirees. UNITRE has been instrumental in helping us organize public engagement events – *Sharing Memories* events – in Italy, whose objective was to present our findings to participants and the general public. Although most of our events took place in Italy, others were organized in the UK.
[16] We use the term 'provincial' to indicate any localities other than the main cities under scrutiny within the chosen regions. This includes mid-sized towns, small towns as well as villages. The term provincial is used across the book to identify participants who were based in such locations in the 1950s.

women (556), between city (565) and province (478) and crossed a full range of class backgrounds (see Table 1.1 for further details on our sample of participants).

In addition to establishing broad headline trends, the questionnaires also provided a foundation for the second phase of data collection, the video interviews. The questionnaires highlighted areas that invited further exploration such as the rituals of cinemagoing, gender etiquette, the role of cinema as a form of education as well as how cinemagoing practices have changed over time. While the questionnaires provided us with a wealth of information, their limitation as an instrument of data collection lay in the impossibility of interacting with the participants. Hence the necessity of the video interviews, which have offered insight into the silences, the gaps and lapses of memory undoubtedly experienced by the questionnaire respondents. To quote Lynn Abrams (2010: 104), the video-interview form makes it 'possible to literally "see" or hear a person accessing their memory store'.

We conducted half-hour topical interviews with 160 Italians from the same eight cities and provincial areas.[17] The video interviews were carried out with the assistance of Memoro,[18] an organization that gathers and shares online memories of older people in audio-visual format. In order to optimize the interviews and to create a degree of consistency across a relatively large sample, only one interviewer was involved in the process and a semi-structured approach was used in the data collection. This ensured that each interview addressed the key areas of enquiry,[19] while giving the interviewee the flexibility to bring in any other memories and topics that fell outside this schema, such as censorship, the relationship between work and leisure, the journey to the cinema and the sensory experience of the venue (see Appendix 2 for interview questions). It is important to acknowledge that the research (both through the questionnaires and the video interviews) was not designed to be representative from a statistical perspective.[20] And yet, it provides representation from eight regions of Italy,

---

[17] See Treveri Gennari et al. (2019) for a detailed discussion of the methodological and analytical issues around the video interviews.
[18] Founded in Turin in 2007, Memoro is a non-profit organization, which now has a presence in a number of countries across Europe, Africa, North America, South America and Asia.
[19] Interviewees were asked about (1) personal details (DOB and place of birth); (2) strongest memories of cinemagoing; (3) relationship between cinemas and other pastimes; (4) meaning of cinema in social relationships; (5) cinema as education; (5) memories related to specific films and stars; and (6) memories related to the cinema as a physical space.
[20] It is also important to remember that most of our participants are self-selected, which means that they are people who probably had some interest in cinema.

**Table 1.1** Socio-demographic characteristics of questionnaire respondents

| | Total |
|---|---|
| **Sex** | |
| Female | 566 |
| Male | 448 |
| Unassigned | 29 |
| **Age** | |
| <60 | 3 |
| 60–69 | 215 |
| 70–79 | 547 |
| 80–89 | 209 |
| >90 | 16 |
| Unassigned | 53 |
| **Family composition** | |
| <4 | 121 |
| 4–6 | 574 |
| >6 | 253 |
| Unassigned | 95 |
| **Education** | |
| No formal education | 15 |
| Year 7 equivalent | 221 |
| Year 11 equivalent | 272 |
| Sixth form | 313 |
| Degree | 143 |
| Postgraduate | 23 |
| Unassigned/not classifiable | 57 |
| Left school | 3 |
| **Religion** | |
| No mass attendance | 50 |
| Less than once a month | 56 |
| Once a month to twice a month | 116 |
| Once a week | 504 |
| Twice a week | 9 |
| More than twice a week | 46 |
| Can't remember | 57 |
| Unassigned/not classifiable | 211 |
| **Politics** | |
| Centre | 172 |
| Left | 153 |
| Right | 83 |

| | |
|---|---|
| Does not want to respond | 186 |
| Not interested | 4 |
| Too young | 275 |
| Unassigned | 170 |
| **Past-time activities** | |
| Going out with friends | 451 |
| Reading books | 355 |
| Listening to the radio | 293 |
| Dancing | 219 |
| Sport | 203 |
| Reading magazines | 144 |
| Going to the theatre | 84 |
| Unassigned | 36 |
| **Did you read the film reviews?** | |
| Yes | 259 |
| No | 428 |
| Can't remember/unassigned | 356 |

Source: *Italian Cinema Audiences* dataset.

exploring key socio-economic characteristics, including north and south, urban and rural, industrial and agricultural, continental and insular.

Qualitative analysis of both questionnaires and video interviews was carried out using a data-driven codebook. The codebook was initially developed through a phase of 'repeated examination of raw data' (DeCuir-Gunby et al. 2011: 138) provided by questionnaire responses. As five researchers were involved in the coding process, a high degree of consistency was ensured through very detailed codes (ibid.), including main thematic codes, subcodes and examples of coded content. The questionnaire codebook was adjusted, in the second phase of the project, to reflect the further thematic areas that emerged in the video interviews.[21] Intercoder reliability was established following a 'group consensus approach' (DeCuir-Gunby et al. 2011; Harry et al. 2005) for both codebooks. Throughout this process 'some codes were condensed into one and new codes were developed' (Harry et al. 2005: 6). Coding of both questionnaires and video interviews was performed through Nvivo, a software for the analysis of qualitative and mixed-methods data. This process was complemented with short written portraits for each participant in order to identify how the construction

---

[21] See Appendix 3 for a list of the thematic areas analysed in this book.

of the self in the narrative is presented, as well as ways in which memories are narrated.[22] Furthermore, the portraits have been a useful additional analytical tool, as we made the decision not to transcribe the video interviews because of the inevitable loss of oral and visual components (body language, facial expression, tonality) transcription would cause. Arguing for the importance of non-verbal communication, oral historian Jeff Friedman (2014: 291) states that 'in addition to the individual semantic meaning of the words spoken in an interview, the role of the body constitutes a factor in the expression of experience conveyed' by the interviewee. By incorporating this element of embodied expression within the analysis throughout this book, the approach applied here also allows for a more reflective style of critique that considers how the ICA's video interviews fall within the field of visual methodologies. Sarah Pink (2012: 3) notes that recently the visual has become 'more acceptable, more viable and more central to qualitative research practice' in the humanities. In applying this approach to our analysis of the video interviews, we aim to show how the use of this audio-visual medium as a 'tool' of research and a form of data collection can 'enable routes to [new] knowledge' (ibid.: 7) about audiences and cinemagoing practices.

## Contextual data

The data collected in the questionnaires and video interviews has been augmented by contextual data including programming information and box-office takings, exhibition data and archival and press material from the period. Sourced from major city-based daily newspapers, the programming data has been collected through cinema listings in January 1954 from the eight cities under scrutiny.[23] Moreover, in the case of Bari, a full year of programming (1952) was gathered in order to carry out an in-depth case study of a mid-sized city. Naturally, this snapshot comprises films at various stages in their life cycles, ranging from new national or international releases opening at relatively upscale first-run cinemas

---

[22] These include details on the general background of the interviewee, key concepts and key experiences linked to cinemagoing as well as modalities of delivery and non-verbal communication. We would like to thank Martin Barker (a member of our advisory board) for suggesting this analytical tool.

[23] We have chosen 1954, as it was one of the best years in terms of national production and exhibition (Bizzarri and Solaroli 1958: 90–4).

for multiple weeks to films nearing the end of their lifecycle, screened in small neighbourhood cinemas, perhaps for just one day. Moreover, box-office reports of first-run cinemas recorded in the biweekly publication of the exhibitor's association (AGIS-ANEC) *Bollettino dello Spettacolo*[24] were used in order to analyse film popularity, through the use of the Popularity Index, the analytical tool developed by John Sedgwick, who has contributed to the ICA project with his expertise in the business and economic history of film.

Exhibition data on cinemas in the main eight cities under scrutiny was gathered through a variety of sources, with the aim of providing a snapshot of the exhibition sector in the 1950s, and included information on cinema locations, owners and managers, capacity and run. *Società Italiana Autori Editori* (SIAE) was the main source for the list of cinemas, alongside ACEC – *Associazione Cattolica Esercenti Cinema* (Catholic Exhibitors Association). SIAE was a partner of the ICA project and contributed with extremely valuable archival data and insight into the exhibition sector. Further information on location, cinema management and cinema run was also found in trade yearbooks, databases and local editions of national newspapers, as well as books and web publications on local history.

Alongside the above-mentioned sources, archives and libraries across Italy have offered us a wide selection of press material, both from specialized film and trade journals and popular press. These sources have been used to contextualize the memories emerging from oral history data within wider historical discourses on cinema, its reception and consumption. Drawing on triangulation approaches to audience research (such as Barker and Mathijs 2008; Biltereyst, Lotze and Meers 2012), the cross-analysis of this wealth of resources and the oral history has allowed a new approach to Italian cinema history. Cinema memories have, in fact, been read against quantitative data about film distribution, box-office records, cinema attendance, paratextual material and critical readings from the popular and the specialized press.

In order to visualize both the exhibition structure, the programming patterns of selected films as well as the memories of our participants, we have employed different digital geovisualization tools.[25] We have mapped cinemas across all of the eight cities, film distribution and their circulation in different cinema runs and

---

[24] The title of the journal changed to *Bollettino di informazioni* (1945–50), *Bollettino d'informazioni* (1950–2) and *Bollettino dello Spettacolo* (from 1952 onwards). We will be using only *Bollettino dello Spettacolo* to avoid confusion.

[25] We have used the following digital software: Palladio, Prospect, Carto and AtlasCine. See www.italiancinemaaudiences.org for all details.

cinemagoing memories. This has been possible thanks to the AHRC Follow on Funding made available to the ICA team, which helped us create an online digital archive, CineRicordi, where the starting point was the map, co-curated by its users.[26]

## Quantitative results

The analysis of the questionnaires presents quantitative results on cinemagoing practices which – while they cannot be taken as representative for *all* socio-economic categories of cinemagoers in the post-war period – still highlight widespread trends in relation to attendance, frequency, film choices and general consumption patterns.

Table 1.1 highlights a representative spread among participants in terms of gender, age, education and religious practice. The responses to the question about politics reflect caution from some participants who refuse to articulate their political allegiance, while at the same time reminding us that a section of our respondents was too young at the time to be involved with politics. Finally, the responses about leisure activities in the post-war period confirm the wide popularity of cinemagoing in comparison to other pastimes.[27]

Table 1.2 shows that cinemagoing was a popular practice in post-war Italy, with cinemagoers attending venues mostly once or twice per month, predominantly with friends and family, generally at the weekend and in neighbourhood and city centre cinemas. One significant figure that emerges from Table 1.2 is the high percentage (93 per cent) of female respondents who remember going to the cinema in the post-war period, only 0.65 per cent less than male participants. This finding takes on particular significance when viewed in the light of existing scholarship based on previous coeval national surveys, mentioned earlier, such as Mariagrazia Fanchi's (2010) study of post-war women's cultural consumption, which claims that female cinema attendance was significantly lower than its male counterpart. Fanchi's observation that the beginning of the 1950s was marked by women's 'departure from cinemas' (ibid.: 306) could help us interpret our oral history data. The dominance of female respondents, who (to various degrees) present themselves as active cinemagoers in the 1950s, can be read as a sign that our participants were

---

[26] All the geovisualizations are available at www.italiancinemaaudiences.org and www.cinericordi.it.
[27] See results about leisure activities in Tables 1.1 and 1.2 on cinema attendance.

self-selecting members of the audience with a stronger interest in cinema. On the other hand, though, official statistical data can also be questioned and better interpreted with the support of the oral history. For instance, the claim that cinemagoing in the mid-1950s was a practice 'concentrated in northern Italy' and 'an urban experience, typical of a few larger cities' (Fanchi 2019: 389) is entirely based on SIAE national data on numbers of cinemas and cinema attendance in those venues. However, SIAE data only reflects the main commercial exhibition sector, as it does not take into account alternative types of cinemas and film consumption that emerge from our oral history. Viewing in courtyards, public and private gardens as well as improvised pop-up cinemas and screenings in barns are all practices that our participants living in small towns and villages remember vividly.[28]

Table 1.2 also shows that film choice was determined overwhelmingly by genre, actors and, to a lesser degree, by advertising and word of mouth, and arguably hardly ever by film reviews, which were read only by 24.8 per cent of our questionnaire respondents. This finding is also borne out by the video interviews, in which many participants explain that they often had few possibilities of knowing what a film was about before seeing it, but the presence of a favourite star could certainly influence their choice, if indeed a choice was available, highlighting how in some cases the star image alone was enough to increase a film's box-office appeal. The top four favourite stars – as well as favourite films – reflected the predominance of Italian and American film production in post-war Italy and are discussed in some of this book's chapters.

In spite of the significance of stardom for Italian audiences, the number of people who collected memorabilia or wrote to actors is remarkably low. As we have argued elsewhere (Hipkins et al. 2016: 223) this fact could be linked to a sense of the distance Italians felt from the world of the screen. In this book we present further analysis of these figures in relation to several issues, including genre, stardom, space/place experience, the relationship between cinema and other forms of leisure and gender identity formation. And yet, further analysis and cross-tabulation of this data are necessary in order to fully explore our participants' responses and paint a more detailed picture of the multifaceted nature of the cinemagoing experience in post-war Italy.[29]

---

[28] For a further discussion of rural cinemagoing practices, see Hipkins et al. (2018).
[29] All questionnaire responses are freely available to download at https://www.cinericordi.it/page/risorse/ricerca.

**Table 1.2** Cinemagoing habits and preferences of questionnaire respondents

| Cinema attendance | Total |
| --- | --- |
| Yes | 977 |
| No | 52 |
| Unassigned | 14 |
| **Years of cinema attendance** | |
| 1950–6 | 438 |
| 1957–60 | 646 |
| 1960s | 7 |
| Unassigned | 33 |
| **Attendance frequency** | |
| Less than once a month | 201 |
| One to two times a month | 630 |
| Once a week | 344 |
| More than once a week | 114 |
| Can't remember | 1 |
| Never | 1 |
| Other | 100 |
| **Ticket price** | |
| Too expensive | 126 |
| Right price | 409 |
| Cheap | 105 |
| I didn't pay | 198 |
| Other | 22 |
| Can't remember | 171 |
| Unassigned | 20 |
| **Which day?** | |
| Saturday | 183 |
| Sunday | 481 |
| Both Saturday and Sunday | 10 |
| Weekday | 95 |
| Any day of the week | 283 |
| Can't remember | 1 |
| Unassigned | 36 |
| **With whom?** | |
| Friends | 562 |
| Family | 322 |
| Partner | 250 |
| Alone | 51 |

| Other | 1 |

**Cinema run**

| First run | 240 |
| Second run | 351 |
| Third run | 230 |
| Parish cinema | 223 |
| Open-air cinema | 65 |
| Film societies/film club | 38 |

**Cinema area**

| In own neighbourhood | 280 |
| In another neighbourhood | 75 |
| In the city centre | 286 |
| Other | 48 |

**Favourite film genres**

| Adventure | 23% |
| Love | 21% |
| Comedy | 19% |
| War | 11% |
| Musical | 11% |
| Neorealist | 10% |
| Melodrama | 3% |
| Western | 2% |

**What made you decide on the film?**

| Actors | 575 |
| Genre | 607 |
| Street publicity | 289 |
| Recommended | 204 |
| Church posters | 77 |
| Film nationality | 80 |
| Press publicity | 280 |
| Anything available | 136 |
| Other | 98 |
| Unassigned | 40 |

**Did you read the film reviews?**

| Yes | 259 |
| No | 428 |
| Can't remember/unassigned | 356 |

**Favourite female stars**

| Sophia Loren | 171 |

(continued)

**Table 1.2** (continued)

| | |
|---|---|
| Anna Magnani | 123 |
| Gina Lollobrigida | 98 |
| Elizabeth Taylor | 43 |
| Unassigned | 162 |
| **Favourite male stars** | |
| Amedeo Nazzari | 84 |
| Marcello Mastroianni | 67 |
| Gregory Peck | 60 |
| Gary Cooper | 60 |
| Unassigned | 143 |
| **Favourite film** | |
| *Gone with the Wind* (Victor Fleming, United States, 1939) | 116 |
| *Roma città aperta* (*Rome Open City*, Roberto Rossellini, Italy, 1945) | 48 |
| *Ben Hur* (William Wyler, United States, 1959) | 44 |
| *Ladri di biciclette* (*Bicycle Thieves*, Vittorio De Sica, Italy, 1948) | 38 |
| Unassigned | 94 |

Source: Italian Cinema Audiences dataset.

## Summary of chapters

Part 1, 'The Activity of Cinemagoing', opens with a chapter where we focus on our audiences' close connection with the space of film consumption, as their memories are used to provide information first on cinema exhibition processes, such as multiple programming and film turnover. By triangulating audiences' memories with archival data and exhibitors' trade-press material we shed light on the spatial distribution of films and audiences' access to different genres, nationalities and stars around the country. Second, through the use of geographical visualization tools and of topographical memories of the audiences, we offer a new understanding of the relationship between cinema and space within the Italian context. In our third chapter we broaden the concept of entertainment as pleasure by including the audience's experiences outside the cinema. Extra-theatrical experience, in fact, is equally important in the memories of Italian audiences, as they refer to experience inside and outside the cinemas as part of the same practice of cinemagoing. The chapter explores aspects as diverse as silence and noise, courting and molestation, but also food consumption, family dynamics, inattentiveness, social experiences and isolation.

Part 2, 'Films: Genre, Taste and Popular Memory', addresses recent calls to reconsider the role of the film itself in the history of film audiences, by thinking about genre, taste and popular memory. Chapter 4 analyses the different conceptualizations of specific film genres from the perspectives of cinemagoers, the press and the film industry. Through triangulation, the chapter contextualizes oral history data with press material and programming data with the aim of determining the extent to which audiences' understandings of genres corresponded to and were influenced by press and industry discourses. While highlighting the role of memory work in relation to genre preferences in the case under scrutiny, we show the importance of using genre as an analytical tool in order to paint a more accurate picture of historical film consumption through oral history accounts. In Chapter 5 we examine how our understanding of one major film from the Italian post-war cinematic canon can be enriched by an engagement with audience memories. The film *Roma città aperta* is repeatedly mentioned by our interviewees, as a favourite, and example of the post-war revival of Italian cinema, neorealism. We argue that this particular film's significant place in film (and Italian) history makes more sense in the context of how it is remembered and narrated by some of its first audiences, as a way of making sense of the recent (often unspeakable) past, through engagement with affect and place.

Part 3, 'Gender and Cinemagoing', devotes attention to gendered modes of cinematic engagement. In Chapter 6 we attempt to 'recover' a largely hidden aspect of Italian cinema history. Understanding girlhood as a historically contingent notion (Dyhouse 2013), the chapter considers how girls went to the cinema, particularly the collective nature of that experience, and how they negotiated the risks it presented. We consider which films and stars they saw there, and how they process and narrate those 'girlhood' memories now. The chapter considers women's memory narratives in the context of their life cycle, as they revisit patterns of cinemagoing in relation to key life stages, such as dreams of romance, and finally reflect critically on their imagined futures as women. Turning to the relationship between female spectators and stardom, Chapter 7 uses an audience perspective to reassess the dominant discourses that surround female stars within the narrative of Italian cinema history. An integrated framework (consisting of archival materials, audience questionnaires and video interviews) illustrates the central role that stars played in eliciting active forms of identification among Italian audiences. While helping to assess the appeal of particular stars, the analysis of the audience–star relation also sheds light on broader concerns within Italian post-war society such as the emergence of consumerism and the formation of gender identity. Chapter 8 examines how cinema operates within the video interviews as a vector for the construction of particular kinds of male identities. The versions of the self that are composed in the oral history interview by men looking back on the place of cinema in their younger lives illustrate not only the power of cinema, both in terms of its imagery and iconography of stardom, but also the cultural place of cinema in Italian society in the 1950s and 1960s, in making available to these men ways of imagining themselves as a man, or offering shared cultural values within which they could locate themselves. Our conclusions return to our original research questions by evaluating both the main findings of the project and its contribution to wider discourses around memory, while looking at the complexity of emotions felt by older people around the history of their everyday culture. Furthermore, we examine how our research has had an impact on communities of older people in Italy and how we are reaching out to engage positively with the affect and desires generated by this project.

Part One

# The activity of cinemagoing

2

# Cinemas, exhibition practices and topographical memories

The Italian Cinema Audiences (ICA) project has aligned itself with other projects of similar kinds in its findings that memories of cinema venues are stronger and more vivid when compared to memories of films, stars, plots or sets, demonstrating 'the affective bonds between people and their surroundings' (Madgin et al. 2016: 677). This close connection with the space of film consumption – whether it was a dedicated luxurious theatre, a garden, an open-air cinema or a fleapit – will be the focus of this chapter. Italian audiences' memories will be used here to inform us first on cinema exhibition processes which took place in the 1950s and which so far are left almost unexplored in Italian cinema history. Multiple programming, film turnover and cinema chains will be investigated in order to analyse practices, strategies and structures of a distribution and exhibition system which, while not sophisticated, was very effective across the national territory. Triangulating audiences' memories with archival data and exhibitors' trade-press material will shed light on the spatial distribution of films and audiences' access to different genres, nationalities and stars around the country. Second, the use of geographical visualization tools in combination with memories has brought about a new understanding of the 'spatiality of the experience of cinema more generally' (Allen 2011: 80). This was achieved through engagement with audiences' topographical memories, which guided us through the geography of cinemagoing, forcing us to 'be as attentive to descriptions of journeys and places as we are to mentions of movie titles and stars' (Bowles 2009: 85).

This chapter reflects upon the use of digital technologies in a new exploration of the history of Italian cinema (both in the form of geographical and emotional maps) to investigate how spatial reference is used in oral history narratives. The significance of spatial historiography is axiomatic in several areas of research in the humanities: it provides new approaches to 'interrogate textual patterns even in the absence of texts' (Vélez-Serna and Caughie 2015: 164). It offers insights into the analysis of sources (Hallam and Roberts 2011) and, overall, has contributed to 'a greater awareness of place' (Ayers 2010: 1). Within the context of memory studies and cinema studies, space has been an integral part of the process of recollection, and spatial reference has been used in oral history narratives to help audiences to reorient themselves in the disorienting experience of reminiscence. This chapter will reflect on the significance of space for the ICA participants in relation to cinemagoing and will provide some examples of how geographical visualizations can contribute to a better understanding of that experience.

## The exhibition sector in Italy in the 1950s: Spaces of film consumption

The variety of film exhibition offered Italians a varied exposure to movies produced at the time, both in the country and abroad. Unlike other European countries, 'Italy saw a constant rise in consumption and number of new cinemas' (Nicoli 2016: 187). According to the data collected by the SIAE (Statistica Documentazione Annuario dello Spettacolo, 1960 – see Table 2.1), the number of cinemas open to the public increased significantly over the post-war period: if

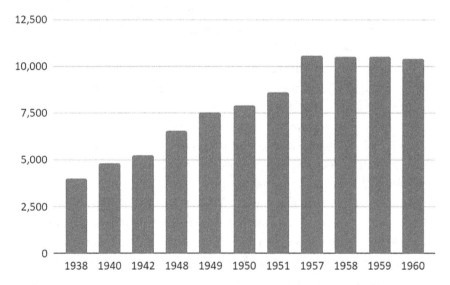

**Table 2.1** Cinemas in the years 1938–60 (from Statistica Documentazione Annuario dello spettacolo 1960)

in 1938 there were only 4,013 cinemas across the country, by 1960 this number had almost tripled, with 10,393 venues available for more than 50 million Italians. This rapid development of the cinema sector was also a consequence of the 'reinforcement of the cinema industry (the first Italian associations, such as AGIS and ANEC were born at the beginning of the 1940s)', allowing the 'spreading of cinema halls ... from big urban centres to the new suburbs and the countryside' (Giusti 2007: 15).

However, the geographical distribution of cinemas was certainly not even (Fanchi 2019: 389). While the north of the country had a more established range of cinemas across all major cities and towns, the south of the peninsula did not have the same number.[1] Published in 1954 in the *Bollettino dello Spettacolo* (20 August 1954: 5), the insightful article titled 'Il censimento di cinema e teatri nelle rilevazioni statistiche della SIAE', however, reminds us that in the post-war period more cinemas were being built in the south. It highlighted, in fact, that while in the north of the country this process of renovation was slowing down in the years up until 1954, in the centre and in the south it carried on at a steady pace. The article also highlights both the inadequate technological infrastructure of these cinemas (where at least ten per cent of the venues did not have proper equipment and used projectors borrowed from travelling cinemas) and the intermittent nature of the programming: out of all commercial cinemas only 70 per cent operated for a full season, 8 per cent were small cinemas with no more than two hundred seats and the remaining 22 per cent were open-air cinemas in city centres – with 1,000–2,500 seats – or smaller cinemas in touristy towns, active only in the summer season.

However, audiences were keen to access local cinemas or travel long distances from rural areas or peripheries into more affluent districts or city centres in order to watch their favourite films. Cinemas in the major cities of Italy were divided into three tiers – first, second and third run – according to geographical location, the type of films shown, the difference in ticket price, facilities and target audiences (see Nicoli 2016: 192). In smaller towns and

---

[1] Out of 7,896 cinemas in 1950, for instance, 4,585 were located in the north of the country, 1,541 in the centre, 1,234 in the south and 536 in the islands. This situation remained unchanged if we see that in 1960 out of the 10,393 cinemas 5,800 were in the north, 1,951 in the centre, 1,655 in the south and 987 in the islands (*Statistica Documentazione Annuario dello Spettacolo* 1960). Forgacs and Gundle (2007: 31) also point to very uneven distribution in regions of the south: while cinema construction grew rapidly in the 1950s in Calabria, e.g. 37 per cent of towns in the region still had no cinema in 1958.

villages, cinemas were just 'cinemas', with a distinction made between commercial and parish ones: a distinction that was reflected in the memories of the audience. Indeed, some participants from rural areas (e.g. Lucia, b. 1936, Cagliari province, or Giorgia, b. 1940, Palermo province) admitted to not knowing of the existence of first-run cinemas. The extensive network of parish cinemas has been explored in several academic works (Fanchi 2006; Treveri Gennari 2009a). Participants have very vivid memories of this experience: audiences were regular attenders of the Catholic venues that were widespread across the country, especially in rural areas where commercial cinemas were more scarce.

These different typologies of cinemas and the geographical distribution of them are not only significant for different types of audiences but also for the programming scheduled. Nicoli (2016: 193) identifies different types of film on offer in the post-war period, ranging from 'very low-profile productions aimed at the provinces, to medium-high level productions, and the big super-productions aimed at capturing public attention'. This is echoed by Di Chiara's study (2013: 11) of the Titanus production company, which identified three types of works: 'the most ambitious works for the circuits of big cities; the medium-level movies with a ... spectacular impact; and the low-budget products for second and third-run cinemas'. This also emerged in the survey 'Italiani ma distensivi: i film graditi agli esercenti' conducted in 1954 among cinema exhibitors and published in *Rassegna del Film*, indicating that certain types of audiences in different cinema runs seemed to appreciate different genres, such as melodrama, on the outskirts of cities (1954: 16). One female exhibitor, Maria Doglione Montesano, even affirmed that her audience liked musicals and romances, not neorealism, admitting that they were less educated than first- and second-run cinema audiences. It does not come as a surprise when members of the audience, such as Adalberto (b. 1935, Milan) and Alessandro (b. 1942, Rome province) describing their cinemagoing experience both in a big city like Milan and in a small town like Olevano Romano (population around five thousand people at that time), define films, rather than cinemas, as being of 'first, second or third run'. They thus categorized both films and venues according to the same distinction. Films were of 'first run' when they were screened earlier than other films, but also 'first' represented for Antonio (b. 1938, Milan) the quality of the venue, the promptness of the release and the higher quality of the audience (selected by a less affordable ticket price). Adolfo (b. 1940, Milan), another participant, clarifies this distinction even further: when talking about the cinemas in his city, Milan, he distinguishes between the periphery, where 'more simple films' (such as the Totò comedies) were screened, and the city centre, where epic films were screened alongside 'films by culturally more advanced' directors, such as Michelangelo Antonioni. Antonio (b. 1938, Milan) adds also that second- and third-run cinemas could not guarantee the same safety as the others: in these cinemas, he suggests, women were not

> safe from ... harassment, harassment. Every now and then I would hear the noise of a slap, especially in second and third-run cinemas. Because of the third run, you know, those poor people who had little money, at a certain point when they saw a beautiful girl ... they could not resist letting their hand wander.[2]

While the issue of behaviour and etiquette within the cinema is the topic of the following chapter, it is important to note that a clear distinction between venues according to types of spectators, programming and affordability is certainly present in the memories of our audiences.

The programming distinction between centre and periphery, or between first, second and third run, is also evident when looking at the cost of cinema tickets. If by simply referring to the SIAE data the average price seems not to vary significantly,[3] this discrepancy is perceived more intensely by audiences. Several participants remember choosing a cinema according to the ticket price, comment on high costs which made them find creative ways around it, such as going with a family member who had free access because of being in the army, or being friendly with the projectionist. The high cost of a cinema ticket forced Enea (b. 1935, Milan), for instance, to take advantage of the free Sunday morning screenings to access first-run cinemas in Milan, which would be otherwise financially prohibitive. Others comment on the fact that Italian families at the time were bigger, and taking all the children to the cinema was only a treat they could afford on very special occasions. The choice of second-run cinemas was often a compromise to access entertainment at the expense of poor-quality sound and image, as well as a disruptive environment. Alternatives involved two people going but paying only for one ticket, or at times not paying at all. The

---

[2] The original expression in Italian is *mano morta* (dead hand). However, we have decided to translate this expression with 'wandering hand'. See Chapters 3 and 8 for further discussion of this behaviour.

[3] Tab. 30 – Cinema – Numero dei giorni di spettacolo, numero dei biglietti venduti, spesa del pubblico, prezzi medi e spesa per abitante, nelle principali città d'Italia (Statistica Documentazione Annuario dello Spettacolo, SIAE, 1960).

*Bollettino dello Spettacolo* repeatedly published articles during this period about a practice common in Italy at the time: entering the cinema without paying for a ticket. This was known as *portoghesismo* (behaving like the Portuguese) and the term indicates those who – according to specific arrangements with the exhibitors – were excused from paying for their tickets (such as police officers and members of the armed forces, etc.) as well as those who illegally managed to find ways to get into the cinema without paying. To these two categories was added a new one, a special way of being Portuguese, which was defined as the *spettatore ad oltranza* (spectator to the bitter end), who decides to use the ticket purchased to its maximum profit by remaining in the cinema beyond the end of the performance (S. 1956: 1).

This phenomenon of *portoghesismo* was vigorously denounced on the pages of the trade paper *Bollettino dello Spettacolo*,[4] as it had a profound financial impact on the exhibition sector. An article titled 'Per i portoghesi' (1950: 2) aimed to explain precisely what type of categories were allowed to enter the cinema for free and with a special reduction. However, in the following years, several articles were published to expose this practice again, to the point that 'L'italiano non paga' (1955: 3) claimed that this established practice was seen by Italians as an 'acquired right' that was almost impossible to eradicate.

It would be impossible to describe the exhibition landscape in post-war Italy without mentioning the *arene* (open-air cinemas).[5] These types of cinemas offered opportunities for audiences in small towns and villages in tourist areas to experience film viewing, while allowing travellers on holiday to carry on watching their favourite movies. While they were active only in the summer season, they played a substantial role for the audience, who remember them fondly. The case of Rome – while constituting an exception due to the extremely high number of cinemas available to the Roman audiences in the 1950s – is at the same time a good example for us to understand the impact of open-air cinemas on the local population across the main cities. If Romans had 172,909 seats available in the city during the rest of the year, in the summer an additional 29,494 seats (17.05 per cent) were made available to them through the open-air venues (SIAE 1957; ACEC Sale parrocchiali). It is true that this number must take into account the closure of

---

[4] See, for instance, 'Lettere in Redazione. Sempre sui portoghesi' (1955: 5); B. (1956: 1); De Luca (1956: 3); B.B. (1954: 5); Bru (1952: 5); and B. (1950: 1).

[5] On open-air cinemas, see Mosconi and Piredda (2006).

regular cinemas during the summer months, as indicated by Augusto Fragola (1954: 3) in 1954 when trying to clarify the dispute around the opening of new cinemas in respect to the ratio of seats to population (1: 12–20). Therefore, while the acceptance of a new open-air cinema would only need to count the ratio of seats available in the summer period, other regulations were forced on the *arene*. For example, the reminder in the article 'Comunicazioni della Presidenza' published in the trade journal *Bollettino dello Spettacolo* in July 1950 (1950: 1)[6] that the rules for programming of Italian films had to be applied to open-air cinemas as well as any other commercial venues is an indication of a type of exhibition that was temporary from an architectural point of view (as the open-air cinemas would not be active all year around), but at the same time fully compliant with the rules governing the exhibition system. The ephemeral nature of the *arene* is certainly an aspect that audiences remember vividly, as memories refer to the discomfort and the precariousness of the seating arrangements, often complemented by chairs taken from home, as remembered by Maria Grazia (b. 1938, Florence province) and Marta (b. 1938, Florence). The other aspect referred to, when reminiscing about open-air cinemas, is the multisensory dimension of the experience, such as the noise of chairs on gravel, or the perfume of the flowers remembered by Maria (b. 1946, Bari province), which – while augmenting the exceptional association of film consumption with holiday time, as in the case of Giorgia (b. 1940, Palermo province) – in some cases generates a 'disruptive' effect. Being outside of the habitual environment of the indoor space, as well as often being transported to more remote areas, made it more difficult for some spectators to concentrate on what was projected and identify with the characters on the screen, as described by Giorgio (b. 1936, Turin).

Cinemas were not only distinguished by their geographical location or architectural features, but their programming was also key to audience decisions. Aspects such as multiple programming, film turnover and cinema chains are investigated in the next section in order to elicit practices, strategies and structures of the distribution and exhibition system and the way audiences remember them. Audience memories, in combination with archival data and exhibitors' trade-press material, can shed light on the spatial distribution of films and audiences' access to different films around the country.

---

[6] With reference to the 20 December 1949 cinema law, article 18, n. 958.

## Cinema exhibition processes: Programming strategies and audience responses

While historical statistical data is ample and readily available for analysis via the *Bollettino dello Spettacolo* and SIAE data, unfortunately programming data is still fragmented, time-consuming and complex to collect and investigate, as it is only obtainable through local daily newspapers in major cities and towns, and much rarer to find for smaller villages, as the local press often did not record programming information.

From the *Annuario dello Spettacolo* (SIAE), information on screening days, ticket sales, tickets per capita as well as box-office expenditure is available. Table 2.2, while confirming Rome, Milan, Naples and Turin as the cities with the highest number of cinemas, reflects the disparity of distribution between the north and the south of the country, as well as the dominance of the capital city in terms of box-office revenue.

Although the search for statistical data was informative, it did not provide the type of information required to corroborate and enhance audience memories. As a consequence, a decision was taken to collect samples of programming data for January 1954 in the eight cities included in the project. This is certainly not comprehensive enough to allow for a thorough investigation into programming strategies and film consumption patterns. However, it offers a snapshot of what films were available at a moment in time to audiences in different parts of the country. Importantly, it also indicates the intensity of film turnover in the cities under scrutiny, which gives us an idea of how films were distributed, exhibited and consumed in post-war Italy.

John Sedgwick, consultant on the ICA project, has analysed this dataset. As is evident from Table 2.3, it offers a new means of comparing programming across the north and south of the country, centre and the islands as well as for each individual city.[7]

The first significant discovery emerging from Table 2.3 is the fact that the programming data provided on the pages of the main local and national newspapers is unfortunately incomplete. It offers, in fact, the only information on a selection of cinemas in each city, rather than all of them (the disparity is

---

[7] Sedgwick's findings have been partially published within a wider study on national and regional patterns of taste (Sedgwick et al. 2019) whose dataset expands up to the 1960s. However, for the purpose of our research, we will be using specifically the 1950s data collected.

Table 2.2 Cinemagoing statistics for Italy's major provincial cities in 1954 (*Annuario dello Spettacolo* 1954)

| City | Population | Cinemas | Screening days | Ticket sales | Tickets per capita | Ticket expenditure | Expenditure per capita |
|---|---|---|---|---|---|---|---|
| Milan | 1,288,571 | 194 | 50,312 | 44,256,380 | 34 | 9,208,001,392 | 7,146 |
| Florence | 390,484 | 73 | 21,202 | 16,038,310 | 41 | 2,572,394,518 | 6,588 |
| Rome | 1,723,099 | 231 | 67,443 | 64,553,920 | 37 | 10,505,216,637 | 6,097 |
| Turin | 747,153 | 119 | 32,959 | 23,343,470 | 31 | 4,425,015,074 | 5,923 |
| Cagliari | 143,380 | 25 | 5,836 | 4,770,620 | 33 | 634,111,966 | 4,423 |
| Naples | 1,042,316 | 111 | 36,672 | 28,198,310 | 27 | 4,230,342,196 | 4,059 |
| Bari | 280,899 | 29 | 10,331 | 8,726,820 | 31 | 1,099,240,391 | 3,913 |
| Palermo | 506,706 | 56 | 21,169 | 13,048,280 | 26 | 1,905,010,493 | 3,760 |

All expenditures and sales are in lire.

**Table 2.3** The intensity of film circulation in seven Italian cities in January 1954 (programming data from local newspapers as well as *Annuario dello Spettacolo* Table 35 on cinema numbers)[a]

| | Rome | Milan | Turin | Naples | Bari | Palermo | Cagliari |
|---|---|---|---|---|---|---|---|
| City population | 1,723,099 | 1,288,571 | 747,153 | 1,042,316 | 280,899 | 541,890 | 143,380 |
| Cinemas in sample population | 137 | 112 | 74 | 69 | 17 | 29 | 8 |
| Cinemas open in 1954 | 231 | 194 | 119 | 111 | 29 | 56 | 25 |
| Population for each sample cinema | 12,577 | 11,505 | 10,097 | 15,106 | 16,523 | 18,686 | 17,922 |
| Film programmes | 1,751 | 1,183 | 708 | 700 | 192 | 285 | 77 |
| Films | 731 | 598 | 435 | 416 | 188 | 243 | 72 |
| Population for each film | 2,357 | 2,155 | 1,718 | 2,506 | 1,494 | 2,230 | 1,991 |
| Screening days | 3,536 | 3,313 | 1,990 | 2,033 | 413 | 691 | 211 |
| Median film exhibition (days) | 2 | 3 | 3 | 2 | 2 | 2 | 2 |
| Max film exhibition (days) | 88 | 102 | 45 | 54 | 8 | 13 | 13 |
| Films screened for one day | 294 | 48 | 33 | 92 | 89 | 63 | 11 |

[a]Florence is not included in this table.

indicated between the number of cinemas open in 1954 and the cinemas in sample population). Despite this limitation, the collected dataset still proves to be extremely beneficial to better comprehend programming dynamics at play in different cities and what was on offer to Italians at a given time in the main cities studied. Moreover, the 'exhibition days' category offers a snapshot of a very intense and intricate cinema market, a fact confirmed by the high number of films that were screened for only one day, indicating the large number of films in circulation for which there was no audience (Sedgwick et al. 2019: 203). This is further borne out by the very low median number of screening days common to each of the cities in the sample. The data suggests a cinema market that is complex, but nevertheless geared to screening those films that audiences did want to see, evident in the maximum number of screening days given over to particular films. It also exposes the fast turnover of less successful films and the exhibitors' need to adjust their programming strategy to their audience's preferences.

When the programming data is combined with the box-office takings, available in the *Bollettino dello Spettacolo*, new findings emerge. Table 2.4 lists the top five films in circulation in the main cities in January 1954.

It confirms the dominance of Italian and American films (Treveri Gennari 2009b).[8] It is clear that Italian films enjoyed a comparable level of popularity to their Hollywood counterparts. Table 2.4 also demonstrates that in cities such as Bari, Palermo and Cagliari, the number of exhibition days was significantly lower than in Naples, Milan, Turin and Rome: smaller populations are less able to sustain films in circulation leading to faster circulation and consequent need for a greater number of films to be screened in their cinemas. What this table does not give us, unfortunately, is the trajectory of film circulation from the main cities, such as Rome and Milan, to other cities such as Naples, Turin as well as smaller centres like Bari, but also across first-, second- and third-run cinemas, which is more difficult to capture from the data available and from the limited time (January 1954) under investigation. While more comprehensive data collection as well as much more in-depth analysis are needed in order to achieve this, for the purpose of this section, it is significant to explore how our participants remember the programming practices and the exhibitors' strategies to attract audiences to their cinemas. This will confirm the relationship between spectators and cinema venues, exhibitors and programming practices. It will

[8] Florence was not included in this analysis.

**Table 2.4** Top five films in circulation in January 1954 (courtesy of John Sedgwick)

| City | Films | No. of cinemas | Exhibition days |
|---|---|---|---|
| **Rome** | | | |
| 1 | *The Prisoner of Zenda* (Richard Thorpe, United States, 1952) | 21 | 88 |
| 2 | *South Sea Woman* (Arthur Lubin, United States, 1953) | 24 | 68 |
| 3 | *Villa Borghese* (Gianni Franciolini, Vittorio De Sica, Italy, 1953) | 18 | 63 |
| 4 | *Plymouth Adventure* (Clarence Brown, United States, 1952) | 24 | 60 |
| 5 | *The Moon is Blue* (Otto Preminger, United States, 1953) | 23 | 57 |
| **Milan** | | | |
| 1 | *Moulin Rouge* (John Huston, United States, 1952) | 21 | 102 |
| 2 | *Anni facili* (Luigi Zampa, Italy, 1953) | 14 | 68 |
| 3 | *Lucrèce Borgia* (Christian-Jaque, France/Italy, 1953) | 15 | 62 |
| 4 | *The Mississippi Gambler* (Rudolph Maté, United States, 1953) | 15 | 60 |
| 5 | *The Merry Widow* (Curtis Bernhardt, United States, 1952) | 13 | 59 |
| **Turin** | | | |
| 1 | *The Greatest Show on Earth* (Cecil B. DeMille, United States, 1952) | 11 | 45 |
| 2 | *The Prisoner of Zenda* | 12 | 45 |
| 3 | *Salome* (William Dieterle, United States, 1953) | 7 | 36 |
| 4 | *The Merry Widow* | 9 | 31 |
| 5 | *The Robe* (Henry Koster, United States, 1953) | 1 | 27 |
| **Naples** | | | |
| 1 | *Lucrèce Borgia* | 11 | 54 |
| 2 | *Salome* | 10 | 52 |
| 3 | *Anni facili* | 10 | 50 |
| 4 | *…e Napoli canta* (Armando Grottini, Italy, 1953) | 12 | 45 |
| 5 | *The Prisoner of Zenda* | 8 | 43 |

**Bari**

| | | | |
|---|---|---|---|
| 1 | *Vortice* (Raffaello Matarazzo, Italy, 1953) | 2 | 8 |
| 2 | *Robin Hood* (Michael Curtiz, William Keighley, United States, 1938) | 1 | 7 |
| 3 | *Pane, amore e fantasia* (Luigi Comencini, Italy, 1953) | 1 | 7 |
| 4 | *Un turco napoletano* (Mario Mattoli, Italy, 1953) | 2 | 7 |
| 5 | *Frine, cortigiana d'Oriente* (Mario Bonnard, Italy, 1953) | 1 | 6 |

**Palermo**

| | | | |
|---|---|---|---|
| 1 | *Pane, amore e fantasia* | 3 | 13 |
| 2 | *Sul ponte dei sospiri* (Antonio Leonviola, Italy, 1953) | 4 | 11 |
| 3 | *Una di quelle* (Aldo Fabrizi, Italy, 1953) | 2 | 10 |
| 4 | *Roman Holiday* (William Wyler, United States, 1953) | 2 | 10 |
| 5 | *Balocchi e profumi* (F. M. De Bernardi, Natale Montillo, Italy, 1953) | 3 | 9 |

**Cagliari**

| | | | |
|---|---|---|---|
| 1 | *The Story of Three Loves* (Vincente Minnelli, Gottfried Reinhardt, United States, 1953) | 2 | 13 |
| 2 | *Giuseppe Verdi* (Raffaello Matarazzo, Italy, 1953) | 1 | 10 |
| 3 | *The Prisoner of Zenda* | 1 | 8 |
| 4 | *Cavalleria Rusticana* (Carmine Gallone, Italy, 1953) | 2 | 6 |
| 5 | *South Sea Woman* | 1 | 6 |

also corroborate the unevenness of the 'geographical distribution of cinema consumption' (Fanchi 2019: 389).

As Charles R. Acland (2005: 62–3) states, the 'schedule is essential to the routinization of filmgoing' and our participants vividly remember both the habitual and the unruly practices that regulated their leisure time. The 'temporal boundary' (Acland 2005: 64) of the leisure activity is remembered through several dimensions: as the schedule and the running time of the actual films; as the days and the length of the theatrical run; as the time lag between premieres in major cities and circulation through smaller areas. When remembering the days and the length of the theatrical run, audiences mention programming choices associated with specific days of the week to attract different types of spectators, a practice used by experienced exhibitors in search of maximizing the profit of their offerings. Cities like Milan or Turin offered less affluent audiences the possibility to see new films for free on a Sunday morning in specific first-run cinemas, like the Astra and the Odeon (Enea, b. 1935, Milan), and the same films both in third run, even if for only a few days (Francesco, b. 1933, Torino province). When looking at the case of a big city like Rome, the distinction in terms of length of theatrical run between a luxurious city centre cinema and a third-run venue in the outskirts is significant, as illustrated by Figure 2.1 (see Treveri Gennari and Sedgwick 2015), in which each coloured dot represents a cinema and each colour groups cinemas which had different turnovers of films. It clearly shows how a film could stay in a first-run cinema for over a month and in a third run for one day.

This, however, was not an experience shared systematically in all areas (Fanchi 2019). Taking a second-tier city like Bari as an example, we have analysed a different set of data (the offer available in the year of 1952). This has revealed that, out of the total number of 1,473 films, 48 per cent would change every day, and 25 per cent every second day, with an average lifespan of three days. This inconsistency across different geographical areas is obviously reflected in the memories of the audiences, and while in a major city one could, 'depending on the time of the shows, move from one cinema to another to see two or three films on the same day' (Adolfo, b. 1940, Naples province), in rural areas, 'if you were a film enthusiast, you had to travel across small centres to find the films you wanted to see' (Antonio, b. 1941, Bari province). Audiences' journeys to the cinema will be further discussed in the next section.

Within this context the memories of the exhibitors are also useful, as they demonstrate how well they knew their customers and how much they tried to respond to their needs, as in the example of a female exhibitor in Puglia. Maria Gabriella (b. 1942, Bari province), who ran a family cinema with her brothers, was very knowledgeable when describing her audiences, who were predominantly male, because female audiences could not attend the cinema at the weekend, as the venues were crowded, full of fights and sexual encounters. This high level of competence allowed exhibitors to programme their films with great ability and in a very strategic manner. This was at times remembered by more perceptive audience members, like Antonio (b. 1941, Bari province), whose proximity to the film industry (his brother had worked with the film director Sergio Leone

Cinemas, Exhibition Practices and Topographical Memories        41

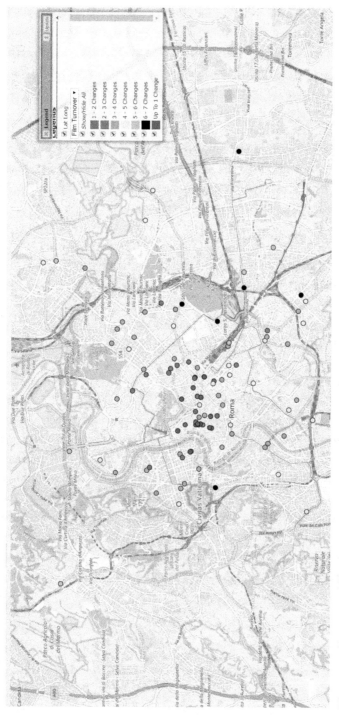

**Figure 2.1** Turnover of films in cinemas in Rome (*Italian Cinema Audiences* geovisualization).

and he was himself involved in the industry) made him more alert to some of the processes of film distribution and circulation: Antonio describes that sometimes an extra film was added to the programme to attract people to the cinema, and while this was often a cheap product, it might provide audiences with the opportunity to see some of the classic filmmakers, such as Fritz Lang. As Maria Teresa (b. 1942, Milan) states, 'By selecting the films, they [the exhibitors] selected the audience.' Another participant, Edoardo (b. 1938, Turin), remembers that the cinema Corso in Turin showed only Metro Goldwyn Mayer (MGM) films.

The discrepancy in film availability becomes a more significant issue when looking at the time lag between premieres in major cities and circulation through smaller areas. In regard to this, audiences talk of the waiting time for the arrival of a successful film in their area. This could range from a week to several years, as Carmen (b. 1936, Naples province), Dada (b. 1932, Milan province) and Luciana (b. 1943, Naples) remind us in relation to the waiting time on the outskirts of a big city like Naples or in a town of only five thousand people.[9]

## Topographical memories, spaces and emotions

The use of geographical visualization tools in the ICA project in combination with an analysis of spectators' topographical memories has guided us through the geography of cinemagoing, forcing us to investigate how participants describe their journeys to and from the cinema and what this geographical memory means to them (see Ercole et al. 2017; Kuhn 2002: 35). Beyond the analysis of the post-war Italian exhibition sector – summarized in the first section of this chapter – our interest lies in the relationship of this sector with the audiences. As Holohan (2017: 2–3) states, 'Critical focus has been brought to bear on the cultural and economic processes and interpersonal relations through which spaces and places achieve their particular character and meaning in our social and emotional lives.' As spaces and places, cinemas are no different, and by connecting the spaces and their stories, we aim to move away from a type of space that Michel Foucault (1980: 70) defines as 'dead', and 'fixed', and develop story maps,

---

[9] See also the survey published by Gerosa (1954) 'Scene della nostra vita in provincia' in *Rassegna del film*, where an interviewee from S. Giovanni in Persiceto (Bologna province) remembered a waiting time of fifteen to twenty days to reach their town after the films arrived in Bologna, and another from the town of Moncalvo in Piedmont lamented that young people now had motorbikes and could go to Asti to the cinema to see newer films, so attendance in the local cinemas was falling.

which 'are records of specific journeys … They are deep maps too, that register history, and that acknowledge the way. memory and landscape layer and interleave' (Macfarlane 2007: 141–5). As part of this process, we have asked ourselves questions about audiences' journey to and from the cinemas they visited, about the choices they made and the reasons behind those choices.

Drawing from the work of Colin Arrowsmith and Deb Verhoeven (2011), Kate Bowles (2013) and Jeff Klenotic (2011), we were also inspired by research published in 1979 by Roger Hart, 'Children's Experience of Place', an empirical study of the development of children's place experience and their active engagement with their environment (New England). In particular, Hart's concept of spatial exploration in relation to gender was a starting point to look back at our data and – more specifically – at a theme we had called 'topographical memory', from which we were able to extract some enlightening findings. We have discovered, in fact, that the video interviews lead to a richer understanding of the spatial and geographical dimensions of memory, as we, for example, analyse how our participants reconstructed their journeys around their cities, or try to remember the location of a particular cinema. How was this journey described? Was the journey the same in big or small cities, for children or young adults, for female and male audiences? As opposed to empirical data, mapping memories means mapping uncertain data, a concept similar to mapping literary spaces, as often divergences occur between real locations and what participants remember. This imprecise geography common to literary spaces as well as to memory needs different approaches, where the precision of the map is put against the imprecision of the emotions, and 'emotionally heightened spaces' can be identified (Anderson and Smith 2001: 1). One of our interviewees, Franca (b. 1938, Rome) vividly recreates these emotionally heightened spaces when narrating her cinemagoing experience in 1950s Rome:

Interviewer: Franca, do you remember the names of some cinemas or the itinerary to get there? Or if you were loyal customers of a cinema …

FP: Yes, when I moved to Rome, there was a small cinema, the Cristallo, on the way down Via Sforza, near Santa Maria Maggiore, where we lived. It was a cinema where we saw many films, but it was near home, so we didn't get to enjoy a long walk. Instead, for the Cinema Trevi, where we could enter for free, thanks to the usher who knew us, we arrived there after a long walk. We could see Rome, we passed through the tunnel, or we took the stairs near it to see the Quirinal

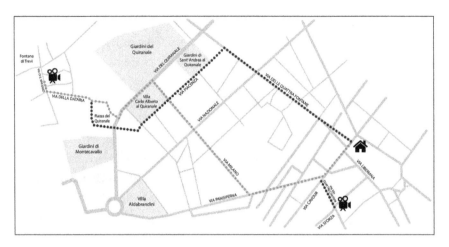

**Figure 2.2** Mapping Franca's journeys to the cinema (*Italian Cinema Audiences* geovisualization).

>Palace. Then, we went down the steps and saw some places, and the few tourists who were there. There were few cars, we could walk and take long strolls. It was a long walk up to the Trevi, I went with one of my friends. We still remember these moments, when we meet and we think about how long the walk was and how we did not notice it. Afternoons like these were great, we had a wonderful life.

When mapping Franca's journey to the cinemas in Rome, the geographical visualization shows not only the choice she had within her neighbourhood but also how she was able to walk what she describes 'a fair distance' (1.6 km) across different parts of this specific neighbourhood in order to go to the cinema (Figure 2.2). This is an unusual practice not just across Italy, but in cinemagoing memories more broadly, as Sam Manning (2016: 544) notes, for example, in the case of post-war Belfast, where many 'early memories of cinemagoing were linked to a small geographical area and were largely confined to the cinemagoing options available locally'.

However, in Franca's emotionally heightened memory of her geographical surroundings her travelling across the city is described as a real journey. This mode of description is not exclusive to Franca, as several other participants who lived in big cities have similar recollections. Franca's narration is detailed about the environment, which is described with no cars, few people around and only some tourists. In Franca's mind, she is almost like a tourist herself, who travels by foot and experiences the city through the journey to the cinema. The two cinemas she refers to (the Cristallo, close to home, and the Trevi, far away) serve – in fact – different but very precise functions. The first one is home: Franca's statement that 'you get out of the house and get into the cinema' makes it like an extension of the house itself and a physical place of shelter. The second, on the other hand, represents the adventure, the opportunity to explore, to become a visitor in her own city. Franca, in fact, reminds the interviewer that she had moved to Rome not long before, almost highlighting her role as a foreigner in her own urban environment. When trying to comprehend how Rome could have been as a city to explore in the 1950s, Franca's description seems to undermine a broad social discourse on the relationship between women and urban environment, reproduced in well-known photographs such as Ruth Orkin's *An American Girl in Italy* (1951) or Mario De Biasi's *Gli italiani si voltano/The Italians Turn Around* (1954). Franca's account, in fact, is refreshing in challenging the deep-rooted popular idea of the Italian public space as belonging to the male gaze. It is closer to what Virginia Woolf (1930) calls 'street haunting' in an essay by that name, where she describes 'the greatest pleasure of town life ...: rambling the streets of London'. The street haunting to which Woolf refers is, however, not purposeless (as in the case of the *flâneur*) but led by an object: a pencil to buy. This is very similar to Franca's description, where the final aim represented by the pencil in Woolf's case is replaced by the cinema to attend, as an excuse to become 'part of that vast republican army of anonymous trampers' (Woolf 1930). The female *flâneur*'s transgression is precisely indicated in Franca's description. Obviously as a woman, the *flâneuse* does not have the 'same freedom to stroll the streets as her male counterpart' (Dreyer and McDowall 2012: 30). This limitation, however, does not restrain the desire to explore the city streets, as the female *flâneur* is able to achieve that with subterfuge: by using a final aim to do so, by being accompanied, by going out in the daytime and by moving in central areas rather than in dark corners of the metropolis. Franca's spatial conditions, in fact, are delimited by the city centre, where the liveliness of the area protects her from the dangers of the suburbs and the purpose of going to the cinema offers her an excuse to explore without pushing the boundaries of her transgression.

While the *flâneuse* has been explored over the years (from Marianne Breslauer's *Défense d'Afficher* in 1936 to Lauren Elkin's *Flâneuse: Women Walk the City in Paris, New York, Tokyo, Venice, and London*, published in 2016), the dimension of the transgression, the role of the urban space and the desire to see and be seen as the female *flâneur* are all aspects less well investigated within

Italian culture. Our audiences' memories allow us to give voice to what Janet Wolff (1985) calls 'The Invisible Flâneuse', since nearly all the major texts on the experience of living in and walking through cities have been in masculine voices. Franca's experience reflects the *flâneuse*'s use of 'the street as corridors and not as a destination itself' (van Nes and My Nguyen 2009: 1). It also shows that female desire of gaining independence and negotiating public spaces by strolling through the city was as much an Italian phenomenon as elsewhere, and at odds with what Fanchi (2019: 390) terms the 'masculinization of cinema audiences ... spurred by both the Catholic Church and left-wing political groups, which joined forces to keep women inside their domestic walls'.

These geographical spaces, however, are not the same for all audiences, as moving around smaller towns and villages was more problematic for female spectators. Eugenia (b. 1925, Cagliari), for example, could not travel as far as Giorgio (b. 1929, Cagliari) in the same city. This discrepancy has been monitored across all the data available and is more evident in smaller centres, in the south of the country and certainly in rural areas. Another Sardinian participant – Ida (b. 1943, Cagliari province) – living in a village of just over three thousand inhabitants which only had one cinema at the time, started travelling to Cagliari (and only accompanied by a male relative) from the 1990s, when the local cinema had closed down. A longer journey was not contemplated at the time for a young woman to take in order to go to the cinema with friends, let alone by herself. This was not only an experience remembered by female audiences who were very young and lived in the rural south of the country. Luciana (b. 1943, Turin) remembers her experience in Turin, where her brother-in-law threatened her when he heard she had gone alone to the cinema at the age of 21. Male spectators, like Alessandro (b. 1942, Rome province) and Franco (b. 1938, Rome province), were able to travel more extensively and therefore had access to different cinemas and a wider range of films. Certain restrictions, in fact, were completely unknown to male audiences. If one analyses Franca's testimony, this gender imbalance becomes more evident.

I: So, what are the strongest memories you have of the cinema of those years, that is until the early '60s? Memories ...

F: The memories, when I was in Canterano, we would go to a cinema in Subiaco, sometimes ... this, now, you'll even laugh ... sometimes we'd go by donkey.

I: On the back of ...

F: On the back of a donkey, because my father had land very close to the town of Subiaco, that is, he was bordering ...
I: But the distance, let's say, how far was ...?
F: If we had to go by the provincial road, the distance ... 11 kilometers.
I: So, a lot.
F: But we passed through the countryside ... 3–4 kilometers and we would arrive in Subiaco.
I: An hour by mule.
FM: One hour, one hour and a half, so ...
I: Sure, sure.
FM: We went with others, not just me, eh.
I: So with several mules or all of them ...?
FM: Donkeys, almost all of them donkeys. We ...
I: You were in a group, let's say.
FM: We would make up a group ... 'We want to go to the cinema to see something' ... that there was nothing there. The countryside ...

This is a story of male friends, allowed to travel for almost two hours on a donkey to reach the closer village to go to the cinema. A similar story was never recounted by a woman, supporting the gender-related differences that operated in terms of socialization for boys and girls in relation to 'parentally defined' ranges of spatial activities (Hart 1979: 43) (see Chapter 8 for further discussion of this). Obviously, the patterns are more complex than this spatial analysis might suggest but on the whole, marked differences are found between the spatial range of male and female leisure activities.

Going back to the original questions about the reasons for audiences' journeys to and from cinemas, it appears that the travelling is often justified by the participants in different ways. Franco explains the need to embark on a long journey to reach a town with a cinema because 'there was nothing' in his own village. While he justifies his brother's presence because without him, he would not have access to the only form of transport available (the donkey) to reach the neighbouring village, he also describes his journey as a collective experience, where friends were an integral part of that leisure activity (or adventure). In her story, Franca explains that her reason – or the excuse – to get to the cinema further away from home was that she knew the usher and she could get in for free. However, the way she describes her journey makes it a more important part of this experience, one that is worth taking into account. In both cases, the environment seems to be at the same time a tool for discovery and an 'instrument for socialization' (Hart 1979: 345), which both lie at the heart of the experience of cinemagoing.

As our broader aim in the ICA research has been to interrogate our own project, by using, for example, the archival material on cinemas embedded in the map, we have created an 'affective narrative space' (Wood et al. 2010: 180) in which emotions and memories are valued for what they can tell us about our participants' cinemagoing experience in 1950s Italy, as well as how they currently reminisce about that experience. However, as Caquard and Cartwright (2014: 103) state,

> The cartography of emotions remains a major challenge due to the dehumanizing character of maps, at least in their conventional form. The map is a rationalized representation of place that is rather limited for conveying emotions.

Following Caquard and Cartwright's warning, the ICA project has attempted in its work with maps to understand them as a process and not as a finished result. This has been possible with the online digital archive, CineRicordi, where the starting point is the map, co-curated by its users. This was a choice carefully made to resolve that 'implicit duality' of production and consumption of the map only possible 'if users become involved in the production process' (Del Casino and Hanna 2006: 35, 40). This methodological decision has allowed participants to contribute to the maps with both their memories and the physical and tangible traces of those memories: digitized artefacts related to cinemagoing belonging to the members who used to attend cinemas in the 1950s. This process has the intention of 'linking maps with narratives' (Caquard and Cartwright 2014: 105), which results in a living archive of Italian cinema history. It also ensures that the maps 'are ... always mappings; ... always in the process of becoming' (Kitchin and Dodge 2007: 331).

## Conclusion

Sébastien Caquard and D. R. Fraser Taylor's editorial in *The Cartographic Journal* (2009) on cinematic cartography formally recognized the interactions between geography and cinema. However, several challenges remain in using spatial methodology in audience studies. We have employed geographical visualization of cinematic data to triangulate historical programming and exhibition data against the oral history and this chapter has confirmed the necessity of making use of this type of visualization in a more systematic manner. By integrating our collected data (questionnaires and video interviews) with new and unexplored archival resources (digitized artefacts related to cinemagoing as well as crowdsourced collections from individuals' private archives), the CineRicordi digital archive applies a 'deep-mapping' methodology to explore and investigate this wide range of data. A 'deep map' – as Bailey and Biggs (2012: 326) describe it, is a process of 'observing, listening, walking, conversing, writing and exchanging … of selecting, reflecting, naming, and generating … [and] of digitizing, interweaving, offering and inviting'. This process obviously allows the research to remain open-ended and continue to invite new contributions and fresh queries. The deep-mapping technique has also enabled us to triangulate oral history, reception and programming data, offering new insights into the relationship between spatial practices of cinemagoing and memories of the same practices. The cartographic dimension of our participants' narratives has demonstrated the importance of space not only in the reminiscence process but also in the way audiences engaged with urban and rural environments, with the space of film consumption, as well as with the journey to and from the cinema. The oral history interviews' significant contribution to spatial historiography illustrated in this chapter is a reminder of the necessity to engage with a wide range of methodological approaches in order to adequately interrogate the data and reach a fuller understanding of audiences' experience of cinemagoing.

# 3

# Only entertainment?: Memories inside and outside the cinema

In Richard Dyer's (1992) book *Only Entertainment*, the emphasis on the primacy of pleasure sets the cinema experience apart from other forms of art. 'Entertainment' is a synonym for pleasure but equally for concepts as capacious as 'escapism, glamour, fun, stardom and excitement', as well as phrases like 'it takes your mind off things' and 'it's only entertainment' (Dyer 1992: 1). Dyer's attention is primarily focused on the industry of entertainment and on entertainment from the point of view of the provider. This chapter will broaden the concept of entertainment by merging it with an audience perspective; it will also expand our understanding of the experience of entertainment, including the audience's experiences outside the cinemas (Allen 2011). Extra-theatrical experience, in fact, is equally important in the memories of Italian audiences, as they refer to inside and outside the theatre as part of the same practice – and memory – of cinemagoing. The chapter will explore aspects as diverse as silence and noise, courting and molestation (Klinger 2006), but also food consumption, family dynamics, social experiences and isolation. The inattentiveness inside the cinema space – a characteristic shared by Italian audiences – for instance, will be analysed here in Butsch's (2000: 288) terms, as a phenomenon that demonstrates both 'independence' and 'familiarity' with the filmic text, and will be part of the many rituals inside and outside the cinemas through which audiences relay their process of recollection.

## Cinema, entertainment and the emotional community of cinemagoers

When looking at entertainment, Dyer's (1992: 21) discussion of 'the complex of meanings in the social-cultural situation' in which entertainment forms are produced must undoubtedly be broadened to include the sociocultural situation in which they are consumed. In order to investigate the role of entertainment for the audience, one needs to shift the focus from the point of view of the provider to the context of consumption. Maltby (2007) suggests that

> an examination of the ways in which the cinema has provided a site and an occasion for particular forms of social behaviour, or of the ways in which individual movies have specified the nature of the site, the occasion, and the behaviour, is an enquiry into the production of meaning, but that meaning is social, not textual.

This approach – at the heart of New Cinema History – has also been the focus of the Italian Cinema Audiences (ICA) project. It has allowed us to position cinema in relation to other forms of entertainment and leisure more broadly (Dyer 1992: 7–8). The ICA responses reflect on the role of cinemagoing in comparison to other leisure activities such as dancing, listening to the radio, reading or playing a sport. If the majority of the questionnaire respondents (977 out of 1,043) affirm they used to go to the cinema, the practice of other activities was not as prominent, and was distributed among going out with friends (451), reading books (355) and magazines (144), dancing (293), playing sport (219) and going to the theatre (84). This confirms statistical data relative to a gradual increase in per capita income among Italians, which is then reflected in increased cultural consumption (Scarpellini 2018). It also corroborates cinema's popularity over all other activities in the period, making it 'the new cultural medium of reference' (ibid.: 23).

The ICA respondents' memories provide further insight into the range of reasons why cinema was chosen over other cultural activities. In certain geographical locations, cinemagoing was 'the only available' pastime (Marina, b. 1950, Rome), while affordability was also a determining factor in cinema's popularity when compared with other leisure activities. In order to understand the significance of cinema in the lives of Italians, we have asked ourselves what function cinemagoing could perform that other popular types of leisure did not. The 'social dimension' of going to the cinema was possibly the main recurrent explanation given by our audiences. Following Tribe's (2015: 3–4) distinction between 'home-based recreation' and 'away from home', our participants stated they preferred the latter, often associating cinema with other sociable forms of leisure, like team sports for example. Playing football, in fact, was for many male members of our audiences, as central to their lives as cinema was, offering insights into the structure of society, as sport as much as leisure 'are processes which themselves have a determining influence over people's lives' (Hill 2003: 2). Giuseppe (b. 1947, Cagliari) describes a sort of continuity between the two activities: 'After playing football and having a snack, I would go to the cinema (as it was dark and you could not play football anymore) and you would meet the friends who would be doing the same thing.' Giuseppe's statement explains that cinema's social dimension was the main attraction and almost a continuation of that sports activity. Cinema was part of a wider form of entertainment, what another member of the audience (Giovanna, b. 1941, Naples province) details as 'always a way to go out', a social act where at times films did not even have a place. It was included in what Giampiero (b. 1949, Bari) describes as the 'normal family routine', as 'embedded in the larger practice … that included socializing with one's peers' (Butsch 2000: 11). This is perhaps why, in the memories of our participants, cinemagoing was often exactly the opposite of that 'concentrated audiovisual attention' to which Hanich (2014: 347) refers when the shift of the audiences' attention is directed to the 'the common intentional object of the film'.

The cinema experience is, in fact, not remembered as described by Thomas Elsaesser (1981: 271) with the viewer 'pinned to his seat' and 'enclosed in a darkened room, cut off visually from the surroundings and exposed to a state of isolation'. It is also not purely, however, as Benjamin (1969: 14) puts it, 'a simultaneous collective experience'. For our audiences, it is an experience at the same time collective and individual, singular and social. It is much closer to Edgar Morin's description (1956 cited in 2005: 97):

> So there he [the cinema spectator] is, isolated, but at the heart of a human environment, of a great gelatin of common soul, of a collective participation, which accordingly amplifies his individual participation. To be isolated and in a group at the same time: two contradictory and complementary conditions.

This description is echoed by one of our participants, Maria (b. 1946, Bari province), who describes her 'experience' in these terms: 'The cinema is atmosphere, passion … The theatre that becomes dark while the first images appear on the screen … being among people but isolated at the same time.' The combination of individual and collective dimensions of cinemagoing described by Maria also reminds us of the idea of the emotional community suggested by Rosenwein as 'a group in which people have a common stake, interest, values, and goals' in order to stress 'the social and relational nature of emotions' (2006: 25). The emotional community of cinemagoers occupies a space which is private and public at the same time, where shared emotions are experienced collectively and their true social dimension celebrated (Shouse 2005). When translated into memories, these emotions remain collective (Halbwachs 1992) and rely 'on the dynamics of groups such as families, social classes, and religious communities', as 'an individual's social interactions with the members of his or her group determine how one remembers experiences from the past and what it is that he or she remembers' (Russell 2006: 796). Moreover, if the 'sole (conscious) aim' of entertainment is to provide pleasure, as Dyer (1992: 19) believes, we can affirm that several of those memories are 'memories closely connected with pleasure, beauty, as well as enrichment and self-esteem, which produce optimistic thoughts and positive feelings during the remembrance' (Treveri Gennari 2018: 42). Cinema is – like other forms of entertainment – 'different, special, a treat' (Dyer 1992: 175) and this exact definition is repeated several times by our participants, who identify cinema as not only 'escape' and 'wish-fulfilment', offering the image of 'something better' to escape into (ibid.: 20), but also as a reward of pleasure. Going to the cinema is described by our audiences as a present (Angela, b. 1939, Milan province), the prize to obtain if one behaved well at home or at school (Antonio, b. 1934, Bari province; Carmen, b. 1936, Naples province) or if one did all the chores in the house (Alfredo, b. 1928, Rome province), as well as a reward for the weekend after a full week of study (Maria Bianco, b. 1931, Bari province).

## Inside the cinema: Rituals and dynamics

Ravi Vasudevan's (2003) idea that cinema is not only 'distinctive' because 'you can't experience it elsewhere, or through any other medium' but also 'continuous with the space in which it is located' points us to our next theme: the cinema itself. This space must be taken into account, as, according to Phil Hubbard (2003: 255), 'we can only understand the appeal of [multiplex] cinemas by considering the embodied geographies of cinemagoing – a leisure practice that involves the consumption of place as well as the visual consumption of film'. The significance of the space of film consumption is evident when analysing the memories of their audiences. We refer here to 'inside' when talking about the cinema itself, the cinema space created by the architecture as well as the relation of this space to the act of watching the films.

The space of film consumption is central in cinemagoing memories, and it allows us to frame cinemagoing as a free-standing activity, as a practice chosen by the audience for its function, its role and its value. Exploring the memories inside the cinema offers the opportunity to better understand the 'etiquette' of cinemagoing, those behavioural codes audiences are aware of, respect, but are – at the same time – often tempted to break. Modes of dress, eating habits, seating arrangements and personal conduct are all unwritten conventions that informed audiences on how to behave in a glamorous first-run cinema in the centre or in a fleapit on the outskirts of the city. The ICA respondents refer – for instance – to the need to wear Sunday clothes when going to the cinema, as it was not appropriate to wear work garments: Paolo (b. 1936, Florence) reminds us that his mother would prompt him to 'dress properly' before going to the cinema, as there was a definite distinction between clothes for every day and clothes for exceptional circumstances, such as going to the cinema.

Two aspects will be taken into account here: (1) the multisensory experience that involves, together with viewing, sound, smell and texture, all in direct connection with the cinema space; and (2) the performance, articulated in two different ways: the act of performing cinema rituals, but also performance against the restrictions, and audiences as performance.

## Multisensory experience

Although 'the idea of "the sensory" has been slower to filter into the methodological consciousness and tools of researchers, than that of "the visual"' (Mason and Davies 2009: 589), the multisensory experience – or what Casetti (2015: 188) describes as the *sensory doing* – is a dimension often remembered by our audiences. This can be articulated, for example, as experiencing the film not only 'through our eyes' but also through 'our entire bodily being' (Sobchack 2004: 63). In his research, Luis Rocha Antunes (2016: 3) associates this multisensory dimension of the film experience predominantly with the viewing of the film itself, indicating that 'there is no such thing – as a purely visual – experience of film. What we see, or what we call seeing, is multisensory in its nature.' However, his approach – as well as others who have been reflecting on the cinematic experience (such as Vivian Sobchack, Jennifer Barker and Laura U. Marks) – does not take into account the context of the act of film consumption, where that multisensory experience is augmented and enriched by its surroundings. And this is what most often audiences remember. We refer here to the smoke of cigarettes, the texture of the velvet chairs in the luxurious first-run cinemas versus the uncomfortable wooden seats of the fleapit venues that would 'produce pain all over your body' – as Dario (b. 1937, Naples) reminds us – the taste of the food bought from the usherettes or taken from home, the sound of the astonishing laughter (Antonio, b. 1938, Milan), screaming (Graziella, b. 1940, Rome), the noise of the peanut shells on the floor of the cinema or of a spectator beating an egg (Graziella, b. 1940, Rome)[1] as well as the sweat of the bodies often too close to each other in overcrowded cinemas (Francesca, b. 1943, Palermo province), the perfume of the flowers in a pop-up outdoor venue or the heat of the summer evenings at the open-air cinema. Vittoriano (b. 1941, Bari) remembers the act of eating lupin beans or chickpeas, displaying that memory in its multisensory nature: the colour (yellow), the texture (slightly burnt and humid, as soaked in water) and the taste are all combined in his description as a 'joy, a pure pleasure'. It is a cinema – as Brian Larkin (2008: 149) states in his study of Nigerian audiences – that 'overwhelms the senses'. That intimate connection between eating, but also smell, place and memory, reinforces the importance of the senses, as a new pleasure is triggered in the moment of remembering. The multisensory experience, in fact, can function as 'an intermediary of memory reconstruction' in the process of reminiscence (Low 2013: 701). The soundscape researcher Helmi Järviluoma (2009) explains this connection between an event and the emotional state at the time of recall, defining this notion of re-experiencing a sonic event as 'hearing-point memory'. Several of these moments took place when we asked our audiences to share their memories at our public engagement events in cinemas, and were critical for the process of reconstructing in the present the memories of the past.

Going back to Hanich's context in which the film experience takes place, our participants' memories highlight how the multisensory experience is very much influenced by the architecture of the cinema, where the surroundings impact on the cinema experience as a whole, and the physicality of the space is intertwined with the spectators' behaviour, the organization of the public experience in many forms, whether it is identification, passiveness or intermittent attention. Thus, the notion of embodiment – according to Vivian Sobchack – is crucial: the spectator is neither ideal nor absolute, but bonded to his/her physicality. Maria (b. 1946, Bari province), for example, describes how she felt important when she could view the film from the gallery: a seating arrangement that made her physical positioning distinct and her experience more special. Elena's (b. 1940,

---

[1] To make 'uovo sbattuto' (beaten egg yolk and sugar).

Milan) memory of watching *Bambi* (James Algar, Samuel Armstrong, United States, 1942) emerges from remembering the balcony of the Cinema Odeon in Milan. As suggested by these examples, the seating has significant impact on the experience itself, and confirms Szczepaniak-Gillece's (2016: 253) idea that 'to examine the legacy of theatre chairs is to untangle the relationships between cinema, physicality, efficiency and film's ties to passivity; this inconspicuous thing encloses an entire history of cinematic bodies and, in turn, a shadow history of spectatorship'.

The physicality of the spectatorship is also linked to the architectural arrangements of the venue, as our participants remember the feeling of crowding on the floor at the front of the auditorium as children (Nicola, b. 1931, Bari), or courting in the back rows of the cinemas as adults (Antonio, b. 1933, Naples),[2] developing a distinct perception – and an embodied memory – of that experience. This process is enhanced during 'the activity of recounting or telling memory-stories … in other words, of performances of memory' (Kuhn 2010b: 298). However, the performance of memory – as Kuhn (2010b: 299) describes it – as 're-enactments of the past … both in and with visual media', is different from the performance of the audience in the cinema, which is the topic of the next section.

## Performance

The 1950s – the period under investigation in the ICA project – were years of major changes in Italy. The rebirth of the economic and social infrastructure was accompanied by substantial transformation in the cultural make-up of the country. The expansion of radio, television and the press was followed by a growing consumption of goods. These radical changes within Italian society created new audiences that started to develop new tastes and became gradually more segmented (Eugeni and Fanchi 2015: 293). However, what the literature on the period doesn't explore is the way this new audience performed within – and outside but in relation to the cinema space. A more traditional type of performance is seen in Italian cinemas through the *avanspettacolo* (variety shows either before the screening or during the intervals between the first and the second

---

[2] 'They were couples, what were they doing? They would go in, throw themselves in the last row of seats, put themselves there … and as soon as the lights went out, they practically didn't think about the film at all, the film.'

part of the film), which often allowed audiences to see their favourite actors live in the cinema space. However, this chapter will concentrate predominantly on the spectators' performance: we will analyse their attitude towards the rules and rituals established in the cinemas, their responses to the restrictions imposed within these spaces, but also their performance outside the cinema venue.

## Cinema rituals and restrictions

When looking at the performance of cinema rituals and the response to restrictions, it is immediately visible how the ICA participants show awareness of certain behavioural codes linked to the experience of going to the cinema. These rituals not only referred to the regularity of the attendance on certain days at certain times, as Emanuele (b. 1937, Cagliari province) states, 'but in principle there were the habitués who went to the cinema anyway, they had their hours'. The practice of cinemagoing included, for instance, modes of dress. Fashioning the body had a profound impact especially as it gratified women's increasing desire for modernization and status outside the home (see Buckley 2006, 2008, 2013; Paulicelli 2008) (see also Chapter 7).[3] This 'embodied social transformation' was also evident within the cinema, a space which represented, in addition to the freedom of hiding within a darkened auditorium, the possibility of seeing and being seen. The cinema space presented itself with a series of codes and conventions. When unsure of the appropriate attitude to display in the cinema, a list of commandments about proper behaviour, printed in the local Catholic weekly newspaper *La Trebbia* in Bobbio (Piacenza), would come to the rescue of the spectators, as in Figure 3.1 (29 September 1956).

Figure 3.1 presents several of the codes articulated by our audiences in their memories: from restrictions on attending cinemas based on gender, tipping the usherettes or interacting with strangers, to how to properly sit and comport oneself within the confinement of the seat, to how to react to inappropriate and immoral films. However, etiquette and good manners have rarely been praised in the memories of our audiences. On the contrary, more frequent were the memories of violation of those rules, of unruly demeanour witnessed by the participants and reprimanded by cinema managers, especially when – as Andrea (b. 1947, Florence province) reminds us – the film had scenes the audiences

---

[3] The relationship between women, modernity and cinemagoing is not exclusive to Italy. See the case of Turkey, discussed in Akbulut (2017).

# Al cinematografo ci si comporta così

D. — Una ragazza può andare da sola al cinematografo almeno di giorno?

R. — No, e di giorno specialmente. I cinema di giorno sono frequentati da molti sfaccendati in cerca d'avventure.

D. — Dovendo conquistare due posti in mezzo a una fila già piena, deve passare prima la signora o prima l'uomo?

R. — Prima l'uomo per farle strada.

D. — E' lecito chiedere alla persona che ci sta davanti e che muove continuamente la testa, di smetterla?

R. — Si può chiederlo e soltanto in casi estremi e con tutto il garbo possibile.

D. — E' necessario dare la mancia alla «maschera» del cinema?

R. — Non è necessario ma è gentile. Le signore se ne asterranno a meno che la «maschera» si sia data molta pena per loro.

D. — La pelliccia o il cappotto si possono tenere sulle ginocchia o si devono lasciare sulla spalliera della poltrona?

R. — Si possono tenere sulle ginocchia ma sistemandole in modo che non disturbino i vicini.

D. — Si può chiedere un fiammifero per la sigaretta al proprio vicino sconosciuto?

R. — L'uomo senz'altro, la signora farebbe bene ad astenersene se mai lo faccia durante gl' intervalli e quando l'altro accende la sua sigaretta.

D. — Se un film è francamente immorale è lecito dirlo ad alta voce?

R. — Le dimostrazioni di biasimo ad alta voce non sono mai molto corrette; meglio alzarsi ed andarsene senza dir nulla.

**Figure 3.1** How to behave inside the cinema (*La Trebbia*, 29 September 1956).

were not interested in. This behaviour presents several readings, and Carmen's (b. 1936, Naples province) description of what happened in the cinema helps us interpret and analyse this behaviour:

> Almost all the films we saw were 'cowboy' films. The seats in this cinema were made of wood and it was mostly attended by males … boys. At that moment in the film when the cavalry arrived they lifted the seats and slammed them up and down causing an ungodly racket. It wasn't enough to wake my sister (who often fell asleep) but it would make me laugh. Although … the first few times it frightened me.

Carmen's memory is not unusual. It is shared by several other participants of the project. It can be deciphered simply as a reaction to social norms (Hanich

2014: 346) where slamming chairs, shouting, dancing in the aisles during musicals, singing and any verbal interactions prevail over the 'quiet attention' dedicated to the film (ibid.: 338). Giuseppe (b. 1942, Cagliari) believes that in some cases, it was almost the main reason to go to the cinema:

> And in the evening, most people would go and see … not so much to see the film, they would go and hear the jokes of these young men who would make fun of each other … jokes for actors, or someone who would spit out or throw nuts. There were all of them. And people would go, they'd put themselves under the gallery, because it was the gallery, to hear these things.

This detailed description certainly contradicts Jacques Aumont's idea that 'one of the characters that define the experience of cinema is an uninterrupted and completed vision' and that 'film is something to be watched in its succession and in its integrity' (Casetti 2015: 192). Films were experienced by our audiences in very different ways, and certainly not in the succession and integrity advocated by Aumont. Allowing the spectators to enter the cinema whenever they wanted – a practice not exclusive to Italy at the time – meant that different sections of the films were reassembled at the end, forcing the audience to watch the films' narrative not in order as Marta (b. 1939, Milan) says. Not being forced to exit at the end of the film also meant that audiences would experience films often in a consecutive loop. Respecting the starting time of the film was seen by Marta as 'a bit constricting, like the theatre', and cinema for her was something less demanding than theatre, something that would not need adherence to norms. A 'reaction to the social norm' is perhaps the most common way in which audiences articulate their memories of this specific type of behaviour. And it is important to respect the positioning of their recollection within the framework of breaking the expected social model. However, infringing the boundaries of 'social norms' brings us back to another form of restriction. Our audiences demonstrate, in fact, that Julian Hanich's (2014: 338) description of 'watching a film' as a 'voluntary action' motivated by one's desire and intentions is not always adherent to the real experience of film consumption. In several cases (and often for our audiences), watching a film is an act chosen by others – at a simple level by parents, friends, family members – or in some cases even imposed, not only due to lack of choice but also for the fact that in parish cinemas, for example, films were not chosen by the audiences, but by those acting on behalf of the Catholic Church.

Surprisingly, the obvious association between restriction and film censorship (whether state or religious) is hardly ever made by the audiences, unless directly addressed by the interviewee (see Treveri Gennari and Dibeltulo 2017). On the contrary, the concept of restriction is described in relation to the act of cinemagoing (family confinement or gender boundaries), as well as to the space occupied in the cinema. Alessio (b. 1929, Rome), for example, divides the cinema into three areas, with precise rules and limitations: near the screen where there was very little space 'for action' as everybody could see what was happening; in the middle, where well-behaved audiences sat and one had to conduct oneself with discipline and self-control; and at the back, where courting, kissing and sexual encounters (see Chapters 3 and 8) replaced the act of watching the film (see also Antonio, b. 1933, Naples). This brings us to the second aspect of the performance category: where audiences are the ones performing and watching other audiences.

## Audiences as performance

By audience performance, what we refer to is more the participatory nature of cinema audiences, which, as Tessa Dwyer and Stephen Gaunson (2017: 522) state, 'can be as unwieldy, wild and dynamic as the films that play on the screen'. Brunello (b. 1936, Turin) describes it as coarseness, which was often expressed through screams, whistling and commenting aloud directly to the screen, while Maria Rosaria (b. 1953, Naples province) states that

> you lived as if you were at the theatre, people … they didn't talk … but they thought they were at the theatre and so they even said a few dirty words … and it was nice.

This behaviour in Italy certainly goes back to the tradition of the opera of the seventeenth and eighteenth centuries but is not dissimilar – for instance – from the way Day and Keegan (2009: 64) describe British theatre audiences, where people 'came to the theatre to see one another and be seen' and the 'rowdy auditorium was its own form of entertainment, offering opportunities for unabashed exhibitionism, flirtation and prostitution, possibly thieving and rioting'.

When Lakshmi Srinivas (2016: 3) describes Indian audiences as 'active', she partly refers to 'an in-theatre experience marked by spontaneity, improvisation and performance that is far removed from the silent absorption of films associated with mainstream audiences in Anglo-American and Western exhibition (multiplex) setting'. This type of performance is not dissimilar from the one remembered by our audiences. However, the loud discussions, courting, molestation as well as all the other activities that took place during the film screening should not be simply read in Butsch's (2000: 10, 288) terms as part of that perceived inattentiveness – a concept used to describe television audiences – that demonstrates both 'independence' and 'familiarity' with the filmic text. While this familiarity is often true in the case of our audiences, who could – as Nicola (b. 1931, Bari) remembers – see the film two or three days in a row, and therefore switch in and out of the film viewing to be entertained by extra-filmic activities, the inattentiveness can also be explained by desire for sociability.

Butsch's description of the theatre, in fact, as 'a place to be seen and see others' (2000: 10) is very much what several participants of the ICA project believed the role of cinema to be: a display, a window, a spectacle. 'It was the opportunity to show off your dress or your new hat' (Mariellina, b. 1921, Bari); 'you had to be perfect, elegant, with your Sunday dress' (Antonio, b. 1934, Bari province); 'we had to take care of ourselves ... as it was the occasion to meet your young love' (Giorgia, b. 1940, Palermo province). These are only some of the many instances of 'a performance within the performance', as Giuseppe (b. 1942, Cagliari) defines it. A performance with its own dress code and ritualities. A performance that at times stretched even further, with spectators entering into a discussion with the screen. So, comments directly addressed to the film's characters are heard by the other members of the audience, who have several performances to choose from. Antonio's (b. 1936, Palermo province) recollection illustrates in an exemplary way this multilayered performance and the relationship between the audience and the screen:

> For example, ... when, it almost always happened, in almost all cowboy films, that the bad guy was hiding behind the door and the guy in white unfortunately did not know ... He would come in through the door and we would desperately try to warn him, 'Watch out! Watch out!', and believe me, it was a show within a show. All of us children, because we were ten, twelve or thirteen years old, who didn't entirely believe that the film was separate from us. There was such an identification that we suggested to the actor ... we thought we were being listened to.

Antonio's description highlights the collective dimension of cinema by using 'we' to describe his group of children (Kuhn 2002: 78). Moreover, he explains how they – as spectators of a young age – did not separate the illusion of the screen from their reality and became extraneous protagonists who intervened in the action of the film. However, the performance in the cinema is not only limited by the interaction between the children and the screen. For older audiences, courting and molestation are two aspects of this performance, which often audiences engage with in their process of recollection. This dimension of cinemagoing was not a novelty in Italy and certainly not exclusive to the post-war period. Already in 1917 in film journal *L'Arte muta* Emilio Scaglione (1917: 14–15) reminded the reader that the cinema in provincial areas helped resolve the problem of relationships, as it encouraged local inhabitants to go out of their homes, getting men and women as close as a few millimetres apart, giving them the opportunity to have their knee brush against their neighbour. And this, all without 'fainting from fear, strengthening women's characters and providing entertainment for the entire family' (1917: 15). However, when asked if it was common to see women going to the cinema on their own, our participants' answers are split according to the respondents' gender. This is especially the case when talking about molestation. While the number of participants discussing this sensitive issue in the video interviews is exactly the same between men and women (fifteen each), the geographical location is mainly limited to cities (only three women and four men from provincial areas). The audiences who share their memories on this topic are predominantly from large metropolitan areas such as Rome, Milan, Turin or Naples, demonstrating the recurrence of a practice more widespread in big municipalities where the offering of cinemas was ampler, the diversity of the audience further-ranging and the possibility of encountering strangers higher. This is reflected in a short farcical pamphlet titled *Manualetto della mano morta* (Brief Manual of the Wandering Hand) written in 1997 but humorously describing a long-standing Italian practice.[4] In the book, Gaudio (1997: 24) affirms that 'incidences of the "wandering hand" are higher than the national average in the areas of accepted modernization, with considerable spread of infrastructure, a modern and efficient service sector, a high level of industrialization'.

More insightful is the content analysis of the responses in the video interviews which we performed on Voyant Tools (an open-source, web-based application for performing text analysis) which reveals an indisputable distinction in language between female and male respondents. Women's terminology is negative,

---

[4] We are grateful to Stephen Gundle for drawing our attention to this publication.

with descriptive terms such as nuisance (5) or bothersome (2), terrible (2), risk (2) or danger (2), as a result of which one is scared (1) or hassled (1) or disturbed (1). The actual description of the molestation is defined as such, as molestation (9) with verbs often portraying the disagreeable nature of the act: lure (2), pick up (2), but also showing the desire to react (2), avoid (3) and the feeling of being ashamed (2). The perpetrators are described not only as maniacs (1) and malicious (2) but also dismissively as morons (2).[5] What also emerges in all these testimonies is the series of unwritten rules expressed by our participants: ensuring that they would not go on their own to second-run cinemas, where friends and neighbours could see them and wrongly interpret their actions; going on their own but hiding it from their parents, being well aware that it was not the thing to do as a woman; as well as bringing 'weapons' (such as a pin) to discourage unwanted attention, as Maria (b. 1931, Bari province) did, or moving seats as often as needed to ensure peace and quiet throughout the film.

Even more striking is the way female participants reconstruct in the present these memories of their past. Theirs is a 'matter of fact' approach, where this male behaviour is regarded as a practice that was as common as it was unwanted, and the female displeasure is only a consideration made retrospectively. The male participants' word frequency and connotation analysis exposes some distinct results. Not only do their descriptions lack the negative words used by their female counterparts, but also they are much more assertive in the way they illustrate their acts as something that just happened (4) or occurred (3), at times described as a victory (1) which would provoke an emotion (2) or a pleasant (2) experience when successful. This almost confirms Gaudio's (1997: 7) definition of 'the wandering hand' as 'a form of courtship in which tactile communication is important or essential'. Our male audiences seem to advocate molestation precisely in the same way, as a legitimate way to seek pleasure (see also Chapter 8). However, when unsuccessful, it is then described as a misunderstanding (2).[6] The term molestation was only used once by our male participants, undeniably indicating a total lack of critical assessment of their past actions. However, harassment becomes harassment when the male respondents are the victims. Within that context, the word 'homosexual' (8)[7] – together with

---

[5] Fastidio (5), fastidioso (2), terribile (2), rischio (2), pericolo (2), impaurita (1), importunata (1), disturbata (1). Molestia (9), adescare (2), abbordare (2), evitare (3), reagire (2), vergogna (2). Maniaci (1), malintenzionati (2), cretini (2).
[6] Accadeva (4), capitava (3), conquista (1), emozionare (2), piacevole (2), equivoco (2).
[7] Omosessuale (8).

'gay' (3) – is used to describe the perpetrator of an unpleasant act, from which our participants had to defend themselves (see Chapter 8). Self-defence became, in fact, part of the performance of the audience, both male and female, who had to adopt a complex range of behaviours in order to be able to enjoy the film without unwanted attention. This – like other types of performance – is not limited to the inside of the cinema space. In fact, broadening Dyer's concept of entertainment means also expanding the experience of entertainment outside the cinema.

## Outside the movie theatre: The expanded cinema, expectations and extensions of the cinematic experience

Nino (b. 1942, Rome) states that 'the show does not begin and end inside the cinema'. This concept of the expanded cinema, referring both to expanded audience expectations and extensions of the cinematic space, is important. The entrance of the cinema, for instance, is described by Maria (b. 1931, Bari province), as the space for opportunities – 'opportunity to meet the boys and exchange a few words' – and by Pietro (b. 1942, Naples province) as a moment of 'expectation', while anxiously waiting to watch the film. Obviously the dimension of the 'expectation' was augmented in rural areas, where a film would take much longer to arrive and the anticipation would build up, enhanced by reviews in local papers and word of mouth from metropolitan visitors (Treveri Gennari and Culhane 2019).

The expectation, however, was felt not only in the waiting for the film to reach different areas of the cities or provincial parts of the country. The physical journey to the cinema constituted itself an expectation – as Daniela (b. 1945, Turin province) reminds us:

> [the journey] to the cinema, which was a foretaste. There was like an avenue of pine trees that led to this building, among other very nice things, very nice, and I remember it was nice to go, wait and then go out and go through this kind of avenue of pine trees commenting with friends ... remembering. It was a detail, let's say, that enriched the evening.

So the act of going to the cinema was special in itself and constituted part of the full experience of cinemagoing. While the journey to the cinema has already been discussed in Chapter 2, here we want to look at the relationship between the audience and the space outside the cinema, as well as what happens once the film finishes. For instance, the foyer of the cinema is meaningful in the process of expanding the cinematic experience: Nino (b. 1928, Rome province) remembers the screening of Walt Disney's *Cinderella* (Clyde Geronimi, Wilfred Jackson, Hamilton Luske, United States, 1950) at the Capranica cinema in Rome, where audiences were brought into the cinema through a purpose-built carriage while a wooden silhouette of Cinderella would accompany them into the main cinema hall. This is a reminder that the expectation for the experience does not start only 'when the lights go down', to quote Armbrust's (1998) article title on cinemagoing in Cairo. For many Italians, cinemagoing represented 'a way to go out' (Giovanna, b. 1941, Naples province) and was strongly connected with other activities. It is a practice, therefore, that cannot be looked at in isolation, because, as Alma (b. 1943, Naples) states, 'there is always a "before" and an "after"'. The concept of extension explores exactly this process of incorporating cinemagoing with other rituals that would take place before and after that cinema experience, like, for example, eating before or after the cinema (Antonio, b. 1938, Milan), going for a coffee to discuss the film or even queuing in line to wait for the ticket. Once outside the cinema, in fact, the long lines – common practice in the post-war period, when cinema attendance was at its highest – 'serve a purpose' (Hediger 2015: 318), not only because the visible queue helps as a form of marketing for the film but also 'it makes the audience visible in a public space'. In fact, while 'audiences tend normally toward anonymity and invisibility … cinema lines make the invisible audiences of the cinema visible. The sidewalk is the stage on which the cinema audience has its entrance into public space' (ibid.: 319). It becomes the opportunity – for example – while waiting to enter the parish cinema, for the priest to investigate the demographic of his audience, whether its members had attended mass or had received holy communion (Mario, b. 1939, Rome).

Moreover, as the pavement is the 'most transient of public space' (Hediger 2015: 319), it offers the ideal platform – once the audience exit the cinema – to expand the film experience itself. It is not only outside the cinema where our audiences queue full of excitement for a film that has finally reached their local venue. It is also outside the cinema where re-enactment of pirate fights, love scenes and other adventures take place. When asked whether she was affected by the films in the way she dressed or behaved, Teresa (b. 1931, Rome) – while denying any influence on her fashion or hairstyle – remembers that the main repercussion films had was on her feelings: 'Going back home I would feel again what I felt inside the cinema, so if it was an adventure film, I felt overexcited, while if it was a sentimental film, I felt like a poet inside.' This prolonging of the film experience, in some cases, was not just temporarily limited to soon after the film screening, but was extended to much later on. Pietro (b. 1939, Florence province), for example, recounts the ritual of discussing the film days after having seen it, in the house of a friend, or in the fields near home, where *Gone with the Wind* (Victor Fleming, United States, 1939) was talked about for several days.[8] This relationship with the text beyond the end of the screening is shared with British audiences, as confirmed by Annette Kuhn (1999), and Jonathan Gray (2010).

When looking at the outdoor dimension of the cinematic experience, Nichols's (2017: 2) approach is appropriate to better comprehend the relationship between audiences, film, cinema spaces and a temporal and spatial outside:

> If we imagine the experience of going to see a film as a fixed point on a timeline the cinematic experience can extend before and after that fixed point. This means that in the lead-up to seeing the film, as well as after seeing the film, anything that the spectator experiences in relation to that film adds to their overall cinematic experience.

The ICA participants have extensive memories of 'before' and 'after' fixed points, confirming the significance of those moments and their close rapport with the actual consumption of the film.

## Conclusion

If 'the transition from early cinema to classical Hollywood cinema implies ... a loss of collectivity and an individualization of the audience', the case of post-war Italian cinema spectators is gradually catching up with this global transformation of the cinemagoers' approach to social experience (Hanich 2014: 343). While a steady 'audience segmentation' coincided with the emergence of 'different cultures of taste' (Eugeni and Fanchi 2015: 293), our participants' memories confirm a stronger focus on the social dimension of cinema, as a practice

---

[8] This prolonged experience was also recounted by audiences interviewed at the time: one of the respondents of the survey in *Rassegna del Film* in 1953 ('Donne al cinema' 1953: 9) is worth citing, as she seems to reflect what our participants remember: 'Films such as *The Quiet Man* left me serene for an entire week.'

consumed with family and friends inside and outside the cinema space. This is even more the case, as that 'elision of the space-time of entertainment with that of home, work and other forms of leisure' described by Dyer (1992: 176) had not reached Italy yet. Therefore, our audiences, who needed to travel short and long distances to reach their entertainment, extended that space and time of cinema outside the venues dedicated to the screening of their favourite films. Analysing these expansions of the cinemagoing experience beyond the viewing of the film has allowed us to take into account aspects so far overlooked in the already limited study of Italian audiences of the post-war period. This expanding of the experience beyond the time and place of film consumption sheds light on the multifaceted dimension of cinemagoing memory. The term cinemagoing, in fact, 'conveniently captures the physical mobility involved, the necessary negotiation of community space, the process of consumer selection, and the multiple activities that one engages in before, during and after a film performance' (Acland 2003: 58). Our cinemagoing memories reflect this multifaceted spatial experience.

Part Two

# Films: Genre, taste and popular memory

# 4

# Audiences and film genre

## Introduction

Film scholars have amply demonstrated that genre is a crucial site for the investigation of the relationship between film industries and audiences. For example, Barry Keith Grant (2007: 20) has claimed that 'genres are dependent upon audiences for both their existence and meaning'. Indeed, the film industry capitalizes on the economic potential of genres as easily identifiable and thus marketable labels that, as Barry Langford (2005: 1) puts it, hold out 'the promise of attracting and retaining audiences in a reliable way, so reducing commercial risk'. So in this sense, genres constitute what Robert Altman (1999: 14) has defined a 'viewing contract' in which viewers' expectations are established. And along the same lines, Steve Neale (1990: 46) has pointed out the key role played by spectators: 'Genres do not consist only of films: they consist also, and equally, of specific systems of expectation and hypothesis that spectators bring with them to the cinema and that interact with films themselves during the course of the viewing process.'

And yet, like much film scholarship genre studies have been – and still are – predominantly characterized by a focus on films, or groups of films. This chapter adopts the view put forth by the editors of the recently published *The Routledge Companion to New Cinema History*, Daniel Biltereyst, Richard Maltby and Philippe Meers (2019: 2), who, while recognizing that 'there is nothing wrong with focusing on film style and ideology, on genres and authors, or on textually inscribed spectatorship', claim that such a limited approach has hampered scholars' ability to find answers related to the sociocultural, political and economic functions of cinema from a historical perspective. Specifically, in this chapter, within the context of the relationship between film genres and viewers, we will adopt their suggestion to shift the focus from a study of 'spectatorship' onto 'actual audiences in all their diversities' by examining cinemagoing memories of 1950s Italian audiences.

In the context of post-war Italian cinema, scholarship has been characterized mainly by text-driven studies of specific genres, and a focus on neorealism, in conjunction with an authorial approach which has foregrounded celebrated film-makers such as Rossellini, De Sica and Fellini. This trend within Italian film studies has been criticized by Alan O'Leary and Catherine O'Rawe (2011: 107) with the claim that 'this insidious common sense' had led to 'a dismissive tone in the discussion of genre films, not to mention a disdain for the audience for such films'. A notable exception to this trend is Vittorio Spinazzola's *Cinema e pubblico: lo spettacolo filmico in Italia 1945–1965* (1975). Published over forty years ago, the book discusses popular film genres and stars, along with neorealist films and auteurs. However, Spinazzola's consideration of the audience is based mainly on box office figures, and, at times, on intended spectators, rather than on actual cinemagoers' testimonies.

While recent research has included industry-oriented (Di Chiara 2013) and historical/theoretical frameworks (Noto 2011), the relationship between film genres (of different national film industries) and Italian audiences of this period has been largely neglected.[1] In this chapter we will shed light on this under-researched field of enquiry by analysing memories of cinemagoing and archival materials collected during the Italian Cinema Audiences (ICA) project.

## Methodology and contents

In the first part of the chapter, drawing on triangulation approaches to audience research (such as Barker and Mathijs 2008; Bilterevst, Lotze and Meers 2012) that have informed the ICA project, we will contextualize oral history data with relevant press material, and film industry data related to the 1950s. While providing an overview of the most popular film genres of the time (according to both project participants and box-office figures discussed in trade journals), we will explore the different conceptualizations of specific film genres from the perspectives of the audience, the press and the film industry.

In the second part of the chapter we will carry out a qualitative analysis of oral history data (both questionnaires and video interviews) with the objective of investigating audience engagement with generic film production, while

---

[1] Mariagrazia Fanchi's study (1995) of 'kolossal' (which roughly translates as 'epic') films adopts a viewer-oriented approach to audience research, but it focuses on a single genre.

considering the extent to which demographic variables such as gender and geographical location determine differences in such engagement. Our interpretive framework follows the ICA project's overall analytical approach which draws on Annette Kuhn's (2002: 9) concept of 'cinema memory as cultural memory', articulated in her ethnohistorical study of 1930s British audiences. In addition, in this chapter, our approach to cultural memory is informed by theories (e.g. Maurice Halbwachs' *On Collective Memory* [1992]) that highlight the double nature of the act of remembering as both *collective* and *individual*. Therefore, testimonies will be examined both as personal experience and as manifestations of the collective identity of a specific group – be it in terms of country, region, age or gender. In this context, genre, as an analytical tool, is employed to better understand audiences' engagement with popular cinematic production, and the different meanings and functions film genres have in participants' recollections of past cinemagoing experiences.

## Reconstructing historical film genre consumption in post-war Italy

One of the key aspects that emerges from the memories of our participants is the significance of genre in relation to their experience of cinema. In fact, genre is indicated as the most influential factor in choosing a film: a total of 607 questionnaire respondents out of 1,043, which equates to 58.19 per cent. As Table 4.1 shows, only the category of stars comes close to that of genre in determining film choice.

**Table 4.1** Factors determining film choice

| What made respondents decide on the film | |
|---|---|
| Genre | 25% |
| Actors | 24% |
| Street publicity | 12% |
| Press publicity | 12% |
| Recommended | 9% |
| Anything available | 6% |
| Other | 4% |
| Church posters | 3% |
| Film nationality | 3% |
| Unassigned | 2% |

**Table 4.2** Favourite film genres

| Favourite film genres | |
|---|---|
| Adventure | 23% |
| Love | 21% |
| Comedy | 19% |
| War | 11% |
| Musical | 11% |
| Neorealist | 10% |
| Melodrama | 3% |
| Western | 2% |

Only 49 out 1,043 respondents did not reply to the question about favourite types of film, which in the questionnaire appeared in a multiple-choice question with the following options: adventure, war, melodrama, musical, love, comedy, neorealist and other.[2] Table 4.2 indicates respondents' favourite film genres, with Western films as the most significant in the 'other' category.

The top three favourite genres apply to wide-ranging corpora of films, which, from a taxonomical point of view, cannot easily be positioned within such categories in a univocal manner. This is specifically the case for comedy, which several scholars (see, e.g. King 2002; Schatz 1981) have described as a 'mode' rather than a genre. Below, we will offer some examples of these categories within the specific historical time and national context under scrutiny. While an in-depth discussion on taxonomical issues related to film genres is beyond the scope of this chapter, before embarking on an illustration of how the categories of 'adventure', 'love', 'comedy' and so forth materialize in the memories of respondents, as well as in archival press and industry materials, here we want to call attention to the necessity of highlighting the historical specificity of such categories, definitions and understandings of genres. With regard to this, Neale (1990: 58) has stressed 'the importance of *historicizing* generic definitions and the parameters both of any single generic corpus, and of any specific generic regime. For it is not that more elaborated definitions are impossible to provide, just that they are always historically relative, and therefore historically specific'. Furthermore, while discussing institutional discourses and genre history, Neale

---

[2] The options available were chosen based on the most popular genres available in Italy at the time. The list of available options was adjusted after the pilot project carried out in Rome, where respondents suggested the inclusion of specific genres to reflect what was shown in cinemas at the time.

offers observations on the type of sources that should be examined that seem particularly apt to a study – like the present one – which triangulates audience (oral history) data, industry data and press material:

> Not only do *industrial* and *journalistic labels* and *terms* constitute crucial evidence for an understanding of both the industry's and the *audience*'s generic conceptions in the present, they also offer virtually the only available evidence for a historical study of the array of genres in circulation, or of the ways in which individual films have been generically perceived at any point in time. (Neale 1990: 52, emphasis ours)

We want to start our examination of different conceptions and understandings of film genres in 1950s Italy by noting that generic cinema features significantly in the memories of cinemagoers, as respondents overwhelmingly tend to remember the genre of the films they watched, rather than individual films.[3] But how is genre conceptualized in participants' recollections? Memories of genres are articulated in two main ways. On the one hand, some participants employ canonical definitions such as 'musical', 'comedy' or 'Western'; on the other hand, others utilize alternative ways to talk about genre which are different from normative or scholarly definitions. As we analysed participants' responses, while we have coded terms such as 'love films' and 'comedy' under the thematic category of genre, we have also included loose indications of generic production, such as 'cheerful films' or 'romantic films', to account for non-canonical conceptualizations of generic forms.

A typical alternative way of defining a film genre is the reference to specific stars. For example, some respondents describe their favourite genre as 'Totò films', which indicates a specific cycle of comedies produced in Italy and starring the popular Neapolitan actor Antonio De Curtis (best known by his stage name, Totò). The fact that many respondents signal their preference for comedies by mentioning Totò is not surprising. In fact, the actor was widely associated with comedy in Italian popular culture at the time, and the comedies in which he starred featured in the annual box-office top ten until the end of the 1950s (Treveri Gennari 2009b: 55). The association of Totò with comedy is also articulated in the pages of trade journals. For instance, in a table showing the top ten highest-grossing film genres between 1945 and 1949 in Italy in an article

---

[3] This aspect is not unique to the Italian case. In fact, Annette Kuhn (2011: 85; cited in BilTereyst 2019: 36) has noted that oral history research into cinemagoing has shown that respondents quite rarely remember individual films.

(Ruffilli 1950: 4) in the trade journal *Cinespettacolo*, the caricature of Totò is employed as a symbol to signify comedy. Another popular Italian star, Amedeo Nazzari – who is also the favourite male star based on questionnaire responses (see Table 1.2) – is mentioned in connection with popular generic production of that period: 'Amedeo Nazzari films' is a recurring expression in participants' memories that indicates a cycle of melodramas[4] directed by Raffaello Matarazzo, typically starring Nazzari and Greek-born co-star Yvonne Sanson – according to Morando Morandini Sr and Morando Morandini Jr (2010: 26) 'the most popular couple of 1950s Italian cinema'.

The definition of specific genres or cycles via association with stars in cinemagoers' memories reflects the fact that genre and stardom are strictly linked, and that typecasting of actors or (generically) iconographic connotations of star personae are essential elements in genre film. The key relationship between genre and stardom has been discussed by several film scholars in relation to Hollywood cinema. For instance, Thomas Schatz (1996: 6) has observed that, during Hollywood's studio era, the production system developed around what he variously terms 'star-genre formulations', 'star-genre combination[s]' (ibid.: 139) or 'star-genre formulas' (ibid.: 229). Similarly, Paolo Noto (2011: 136) has claimed that performance and stardom are hugely important in Italian 1950s generic production, as they contributed to the genrification of films: 'I believe … that what is memorable and what circulates in various genre films are performance and attractions, not syntagmatic structures, which, for that matter, are so elastic that they are hardly characterizing.'

Another recurring alternative way in which genres are defined by participants corresponds to what Rick Altman (1984: 10) calls 'the semantic approach', which focuses on 'common traits, attitudes, characters, shots, locations, sets, and the like', as opposed to the 'syntactic approach', which privileges the structures into which genres' 'building blocks' are arranged. For example, 'cowboy films' and 'films with cowboys and Indians' are expressions used by participants to indicate the Western genre. On the other hand, even though to a lesser extent, genre films are defined by respondents by making reference to the kind of emotional response that they elicit. For instance, popular Italian melodramas are described as *strappalacrime* (tear-jerkers or weepies), and comedies are identified as *film da ridere* (films that make you laugh). The similarity of comedy and melodrama

---

[4] For an in-depth discussion of 1950s Italian melodrama, see Morreale (2011).

within this context is not surprising. Like comedy, as we have mentioned above, melodrama too has been described as a mode rather than a genre (Williams 1998). In relation to this, King (2002: 2) has rightly pointed out that comedy shares common traits with 'the weepie' in that each genre is 'defined to a significant extent according to the emotional reaction it is intended to provoke'.[5]

Overall, participants' use of multiple labels to describe films reflects genres' inherent hybrid and flexible nature. This, at times, results in a tendency to apply overarching terms to a variety of films, which would otherwise be included more rigidly within one generic category according to industrial, critical or scholarly taxonomies. For example, the terms 'action' and 'adventure' are used by a number of respondents to describe *Stagecoach* (John Ford, United States, 1939), which is overwhelmingly classified as a Western.[6] The term 'adventure' is also used in conjunction with epic films, such as *Ben Hur* and *The Ten Commandments* (Cecil B. DeMille, United States, 1956), swashbuckler films, such as *The Three Musketeers* (George Sidney, United States, 1948), pirate films, such as *The Black Pirates* (Allen H. Miner, United States, 1954), and war films, including *The Bitter Tea of General Yen* (Frank Capra, United States, 1933). The word 'adventure' appears frequently in relation to questionnaire respondents' favourite film, *Gone with the Wind*, a highly hybrid text, which is usually included (by both scholars and critics) under the categories of romance, epic, historical film or *drammatico* (dramatic), as it appeared in the film listings of the Roman edition of the newspaper *L'Unità* (1953: 5).

A triangulation of sources can help us determine the extent to which audiences' conceptualizations of genres corresponded to and were influenced by press and industry discourses that circulated in Italy at that time. As Barbara Klinger (1997: 118) has noted, discourses on films that appear on newspapers and magazines (which, we would argue, should include trade journals) provide crucial evidence 'about the terms governing a film's cultural circulation', while shedding light on 'the critical standards and tastes within the aesthetic ideologies and social preoccupations of a given historical moment'. And yet, the alternative conceptualizations and understandings of genres that emerge from the oral history data under scrutiny suggest that 'critical standards and tastes' voiced

---

[5] Within the context of Italian cinema, Elena Mosconi (2002) has highlighted the generic flexibility of the melodramatic mode in her study of a previous cycle of popular films, directed by Mario Mattoli in the early 1940s, whose narratives revolve around everyday passions.

[6] The Rome edition of left-wing Italian newspaper *L'Unità* (1960: 6) labels the film 'a classical Western film'.

by film critics or industry professionals did not necessarily dictate audiences' reception – in the broadest sense – of films. The fact that some respondents employ flexible and non-univocal definitions of genre, in comparison with more rigid classifications in the press and trade journals, indicates, if not a conscious resistance, at least a degree of impermeability to 'official' discourses, or even a deliberate disregard of them. This aspect is also corroborated by our quantitative findings showing that 41 per cent of questionnaire respondents claim that they did not read film reviews, while over 24 per cent claimed that they did and around 34 per cent could not remember.

An example of such more fixed and univocal generic categorization in the press can be found in the newspaper *L'Unità* (1953: 5), published in Rome, which provides a legend that explains the abbreviation included next to each film title in the cinema listings. The genres in question are comedy, adventure, sentimental, satirical, drama, Western and musical. Only one label is applied to each film in the listings. However, not all Italian newspapers adopted the same approach to genre classification. Unlike *L'Unità*, some newspapers reveal a less rigid approach, one that takes into account generic hybridity. The newspaper *La Stampa* (1956: 4), published in Turin, provides an example of this in relation to the Italian-French co-production *Je suis un sentimental* (*Headlines of Destruction*, John Berry, France/Italy, 1955) which was described as 'a detective adventure in a comedy mood'. Similarly, *L'Unione Sarda* (1954: 4), published in Cagliari, defined *April in Paris* (David Butler, United States, 1952) as a 'musical romantic comedy'.

At the same time, respondents' memories reveal that some viewers' reception and understanding of films were mediated, if not influenced, by official public discourses on genre. A significant example is that of the term *colossal* (also known as 'kolossal'), which appeared in different variations on newspapers and specialized press. *La Gazzetta del Mezzogiorno* (1953: 4) defines *Gone with the Wind* as *il supercolosso M.G.M.* (M.G.M's super epic); *Il Mattino* (1954: n.p.) describes *Quo Vadis?* (Mervyn LeRoy, United States, 1951) as *colossale*; *La Nazione* (1954: 4) labels *Ivanhoe* (Richard Thorpe, UK/United States, 1952) a *colossal technicolor*; *The Ten Commandments* is defined as a *colossale produzione* (epic production) in *Il Giornale dello Spettacolo* (1957: 2), the trade journal of AGIS (the Italian National Show Business Association). The term *colossal* is employed widely by respondents, and in its Italian usage it can be understood as a cross-generic term that defines a style of film-making which is applied to spectacular big-budget films, such as historical or religious narratives. Films frequently identified by participants as *colossal* include *Ben Hur* and *The Ten Commandments*. The term loosely corresponds to the English 'epic'; however, both in newspapers and in trade journals it appeared in connection with spectacular productions of different genres.

Our analysis of trade journals published at the time (specifically *Cinespettacolo* and *Il Bollettino dello Spettacolo*) focuses on comparing industry-oriented generic taxonomies with respondents' conceptualizations, with the aim of shedding light on points of contact and divergence. What has emerged through this investigation is that the Italian film industry's categorizations were really complex and articulated according to a number of genres and subgenres, which, in addition to the fact that such categorizations changed quickly in short periods of time, makes it impossible to compile an exhaustive classification of genres. For the purposes of this chapter, it must be noted that, in comparison to generic labels appearing in the press, trade journals' definitions – although in many cases they overlapped with newspaper ones – seem to diverge from audiences' conceptualizations of genres to a higher degree. An example of such divergence between audiences' and industry's understandings of genres is the film *Chi è senza peccato* (*Who Is without Sin*, Italy, 1952), directed by Raffaello Matarazzo and starring Amedeo Nazzari and Yvonne Sanson. In *Cinespettacolo*, Alessandro Ferraù (1954: 3) classified the film as 'popular drama'.[7] As we have indicated above, this type of film belongs to a specific cycle of melodramas directed by Matarazzo and starring Nazzari which is discussed by project participants in terms of 'Amedeo Nazzari film', 'tearjerker' or *film passionali* (films of passion).

What is interesting about this point of divergence between industry and audience definitions is that it sheds light on the divide between discourses circulating among industry professionals and among film consumers. A clear elitist detachment transpires on the pages of trade journals that comment on why some genres are more popular than others with Italian cinemagoers. For example, an article in *Cinespettacolo* (Ruffilli 1950: 3–6) laments the lack of success of neorealist films – 'the only real expression of film art'. Here, the author, Weiss Ruffilli, discusses the most successful genres in terms of box-office intake between September 1945 and June 1949. He reports that the highest-grossing genres produced in Italy are 'farces, musicals adapted from popular operas, films in which working-class passions are displayed, and adventure films' (ibid.: 3).

---

[7] It is worth noting that the term *melodramma* (melodrama) was not in common currency at the time in Italy in relation to cinematic production.

Ruffilli explains the (box-office) 'failure of neorealist cinema in Italy'[8] with the claim that 'one cannot produce with the intellect, for the elites. One must produce for the masses, for the people, for the simple souls, for the unrefined brains. ... It is sad, but it is true' (ibid.: 6).

The author's contempt for the masses who consume 'popular' cinema needs to be read within the context of a wider debate that took place in the pages of newspapers, critically oriented film magazines and other press media, which saw many film critics conceiving neorealism as a cinematic form of high artistic expression that was constructed in opposition to genre films – which embodied popular mass entertainment[9] – and, by extension, to their audiences. Catherine O'Rawe (2008) offers a critical overview of this debate, both within specialized press of that time and in subsequent film scholarship, while analysing a series of exchanges – the 'Inchiesta su cinema e pubblico' (survey on cinema and audiences) – that were published in *L'Unità* between December 1955 and May 1956. These addressed issues about the reasons why some genres (frequently exemplified by Matarazzo's melodramas) were more popular among audiences, and how the divide between critics and the public could be bridged (ibid.: 186). Importantly, O'Rawe (ibid.: 189) highlights that discussions of the public's relationship to the cinema were marked by a 'language of trauma' which evoked a 'wounding of the spectatorial body' through the consumption of popular films that might seem soothing to the body and spirit, but are, actually, dangerous and toxic. Clearly, the underlying assumption behind these critics' attitude was that the audience was a passive entity that needed to be educated.[10] Such a view is certainly not unique to the Italian context. If, on the one hand, it mirrors the much-discussed opposition of cinema as (highbrow) art versus cinema as (lowbrow) mass entertainment, on the other hand, it is in line with audience studies which have focused on negative 'media effects', specifically those studies informed by the so-called 'hypodermic needle model' which sees the public as a totally passive body that unwittingly absorbs 'injected' dangerous media messages. This approach has been critiqued by many scholars, including Martin

---

[8] Some commentators paint a more nuanced picture of neorealist films' box-office performance. For example, Spinazzola (1975: 19–20) claims that a number of neorealist films – including *Roma città aperta*, *Paisà* (*Paisan*, Roberto Rossellini, Italy, 1946) and *Ladri di biciclette* – achieved 'notable economic results' between 1945 and 1950.
[9] For a detailed discussion around this topic, see Noto (2011).
[10] For an in-depth investigation of the ways in which audiences were perceived and portrayed in a patronizing manner by 1950s film critics in Italy, see Noto (2018).

Barker (1998, 2003) and David Gauntlett (2006), who have argued that one of the many faults of the media effects model is that it assumes superiority to the masses.

Through triangulation, we have also aimed to determine whether the film genres remembered by respondents correspond to top-grossing genres of the time, and their industry categorizations. In order to do this, we have examined box-office figures reported in *Il Bollettino dello Spettacolo* and *Cinespettacolo* in the 1950s. As the box-office success of specific genres changed over the course of a decade – along with generic definitions – and providing a full account is beyond the scope of this chapter, here we will focus on some illustrative examples. An article by Alessandro Ferraù (1954) in *Cinespettacolo* examines the box-office performance of 123 Italian films in the June 1952–June 1953 season, according to genre. The interest of the article for our analysis is that it provides a list of genres, from the point of view of industry professionals, that are typical of the Italian film production of the time. At the same time, it allows us to highlight how these categorizations depart from the ones used by audiences. The list in question includes popular drama, historical, swashbuckler films, comedy, musical, drama, patriotic, sports films, religious, based on plays and novels, neorealist and anthology. The 'popular drama' is the most successful genre and includes films directed by Raffaello Matarazzo and starring Amedeo Nazzari and Yvonne Sanson, which, as mentioned above, are largely described by project participants in a different way.

The analysis of the second top grossing category, which includes both historical films and swashbuckler films, is also revealing when it comes to comparing the most popular film genres of the time, according to project participants' memories, on the one hand, and historical box-office figures, on the other. In relation to this category Ferraù (1954: 4) notes how 'historical films' produced in Italy and in the United States are similarly popular with cinemagoers. He goes on to discuss examples of American historical films that are somewhat similar to Italian productions of this type, including *The Robe* (Henry Koster, United States, 1953) and *Quo Vadis?*. Although some respondents describe *Quo Vadis* as a historical film, others label it as a 'colossal' film along with *Ben Hur* and *The Ten Commandments*; one participant even defines it a 'costume film'. It must be noted that the popularity of *Ben Hur* and *The Ten Commandments* is reflected in cinemagoers' memories as they both appear among the favourite films mentioned by questionnaire respondents. (See Table 1.2 for details of the top four favourite films.)

Beyond highlighting the discrepancies in conceptualizations and definitions of the most popular genres in the memories of our respondents and in the archival industry data, this example raises issues around the comparability of these different sets of data, specifically in relation to the fact that industry data offers a synchronic snapshot of film popularity in the past, while oral history offers a reconstruction (Rigney 2005: 14) of the past through memory.[11] This methodological challenge is particularly evident in the case of the adventure genre, which is questionnaire respondents' favourite. As we have indicated above, this category is used in rather flexible ways by audiences, with the terms 'adventure' and 'adventurous' being associated with a wide variety of (mainly American) films, ranging from *Duel in the Sun* (King Vidor, United States, 1946) to *Gone with the Wind* to *20.000 Leagues under the Sea* (Richard Fleischer, United States, 1954). In contrast, this category was used in a more rigid and more selective manner by the industry. For example, in an article in the *Bollettino dello Spettacolo* (Ferraù 1956: 3) that examines Italian films grossing over 200 million *lire* in the years 1954-6, the genre 'adventure' is separated from 'swashbuckler films' and 'historical films' – two genres which frequently overlap with 'adventure' in participants' accounts. For example, *The Three Musketeers*, arguably a hybrid text between adventure and the swashbuckler genre,[12] is defined as adventurous by many respondents. Press material seems to be closer to audiences' formulations of genre in this case. For instance, the newspaper *L'Unità* (1953: 5) includes a coeval musketeer narrative, *At Sword's Point* (Lewis Allen, United States, 1952), in the adventure genre.

The triangulation of sources has highlighted both points of contact and points of divergence between official classifications of genre, in the press and industry material, and alternative conceptualizations and understandings formulated by audiences. Given the elusive and hybrid nature of genres, this variety of definitions and notions is not surprising. What is relevant to our study is how this methodology has allowed us to establish the extent to which top-down definitions of genre, articulated by both industry professionals and critics, influenced the way in which cinemagoers received, consumed, understood and remember film genres today. While some viewers absorbed 'official'

---

[11] For a more detailed discussion of methodological and analytical issues related to memory and oral history within the ICA project, see Treveri Gennari et al. (2019).

[12] The title of James Chapman's 2015 book, *Swashbucklers: The Costume Adventure Series*, is illuminating in this regard.

or 'critical' discourses of genres, others did not. Altman's observations on the privileged role played by film critics offer an explanation of the difference in generic conceptualizations adopted by film critics, as well as those who wrote on publications targeted at industry professionals (specifically exhibitors), and the so-called masses of cinemagoers:

> Critics are assumed to have the power to rise above the very audiences with whom they viewed the films they write about. … Though originally developed to empower critics, who were thus all the better able to look down from their cultured heights on the masses, the distancing of critics from the genre audience has had the effect of excluding them, at least in theory, from the active constitution of genres. (Altman 1999: 28)

By bringing cinemagoers' accounts of generic film consumption to the forefront, this chapter aims at offering an alternative critical perspective, whereby audiences' role is seen as 'active and engaged rather than theoretical and objective' (Altman 1999: 29).

## Modalities of Generic Engagement

In this section we will offer a qualitative analysis of the project's oral history data (both questionnaires and video interviews) with the aim of establishing differences in audience engagement with generic film production. This is based on the assumption discussed at the beginning of the chapter that a shift from the study of implied spectatorship to 'actual audiences in all their diversities' implies a notion of audiences not as a monolithic and homogenous entity but as a heterogeneous group of people. The first step of this investigation has been to find out whether there exist any differences based on demographic variables. Table 4.3 presents a cross-tabulation of geographical location and generic preference, as indicated by questionnaire respondents. (Figures shown in percentage in the Tables 4.3–4.5 are based on the total number of responses given to the question about favourite genres.) Geographical location indicates the four main areas of north, centre, south and islands that were used as categories representative of the Italian territory within the project.

The figures in Table 4.3 show that geographical location is not a determining factor in relation to most genres. Slight variations – even if minimal – can be noted in relation to neorealist films, which seem to be favoured by audiences

**Table 4.3** Genre preference by geographical location

| Genre | South | Insular | Centre | North |
|---|---|---|---|---|
| Adventure | 19% | 24% | 25% | 22% |
| Comedy | 20% | 18% | 19% | 19% |
| Love | 24% | 20% | 21% | 19% |
| War | 10% | 11% | 11% | 10% |
| Melodrama | 3% | 3% | 3% | 4% |
| Musical | 10% | 15% | 9% | 10% |
| Neorealist | 13% | 6% | 8% | 12% |
| Western | 2% | 3% | 3% | 3% |

**Table 4.4** Genre preference by urban/provincial location

| Genre | City | Province |
|---|---|---|
| Adventure | 23% | 22% |
| Comedy | 19% | 20% |
| Love | 20% | 22% |
| War | 10% | 11% |
| Melodrama | 3% | 4% |
| Musical | 12% | 10% |
| Neorealist | 11% | 9% |
| Western | 3% | 2% |

in the north and south of Italy, and less so in the centre and islands. However, an examination of open-ended responses in the questionnaires and video interviews indicates that these small variations are not explicitly associated with the geographical areas in which respondents lived in the 1950s.

Our analysis has also included a cross-tabulation of genre preference with urban versus provincial location. This is presented in Table 4.4.

Not surprisingly, as in the case of geographical location, the urban/provincial variable does not determine significant dissimilarities in relation to genre preference. In fact, film consumption played a key role in reducing differences between urban centres and rural or provincial areas in post-war Italy. And specifically, as Forgacs and Gundle (2007: 31) have noted, the increased number of cinemas in small towns and villages was a sign of the rapid cultural transformations that occurred in rural areas in the immediate post-war years. In addition, these results are in line with our project's overall findings on the comparison between

**Table 4.5** Genre preference by gender (male/female)

| Genre | Female | Male |
| --- | --- | --- |
| Adventure | 15% | 33% |
| Comedy | 22% | 15% |
| Love | 31% | 9% |
| War | 4% | 19% |
| Melodrama | 4% | 2% |
| Musical | 14% | 7% |
| Neorealist | 10% | 10% |
| Western | 0.5% | 5% |

rural and urban cinemagoing experiences, which indicate that 'differences are a matter of degree, rather than being absolute' (Hipkins et al. 2016: 224).

Remarkable differences in responses have emerged in a cross-tabulation of genre preference and gender. Table 4.5 shows the extent to which male and female respondents manifest dissimilar generic preferences.[13]

As the figures in Table 4.5 reveal, the most significant dissimilarities in participants' preferences emerge in relation to genres – such as love, war, and Western – that are typically heavily gendered both in their narratives and in their intended target audiences. Overall, quantitative results emerging from questionnaire responses show a generally homogenous generic engagement, with the notable exception of the gender variable.

This finding has begged further examination of the fragmented nature of generic engagement based on the gender of respondents. Qualitative analysis of both questionnaires and video interviews has indicated that cinemagoers' accounts reinforce the heavily gendered generic engagement revealed by the figures presented above, with women favouring female-oriented genres, such as love films and popular Italian melodrama, and men preferring male-oriented American Western, action and adventure films (e.g. swashbuckler films). While this polarized gendered preference, in itself, suggests that generic film-viewing as a mode of cultural consumption can be interpreted through Judith Butler's (1999) seminal notion of gender identity and behaviour as a socially constructed performance, film-goers' reactions to specific genres reinforce this

---

[13] There were twenty-nine unassigned respondents in the questionnaires, but these figures are not included in Table 4.5.

notion even further. For instance, female respondents remember crying profusely,[14] and enjoying doing so, while watching melodramatic and sentimental films – thus performing stereotypically feminine behaviour. Crying is associated with female viewers by male respondents too: for example, Giancarlo (b. 1943, Cagliari province) remembers, 'You would see these little women crying as they shared their tissues with each other to dry their tears.' The fact that women were the target audience of popular Italian melodrama is also revealed by a female respondent, Giorgia (b. 1940, Palermo province), who recalls that the town crier, when announcing cinema programmes, would encourage women in particular to watch these type of films. While a male respondent remembers not liking this genre, as it did not suit the taste of teenage boys, a female one, Irma (b. 1935, Turin province), claims, 'I really liked those that make you cry and move you. *Naturally*, I didn't like Westerns: we leave this to him [pointing at a man – possibly her husband – who was present during the video-interview].' The word 'naturally' here betrays an essentialist understanding of generic preference in keeping with normative gender binary oppositions.

Unlike female participants, male respondents' generic engagement – specifically with male-oriented American adventure and action genres – is one of identification, active participation during the show (e.g. by warning the hero when the 'bad guy' arrives) and imitation. The following memories of watching Western films offered by questionnaire respondents are illustrative:

> In particular [I liked] American Westerns. I would identify more with the protagonist and they were more engaging. (Male, b. 1940, Florence province)

> Once after the show I smoked my first cigarette, imitating an actor from a Western film. (Male, b. 1938, Rome province)

Even if the majority of cinemagoers' memories of film genre are articulated along the lines of normative gender constructions, some (rare) 'subversive' accounts – offered mainly by women – are present. Respondents' narrations of non-normative generic engagement tend to be quite self-reflexive in the description of such past

---

[14] An in-depth analysis of what films and genres elicited tears in male and female viewers is beyond the scope of this chapter. However, it is worth noting that questionnaire respondents were asked what films made them cry. Out of 154 participants who responded to this question claiming that they never cried while watching a film, 108 are male, 41 are female and 5 are unassigned. Although a minority of male participants remember crying in the cinema, both in questionnaires and video interviews, this behaviour emerges as a prevalently feminine one. In this sense, our findings are not dissimilar to Harper and Porter's investigation (1996) of weeping in the cinema in post-war Britain.

transgressions. For instance, Maria (b. 1934, Bari) recounts, 'When I was a girl aged twelve …, when I was in middle school, I was passionate about swashbuckler films. I watched all the films starring Errol Flynn … We were gripped by these films. … We were tomboys … the way we got excited by these swashbuckler films, as they were called.' This particular memory is a telling example of Ann Rigney's argument about cultural memory. Rigney (2016: 67) claims that a mnemonic perspective on culture can uncover 'the intersections between autobiographical memory (relating to one's own experience) and the repertoire of inherited templates that individuals can use to interpret that experience'. While reconstructing the past in the present, Maria uses the 'inherited template' of normative gendered behaviour to interpret her – and her female friends' – experience of loving swashbuckler and Western films. Her comment that they were 'tomboys' is crucial here in highlighting that the consumption of these (male-oriented) cinematic cultural products was a transgression of normative femininity. And yet, the lenient and humorous tone Maria uses in articulating her memory, as well as the fact that she specifies her young age, suggests that this was a tolerable transgression, because it was perpetrated by girls who had not yet entered womanhood.

In relation to this, Jack Halberstam (1998: 5) argues that 'tomboyism generally describes an extended childhood period of female masculinity'. The author claims that this period 'tends to be associated with a "natural" desire for the greater freedoms and mobilities enjoyed by boys' (ibid.: 6). As such, it is not seen as problematic, unless it extends beyond childhood and adolescence. 'As soon as puberty begins, however', Halberstam observes, 'the full force of gender conformity descends on the girl' (ibid.). (A more detailed discussion of girlhood and cinemagoing in post-war Italy is offered in Chapter 6.) Luciana's (b. 1943, Turin) memories of watching Italian popular melodrama as a girl contrasts interestingly with Maria's testimony, as she explains that these films indicated that 'a woman should be pure, she should not betray the man who loves her … these values … really educated me in this thing … how a woman should be'. Similarly, Lizia (b. 1941, Bari province) remembers: 'sentimental films … I watched those because I was a girl, with that kind of upbringing in the past'. This resonates with Halberstam's (ibid.) claim that 'if adolescence for boys represents a rite of passage …, and an ascension to some version … of social power, for girls, adolescence is a lesson in restraint, punishment, and repression'. It must be noted that most of our respondents were children or adolescents in the 1950s, therefore their engagement with cinema is related to phases of gender identity formation in the passage from childhood to adulthood.

Film audience and reception scholarship on gendered engagement – suffice it to mention the work of Annette Kuhn (1984, 1996, 2002) and Jackie Stacey (1994) – indicates that the polarization of generic preferences along opposite ends of the gender spectrum is not exclusive to post-war Italy. And yet, at this time, Italy saw an increased gender-based differentiation of films – a phenomenon that Mariagrazia Fanchi (2016: 229) has defined 'a genderization of cultural products', that went hand in hand with a relocation of women from the workplace to the domestic sphere. Certainly, gendered modes of spectatorship are not only linked to generic preferences but, as findings emerging from our project have highlighted, also to fandom, access to venues and modalities of consumption within cinematic spaces. (Some of our respondents recall that male and female spectators would sit in a separate place in the cinema, as we discuss further in Chapter 8.)

Considering the main aspects of gendered generic preferences in relation to Italian popular melodrama, specifically the Matarazzo films, one can see a trend suggesting that female participants might conform, at least in their recollections, to the authority of patriarchy and its ideological implications related to femininity in 1950s Italy. Especially in the case of the educational role played by Italian popular melodrama, generic preference suggests restraint and repression in the process of gender identity formation for girls and young women. Inward-looking and potentially reactionary representations of Italian femininity in these films[15] are in stark contrast to more emancipated modes of adult femininity as presented in American films, which many female respondents admired, but, nevertheless, perceived as an unachievable dream. And yet, as we shall discuss in Chapters 6 and 7, some accounts reveal how age played a role in female viewers' engagement with young American female stars and characters, whereby identification was a possibility in girlhood. Most male spectators, instead, engaged more actively with models of masculinity offered by outward-looking, typically American genres that featured strong male characters that are vigorous, adventurous and brave. The fact that male respondents identified with and imitated these characters – rather than just hopelessly admiring them – speaks volumes to the freedoms and the degree of agency allowed to men in Italy in the 1950s.

---

[15] In relation to this, Spinazzola (1975: 74–7) describes these films as never questioning male dominance over women, who are defined by their functions of wife and mother.

## Conclusion

In their article on triangulation of sources in historical audience research Biltereyst et al. (2012: 691) reflect on the methodological challenge of 'how to capture the historical audience', on what kinds of 'sources' and 'traces' are available to researchers and how we can interpret them. In this chapter, we have attempted to capture historical Italian genre audiences by shedding light on the specific methodological and analytical challenges of employing and interpreting different types of data and sources related to the category of genre – a category which has been at the centre of heated theoretical debates within film studies in the past decades. At the same time, we have demonstrated that, in spite of such challenges, genre, as an analytical tool, can help us to better understand the relationship between film industry, critics and viewers, on the one hand, and audiences' different types of engagement with popular cinematic production, on the other.

A triangulation of sources revolving around definitions and understandings of genres has allowed us to uncover points of contact and divergence between industry professionals, the press and cinemagoers in the much-debated context of the consumption of cinema as a manifestation of popular culture in post-war Italy. With regard to the discrepancies between archival industry data (box-office performance) and the most successful genres in the memories of our respondents, we need to consider the workings of memory and remediation both at an individual and at a collective level.[16] Or, to use Barbara Klinger's (1997: 123) terms, we need to look at the diachronic life of films. In the Italian context, this means that some films – such as *Gone with the Wind*, *Roma città aperta* and *Ladri di biciclette* – are remembered the most by audiences today partly because they were screened repeatedly over the years in cinemas, as well as on TV later on, and they have gained iconic status in Italian culture. And yet, these films are not representative of participants' favourite genres. Therefore, limiting our scope of inquiry to the synchronic dimension – in this case box-office success at the time of release – of films prevents us from achieving, or even attempting to achieve, the 'total history' advocated by Klinger (ibid.). This aspect, along with the above-mentioned fact that respondents tend not to remember individual films, shows the significance of employing genre as an analytical tool

---

[16] For a discussion of this aspect within the ICA project, see Treveri Gennari et al. (2019).

for cinema history research, because a focus on corpora or groups of films can help us reconstruct historical film consumption and reception more effectively through oral history accounts, in conjunction with other sources.

The qualitative analysis of audiences' memories of genres presented here has revealed starkly polarized gendered modes of engagement with and reception of cinema in the period in question. Indeed, a focus on genre has proved useful in understanding the fragmented nature of audience engagement within the Italian national context in the period under scrutiny. In the memories of our participants, gendered engagement with genre films that circulated in post-war Italy sheds light on audiences' reactions to, elaborations and interpretations of conservative – if not, in some cases, regressive – gender models that promoted patriarchal values at a time when, according to one female participant (b. 1939, Naples province), cinema represented 'an opportunity for diversion' since 'specific restrictions' were 'imposed' on women. Oral history data provides insights into the various roles film genres play in participants' present recollections, as reconstructions of the past through memory work (including modalities of narration) are shaped by 'inherited templates' of interpretation which connect the individual and the collective lived experience of cinemagoing. The above-mentioned example of Lizia, who comments on the fact that, as a girl, she was only allowed to watch sentimental films because that was the norm in her restrictive 1950s female upbringing, offers an illustration of how oral history can play a significant role in explaining or interpreting phenomena – such as the fact that some genres perform better at the box office with male or female audiences – with reference to the real and multifaceted social and cultural contexts in which the filmic experience took place. By foregrounding cinemagoers' accounts of generic engagement, this chapter has provided an alternative (bottom-up) critical perspective, while stressing the importance of shifting from ideal/theoretical spectators to real audiences in an effort to reconstruct historical consumption and reception of generic film production.

5

# 'Back then I believed in the nation – I don't anymore': Revisiting the national film canon through audience memories of neorealism

*'Did you like neorealist films?' – 'Yes and no. They seemed too similar to daily life.'*

(Female participant, b. 1946, Palermo)

*'The knowledge of great loss and destruction was for us the first knowledge.'*

(Hoffman 2010: 407)

## Introduction

In this chapter[1] we take a key film from the Italian post-war cinematic canon, and examine how our understanding of its significance can be enriched by an engagement with audience memories.[2] The film in question is *Roma città aperta* (*Rome Open City*, Roberto Rossellini, Italy, 1945), cited as the most popular Italian film by those surveyed in our questionnaires (see Appendix for the most popular films), and repeatedly mentioned by our interviewees. As the most popular

---

[1] This chapter is based upon a paper first delivered at the University of Warwick 'Rome Open City' conference in November 2015, where it was presented alongside a video essay created by Sarah Culhane. Some of the key participants' responses discussed here are visible in that video essay, so we have made it available at https://www.youtube.com/watch?v=SGXmmmEMsAw&feature=youtu.be.

[2] This chapter primarily makes reference to the 1,043 surveys and 160 interviews upon which this book is based. However, it also draws upon three additional interviews dedicated to discussion of *Roma città aperta*, conducted by the ICA research team: Elena (b. 1934, Bologna), Luciana (b. 1941, Sardinia), Rita (b. 1933, Bologna province); *Romarcord*, the University La Sapienza documentary project recording audience memories in Rome in 2014, with a focus on neorealism and *Roma città aperta*, http://www.romarcordsapienza.com/; and our first pilot project, based on twenty interviews carried out in Rome, undertaken in 2007 to test the methodology (Treveri Gennari et al. 2011).

Italian film cited, and the one from which certain scenes are remembered in the most detail, *Roma città aperta* will occupy the bulk of our analysis, but it forms an important duo with *Ladri di biciclette* (*Bicycle Thieves*, Vittorio De Sica, Italy, 1948) because the two films are often mentioned at the same time, frequently as examples of the post-war revival of Italian cinema, associated retrospectively with neorealism. Both these films have been analysed extensively on the level of textual and authorial significance, and production, probably more than any other Italian films, but the viewers and their responses are absent (Piturro 2008). Yet, as Susannah Radstone has argued, 'the ways that ... images are remembered and become woven into the texture of identity/memory is as much a question of the history of individual subjects as it is a question of films themselves' (Radstone 2010: 336). What we argue here is that *Roma città aperta*'s place in film history makes more sense in the context of a more detailed engagement with how it is remembered and narrated by some of its first audiences.

It is important to begin by saying that although *Roma città aperta* and *Ladri di biciclette* emerge as the two most popular films from our surveys, the numbers of respondents remembering them are fairly modest (garnering just 5 per cent and 4 per cent, respectively), reflecting the diversity of US and Italian titles emerging from our audience memories (often providing an alternative history of cinema, remembering films neglected by scholars), and the tendency for cinemagoers not to remember many titles. Indeed it is worth remembering that the top film, *Gone with the Wind* (Victor Fleming, United States, 1939), received more 'votes' than both films put together with 11 per cent. Furthermore, when questionnaire respondents were asked whether they liked neorealism, approximately 60 per cent responded positively; the remainder either actively dislike the films or do not appear to have any opinion, which we might take for lack of knowledge or a reluctance to comment negatively on films viewed as national classics.[3] As the opening quote from our survey to this chapter suggests, what is most striking is that the reasons for liking *and* for disliking the films are very often the same: that they reflected 'reality' and that they make the viewer sad.

The two films crop up transversally in our video interviews, often more than once, in response to a variety of questions, as first films remembered, as films reflecting reality, as films addressing the war, as films that taught audiences

---

[3] We have noted in our introduction the 'cluster' effect visible in our surveys: often filled out in group situations there is undoubtedly a contamination effect since similar responses come in groups, suggesting certain group responses of positive and negative reactions to neorealism.

something, as films that provoked great emotion or tears, as films featuring great performers, particularly Anna Magnani, as films emblematic of a certain pride in Italian culture after a messy and uncertain transition from fascism and as films that should be remembered by subsequent generations. What is certain is that in the interviews these neorealist films tend to get a more positive response than in the surveys. This may have something to do with the self-selecting nature of our interviewees, a significant number of whom (as noted in the Introduction) present themselves as film enthusiasts and display a familiarity with the official history of Italian cinema. However, it is primarily because in our interviews we did not ask the direct question posed in the questionnaires about whether or not respondents liked or disliked neorealism. Focusing on this 'thicker' description offered by our interviews, we inevitably encounter a more positive account of neorealism that does not fully mirror that stark division in our questionnaire responses.

Nonetheless we do find some clues to understand that division in the fuller accounts of video interviews, and we will put those in dialogue with the questionnaire responses. In addressing these clues we can draw on the theory that what deviates from the standard narrative or is 'absent from history' might actually be the most telling moment (Fanchi 2019: 388).

It is useful to begin by considering the questions we did ask in interview that gave rise to the mention of neorealism and these two films. Most typically in interview these films arose in relation to questions about what cinema offered in terms of education, and whether it was felt to reflect contemporary reality. We consciously posed the latter question to see how spontaneously respondents brought up neorealism, without 'planting' the films or the movement in the dialogue directly (although how successful this was given the semantic link between *neorealismo* and *realtà* (reality) is debatable). We shall address the important links between education and neorealism later, but a significant feature of our study is how frequently in responses to a question about whether films reflected 'reality', that 'reality' was taken to be war and post-war poverty. The frequency is perhaps not surprising given the period in which our respondents were growing up, but it also speaks to the way in which the prominent notion of realism in mid-twentieth-century Italy, neorealism (and going further back to the movements of Verismo and French realism), has strengthened the association of the real with suffering.

As the work of Louis Bayman (2014) on melodrama in Italian cinema has shown what we understand as 'realism' when we talk about neorealism is in fact closely intertwined with melodrama. Perhaps this is nowhere more true than in

*Roma città aperta*, a film that has been hotly contested as 'a historical document via the insistent praise of its authenticity and referentiality' (Bayman, Gundle and Schoonover 2018: 299), and an example of high melodrama (Landy 2004). As Bayman (2009: 52) writes, 'The Resistance struggle, in this film, is melodramatically structured as … an eruption of repressed emotional force from the underground of the realist representation of the city environment.' In fact what lies behind the experience of the long and painful close of the Second World War in Italy included civil war, the deportation of most of Rome's Jewish population to the Nazi death camps and factional tensions within the Italian resistance itself. As David Forgacs suggests, these less than glorious elements are largely absent from *Roma città aperta*, since the film is loaded with particular affective values of noble self-sacrifice and victimhood in its celebration of unified Italian resistance to Nazi oppression (Forgacs 2018: 310). How *Roma città aperta* tells the story of the Second World War is far from neutral, and certainly quite limited, despite all the claims for the film's documentary power. What unites many of our respondents, however, is a continued desire to see Italy's history reflected in it (the verb to 'mirror' is used forty-seven times in this way in the surveys). The film has become so entangled in accounts of post-war Italian history that it is regarded *as* history. Indeed Millicent Marcus observes that, for Romans, the film is a 'primary datum, [of] "extramural" fact' (Marcus 2004: 76). Our interviewees' responses allow us to interrogate that powerful nexus between affect and the idea of the real, as they enable us to understand how these play out in the context of personal narratives, nuanced in particular by factors like age, generation and origin. Furthermore we consider how the subsequent canonization of these well-known films and genres has further affected audience responses to them. As Louis Bayman, Stephen Gundle and Karl Schoonover explain, *Roma città aperta*'s 'singularity accrued only through subsequent political and historical investments that would eventually ensconce the film's status as a classic' (2018: 296). We explore how the film sits between popular memory and official memory, coinciding in these roles, perhaps because of its particular psychic link to a narrative of 'good Italians' (Focardi 2000) and post-war pride in the acclaim the film brought Italy in its status as 'masterpiece' (in the words of one female respondent from Turin, b. 1943).[4]

---

[4] Another good example lies in this male participant's endorsement of neorealist films (b. 1931, Palermo): 'Yes, I think they were something for Italy to be proud of in that genre and that period.'

## *Roma città aperta*: An affective experience of war

Perhaps the most obvious factor defining our interviewees' responses to this film is their age. A handful of our survey respondents cite the film as having recounted their very own experiences, like this female participant, who cites the film as her favourite 'because it made me re-live very sad situations that I experienced first-hand, or feelings I had really had' (b. 1936, Naples). We might immediately pay attention to the use of affective language here, in 'sad' or 'sensations', attesting to the film's power to convey a truth of feeling, as well as events themselves. This strength of feeling also comes across, through the questionnaires, as a reason *not* to like the films too. Some of those who said they did not like neorealism, citing *Roma città aperta* as the film they knew, gave as their reason that it was too close to reality they experienced, repeating the word 'sad'; a male participant explains, 'because the war had just finished and watching scenes experienced first-hand was sad' (b. 1935, Naples), or a female participant, 'I didn't like them much, because we were already so sad' (b. 1941, Rome). In these accounts of its affective power then, very often, a positive or negative response to neorealism comes down to a question of how emotion is processed in relation to its proximity to the real. If, as Bayman argues, 'neorealism shows how the interaction of realism with melodrama is one way to reveal the suffering of ordinary people with vividness and authenticity' (Bayman 2009: 60), then whether audiences read that revelation as a form of cathartic recognition or an intensification of suffering too close to their own lived experience comes to the fore in our research.

The positive response to this affective power is then writ large in the video-interview anecdote of Sergio (b. 1931, Rome), who talks of how in the film he saw repeated the experience he had as a child. Recalling the protagonist, Pina's death scene in *Roma città aperta*, he vividly links it to a similar event, which he and his mother experienced during the war on the very same street in Rome. When Germans began shooting, his mother pulled him inside a doorway, and there he remembers seeing 'the terrified face of this woman, it was like the face of Anna Magnani – I saw that face again in her'. Already in that last phrase confusion seeps in around demonstratives and pronouns; which came first, the woman or Anna Magnani, whose face has become superimposed on that of the woman? In this account, as Radstone has written, 'what emerges is a liminal conception of cinema/memory, where the boundaries between cinema and memory are dissolved in favour of their mutuality and inseparability' (2010: 336). Sergio reinforces this dissolution when he talks about how he experienced cinema 'on his skin', which refers to a haptic relationship with the film that recurs in other accounts of its impact; while his is the most extreme there are linguistic echoes of this across other choices of language heard in other video interviews, 'segnato' (marked) (Giovanna and Luciana) or 'impresso' (imprinted) (Francesco and Rita). Sergio also uses the present tense when he talks about neorealism, claiming, 'you live it on the street', 'you are part of it'. His verbal delivery really stresses the immediacy of the experience conveyed by the film. His reference to feeling like a participant in the film also indirectly references the practice of non-professional casting for which neorealism was famous. Indeed the *Romarcord* interviewers stumble across a lady who does indeed claim to have been an extra in the film.[5]

The fact that these respondents all experienced war as a child, and that Sergio also cites Elsa Morante's novel *La storia* (*History*, 1974), an account of the war from the point of view of women and children, speaks to their own possible 'motor helplessness' that may well have intensified their affective response to the war (Deleuze 2005: 3). Fragments and anecdotes of direct experience of war from childhood tend to be associated with incomprehension and terror, often suspended outside of a broader narrative of experience, as indeed they would have been for children (and often for adults). This moment of unexpected terror can be related strongly to the affective power of Magnani's final scene as Pina, suddenly breaking into a run after the truck taking away her fiancé, arrested by the Nazis, and getting shot dead, the scene our respondents almost always remember best, and to which we will return. In Sergio's account and in that of the female participant cited at the beginning of this section that thrill of recognition bonds them to the film, but equally often, our questionnaires suggest, this memory of intense vulnerability might have been a reason to reject the film.

## *Roma città aperta* and postmemory: Second-hand experience of an unspeakable war

In Sergio's account, as we underlined, there is already an in-built cinematic quality, in which he is both performer and spectator, but primarily the spectator looking upon the suffering of the Other/the woman/Pina/Magnani. Bayman

---

[5] http://www.romarcordsapienza.com/166-2/.

argues that neorealism establishes 'the common realist concern to encourage empathy with the protagonists of a fiction' (2009: 60). The desire to generate empathy is usually associated with addressing and involving those who are not experiencing suffering themselves. This impetus to establish empathy is also a strong element of Karl Schoonover's argument that neorealism's primary address is to an international spectator, angling to engage him or her in Italy's post-war plight (Schoonover 2012: 200). What our interview responses suggest is that this address also reached out to those Italian audiences that were proximal to suffering, but did not experience it first-hand, primarily because of their age. Turning to a later generation that cannot remember the war directly, many interviewees of the post-1945 generation are nonetheless eager to declare their attachment to the film. They sit in an odd proximity to narratives of the war, in the words of Piera (b. 1944, Turin) who explains her liking for neorealist film narratives in our video essay: 'when I was little, the war had finished, but the war was still there, so these films reminded me of something I had experienced first-hand', thus both experiencing war and not experiencing it. This brings to mind Marianne Hirsch's work on postmemory, which, she writes,

> is distinguished from memory by generational distance and from history by deep personal connection. Postmemory is a powerful and very particular form of memory precisely because its connection to its object or source is mediated not through recollection but through an imaginative investment and creation. This is not to say that memory itself is unmediated, but that it is more directly connected to the past. Postmemory characterizes the experience of those who grow up dominated by narratives that preceded their birth, whose own belated stories are evacuated by the stories of the previous generation shaped by traumatic events that can be neither understood nor recreated. (1997: 22)

The 'imaginative investment' in the Second World War experience in Italy characterizes many of our participants' responses to neorealism. One male participant mentions *Roma città aperta* because 'it told us the history our parents experienced' (b. 1943, Cagliari). As Ninetta (b. 1936, Naples) says of seeing *Roma città aperta* at school, 'it was like living that period first-hand'. While we might take issue with Brunetta's claim that *Roma città aperta* and *Paisà* 'are more representative than any other primary historical source' (1993: 409), there is no doubt that that is how the film is being used here. Time and again, through our questionnaires and interviews, the words 'witness', 'real' and 'true' ring out. What can our interviews tell us about how these adjectives get attached to this particular film? Memories of war are second-hand, but coming from close relatives, so the film was felt to have a strongly informative function about what friends and family went through, and thus the strong attachment to this film as document might be related to a desire to understand parental suffering, an empathic mirroring back. As Marina (b. 1950, Rome) says, in response to the question about whether films reflected reality, '*Roma città aperta*, which we studied at school, I wasn't born then, my father was in the war in 1940, my father told me about it, those things were true, neorealism was all true'. This leap from the close relative's experience to an idea of neorealism as 'all true' could be related to what Eva Hoffman describes as Holocaust survivors' children's 'deep identification with the parents', children who have 'inherited not experience, but its shadows' (2010: 411).[6] Where better to connect those shadows to the real than through the cinematic experience?

The particular moment to which these felt shadows of trauma attach is, unsurprisingly, a scene of death. When Rita (b. 1933, Bologna province) says, 'for me, *Roma città aperta* is encapsulated in the image of Anna Magnani running after the truck' (Figure 5.1), she seems to speak for many. This chimes with a respondent from Bari province (female, b. 1937), who cried over 'the touchingly realistic scene of Anna Magnani running after the truck that is taking her husband away'. In contrast with the repeated mentions of this scene, only one respondent remembers 'the execution of the priest' at all, and one respondent even remembers Pina's death sequence as the final one.

Memories of Magnani in this scene, actually part way through the film, occur particularly in relation to her performance, suggesting intense levels of engagement with her character's feelings. As Francesco Pitassio writes, 'her performance is construed as an *overwhelming interruption*' and he describes the scene as an 'affective eruption' (Pitassio 2018: 374). This intensity has rendered it an embodied memory for many, who remember not only crying over the scene (only *Gone with the Wind* and *Catene* (*Chains*, Matarazzo, Italy, 1949) beat the film in this respect) but also re-enact Pina's gesture as she chases the van. This

---

[6] The concentration camps are mentioned by relatively few interviewees. However, for Giuseppe (Milan, b. 1943) they cast a much longer shadow than the suffering in Italy under occupation. He says, 'I dream of the SS at night'. Brought up Communist, in place of Jesus on his wall at home were the portraits of his father's companions who died at Mauthausen. Thus the films that left an impression on him included *Kapò* (Gillo Pontecorvo, Italy/France/Yugoslavia, 1960), which resonated strongly as members of his family on his father's side died in the concentration camps, and *Italiani brava gente* (*Attack and Retreat*, Giuseppe De Santis, Italy, 1964), which he describes as 'emblematic'.

**Figure 5.1** Anna Magnani as Pina in *Roma città aperta* (*Rome Open City*, Roberto Rossellini, Italy, 1945).

confirms the film's ability to stand in for experience by re-creating affect; as Jill Bennett writes, after William James, 'if emotions are not retrievable from memory, they are *revivable*, hence we don't remember grief or ecstasy, but by recalling a situation that produces those sensations we can produce a new bout of emotion. So, in other words, affect, properly conjured, produces a real-time somatic experience, no longer framed as representation' (2003: 27, her italics).

This argument gains weight when we consider that the key scene in this discursive remembering, Pina's death, is marked as a maternal sacrifice within the film: her son is kept back from her dead body by the priest in a famous reverse *Pietà*. In expressing what she learned from cinema, Mariellina (b. 1921, Bari) cites *Roma città aperta* as one that taught her about motherhood and 'women's strength', which has much to tell us about the gendered power of this representation, and gives us a rare insight, given Mariellina's age, into the response of someone who was a woman when she first saw the film. Sonia (b. 1945, Milan) also relates to Pina as a woman with family, asking, 'What didn't poor Pina do, for her brother [correcting herself], her husband Francesco?' using the informal 'la Pina' here, as if Pina is a family friend, reflecting Anna Magnani's familiarity as a star of the people. Magnani's enduringly powerful star persona perhaps also offers some kind of reconciliation, since contemporary audiences were not quite sure that her character was really dead.[7] This scene of maternal sacrifice could arguably become a container for a trauma that was not always spoken in the post-war period. Giovanna (b. 1950, Rome) explains her fascination for the film because when she was growing up, 'people didn't talk about it [the war] much'. For Hoffman, the parent, traditionally the mother, can act as a container for the inchoate in a context of trauma (2010: 408).

What these interviews suggest is that what is not spoken is still felt, particularly in family dynamics, which might explain why the processing of an experience so close and intensely felt attaches to a moment of passionate outburst, precisely a *family moment*, something structured around a dynamic comprehensible in what must have appeared a chaotic political situation. In fact Giovanna's obsession with finding out more about the film, apparent in her recounting the anecdote that Magnani's outburst was really one of a passionate woman irritated with her lover, director Roberto Rossellini, reflects a sense that this scene contains more than the sum of its parts. This 'excess' becomes more explicit in the response of Gianfranco (b. 1929, Florence). The process of remembering a film like *Roma città aperta* functions as a trigger for other memories, especially those related to the war, for example, his memory of a German in Florence stealing the wallets of passers-by, or even the massacre of Campo di Marte in 1944. It is significant that this latter memory is actually of an act of violence perpetrated by the RSI (Italian Social Republic), by Italians on Italians. The infrequency with which such memories occur confirms David Forgacs's hypothesis that by acting as a container, *Roma città aperta* has also shaped collective history, in choosing to emphasize a nation of good Italians, united as victims of Nazi oppressors (Forgacs 2000).

The intense attachment to *Roma città aperta* can and must also be read in the light of the film's critical canonization, and the two elements of attachment to narrative detail and early and repeated exposure to the film exist in a dynamic relation that cannot be disentangled. As Francesco Pitassio writes, 'Pina's death simultaneously epitomized national hardships and the heyday of Italian cinema, merging past events with their fictional representation. From the late 1940s,

---

[7] So much so that one respondent, Gianni (b. 1941, Cagliari province), insistently remembers that in this scene the priest falls down dead, and Anna Magnani comes and picks him up: the exact reverse of what actually happens. This may be an instance of what Portelli describes as 'uchronic memory', which he describes as a way in which oral history stories 'emphasise not how history went, but how it could, or should have gone, focussing on possibility rather than actuality' (Portelli 1988: 46).

public discourse looked back at historical happenings and the collective attempt to reconstruct Italy, while celebrating the glories of neorealism. At the crossroads was the body of Anna Magnani in her most renowned role' (2018: 375). The repeated reference to the scene of Magnani's death might also lead us to wonder whether the repeated showings of the film and extracts from the film on television might not have crystallized and set memories of the period for our interviewees, creating a form of 'prosthetic memory' (Landsberg 2004), as we have suggested before (Treveri Gennari et al. 2011). This does not make the film or memories of it any less valuable, however; indeed, it is crucial not to underestimate its power as an affective, rather than documentary one. As Christian Metz writes, 'Films release a mechanism of affective and perceptual *participation* in the spectator ... they appeal to his sense of belief ... with the accents of true evidence' (Metz 1974: 4). It is on this basis, nonetheless, that the film and its popular reception have a great deal to tell us about how history has sedimented in the Italian national psyche. The significance of the scene of Pina's death in this creation of a 'prosthetic' memory perhaps becomes most significant in the interview with Francesco (b. 1933, Turin province). Under pressure, as we might all be in the face of a taxing question to fish out a memory of a significant emotion or scene from any film seen, what he eventually retrieves just happens to be that most famous scene. Francesco's sudden act of recall is a useful reminder that this scene is the only scene from any film remembered by more than one person across 1,043 questionnaires (six people mention it, despite there being no question about a specific scene). This is a scene repeatedly shown on television, as, precisely, just a scene and not part of a whole film, a fact which emerges from Elena's interview (b. 1934, Bologna) when she says she has never seen the whole film – just that scene on television. We might interpret in a similar way the memory of the posters for the film discussed by Rita (b. 1933, Bologna province). While the original film poster showed Magnani, but emphasized Aldo Fabrizi and the Nazi threat,[8] Rita remembers seeing and then looking for Magnani's famous gesture chasing the lorry. This may be an instance of misremembering that points back to the iconography subsequently imposed on the film, such as the poster used to advertise the restored version of the film in 2014, which Rita also went to see.[9] However, it is also possible that she did see a still from the film

---

[8] The original poster used to promote the film in Italy at the time of its release in 1945 was designed by Dante Manno. See Mel Bagshaw (2003).
[9] http://distribuzione.ilcinemaritrovato.it/roma-citta-aperta.

in the papers at the time, or possibly a cinema lobby, and confused that with the posters. In any case, the comment is interesting because it suggests that either her memory of the film or her first viewing of the film was coloured by a discursive emphasis on this particular scene of sacrifice for the nation.

## *Roma città aperta*: 'A sense of place, a sense of belonging to a place'

If the theory of prosthetic memory is one that 'models the memory-cinema relation as one in which cinema implants memories into passive spectators' (Radstone 2010: 336), taking 'no account of the spectator's negotiation of images', our interviews certainly offer the opportunity to challenge that approach, by moving towards the model of cinema/memory as the 'full two-way exchange' that Radstone proposes. She suggests that Annette Kuhn's account of her personal 'memory work' in particular is a good example of how the individual's reverie and memory of particular films can reveal 'cinema/memory's binding of individuals with a national imaginary and with place' (ibid.: 337). As Kuhn wanders through the London streets and links her reverie to two films about war, poverty and the British national imaginary, she realizes how her 'reverie then combines a primal fantasy with a host of other fascinations (with the recent past, with recent war, with a family romance); and sets these into imaginings in which a sense of place, a sense of belonging to a place, are central' (ibid.: 338).

While our own interviewees' memory work, emerging through interview, rather than written personal reflection, does not possess such intensely subjective qualities as Kuhn's, the main context in which ownership of that shared 'reality' of *Roma città aperta* is reinforced and personalized in interview is in relation to place, sometimes affording a sense of greater personal ownership of the film, sometimes creating distance. Respondents cite certain kinds of response to the film according to their distance from Rome. Neorealism is, of course, well known for its use of real locations, and there is no doubt that this link is felt to intensify connection to this film (and *Ladri di biciclette*) among Roman audiences. Franco (b. 1938, Rome province), for example, cites specific locations, such as Porta Portese, in his engagement with these two films. Several survey participants, from the province and city of Rome, select it as their favourite film because of its link to the city, 'because it spoke of the Rome that I love so much' (a male participant, b. 1939), because 'it was the story of a city like Rome' (a male participant, b. 1939) and because of 'the powerful representation of Rome during the German occupation' (a female participant, b. 1938), and one female participant declares her liking for neorealist films because 'Yes, yes, they told you the truth about the city of Rome' (b. 1937, Rome province). A strong devotion to the film can be perceived among the Roman interviewees in our pilot study: Lucia (b. 1922, Rome) saw the film four times, and Luciano (b. 1940, Rome) saw it four or five times, although the former preferred US cinema in general, reflecting the status of *Roma città aperta* as an exception, as it is for Luigi (b. 1927, Rome), who loved the film, although he did not like neorealism. For those who did experience the war 'first-hand' in areas of particularly acute or lengthy wartime struggle the film is also to be felt to be universal even outside of Rome, as these comments about their favourite films suggest: an 80-year-old woman from Tuscany chooses '*Roma città aperta*, it reminded me of things that had happened in my family', while a 78-year-old woman, mentioned earlier, who selects '*Roma città aperta*, because it made me relive very sad situations that I experienced first-hand' was from Naples.

However, 'cinema/memories', writes Radstone, 'prove to be composites and condensations, belonging wholly neither to the public world of the cinema nor to the personal and interior realm of fantasy' (2010: 338). This is evident in that the urban space of Naples is felt to be sufficiently close to the place reality of neorealism that at least two respondents also claim ownership of these films for Naples: Rita (b. 1935, Naples) claims *Sciuscià* (*Shoeshine*, Vittorio De Sica, Italy, 1946) 'was the reality of Naples', and actually remembers the film as being set in Naples, although it is set in Rome, and possibly she is remembering the 'Naples' episode of *Paisà* (*Paisan*, Roberto Rossellini, 1946), or the quite similar *Proibito rubare* (*No Stealing*, Luigi Comencini, Italy, 1948). Michele (b. 1944, Naples province) cannot remember the name of the film he felt reflected the experience of Naples, but thinks it might have been *Napoli città aperta*![10]

Generally, however, among respondents distant from Rome, in Sardinia, Sicily or Puglia, all areas where the experience of the Second World War was less prolonged, the films provoke different reactions in relation to spatial belonging. One of these is a categorical denial of any sense of connection to her reality, like Maria (b. 1931, Bari province), for example, who says instead that she learned about what had happened during the war in these films. Others hint at other

---

[10] The film is most likely to be *Le quattro giornate di Napoli* (*The Four Days of Naples*, Nanni Loy, Italy, 1962).

kinds of reality represented for them which might point towards a more appropriate neorealist film, like *Riso amaro* (*Bitter Rice*, Giuseppe De Santis, Italy, 1948) for Rosangela (b. 1943) in a rural setting in the province of Turin, or for Giuseppe (b. 1929, Palermo province), who describes watching films that were close to the local reality of the 'mafia and the massacre of Portella della Ginestra' which also used extras from his village (possibly a reference to *Salvatore Giuliano* (Francesco Rosi, Italy, 1962)).

Gender is also an important factor here. Female survey respondents give several interesting reasons for remembering *La ciociara* (*Two Women*, Vittorio De Sica, Italy, 1960), but one female participant from the province of Naples remembers weeping over *La ciociara*, because it was a 'sad story that could have happened in my village', speaking obviously to the film's setting in her region. In response to the question about reality, Marta (b. 1936, Florence) speaks of films that show 'women's problems connected to her life', but these are not articulated clearly, arguably because there is not a canonical language in which to talk about them. Olga (b. 1939, Bari province) is a little more explicit and talks about the reflection of reality in cinema of the time being the mistreatment of, and violence towards, women. She remembers seeing female stonebreakers in films that could be seen in the village, but does not refer to a particular film. Her account seems informed by a feminist awareness, and gestures towards an alternative history that could emerge from a more in-depth examination of women's memories.

While just as many questionnaire respondents from Rome dismiss neorealism as too sad, or boring, as respondents from any other region of Italy, few interview respondents from Rome challenge directly the accuracy and canonical status of *Roma città aperta*, but is worth mentioning the valuable testimony of the female passer-by in the *Romarcord* project, who moves quickly from a question about *Roma città aperta* to explain how she thinks the Jewish deportations missing from the film are a most significant feature of Rome's wartime history. It is also interesting to note that the same series of interviews includes a Jewish man who hasn't seen *Roma città aperta*, but says he has watched TV documentaries about Jewish deportation instead. These constitute the exceptions, but they articulate a consciousness of the film's shortcomings that is not otherwise expressed openly.[11]

---

[11] See Forgacs (2000) for a detailed account of how the film constructs a national myth of unity by omission.

A sense of physical distance from the film's location can also serve to reinforce the film's value as document, and one that perhaps serves to enhance a sense of national belonging. Delia (b. 1936, Turin province) saw Rossellini and De Sica films at the *cineforum* (film discussion club), but says that they presented a version of the war very different to the one she had experienced. She had been evacuated to a small village, so the sight of German round-ups or the struggle to survive was new to her. She experienced those things through neorealist films ('we saw what the world was like'). In fact, she still does not like films 'that are pure fantasy' and prefers realism. As one participant explains, he remembers *Roma città aperta*, because he 'was struck by the detailed description of something that in Sardinia we experienced from a distance' (b. 1936, Cagliari province). Also from Sardinia, Ida (b.1943, Cagliari province) recounts that it was only through watching films like *Roma città aperta* and *La ciociara* that she realized what the war was. Similarly, in interview Rosa (b. 1931, Bari) recounts how films about the Resistance also taught her about how badly other parts of the country suffered during the war, commenting that in Bari they were lucky as it was not as bad. When asked about whether and how cinema reflected reality she cites films about the war that reflected the 'evil' of the Germans. In narrating her reaction to films about the war and the atrocities carried out by the Nazis as a dialogue with herself, she reveals a personal moment of historical understanding: 'No, I said to myself "these are not just things people say"; "No," I said to myself "these things are true."' In this light, we can see that the film is regarded as playing a fundamental role in forging a shared history for a country that in fact experienced war as an extremely fragmented range of experiences, even while 'as an act of cultural memorialization, the film's remembering is by nature always at least in part idealized, and somewhat faulty' (Bayman, Gundle and Schoonover 2018: 299).

## *Roma città aperta*: A reluctant education?

The fact that a 'postmemory' generation often first encountered the film at school has no doubt reinforced its status as official history, since so many respondents describe it that way. This account chimes with Charles Leavitt's hypothesis that the film itself, with its child-centred narrative, aimed to address the 'youth problem': 'the fate of the nation's children after Fascism'. Its ending in particular, he argues, exhorts the viewer to work towards action: 'only if they – the boys, the viewers – understand the message that has been conveyed, the duty that has been imparted, will true closure be achieved' (Leavitt 2018: 368). However, this institutional imposition and putative pedagogical pressure did not always necessarily produce the desired results and perhaps explains some of the negative responses in our surveys, which also included the word 'boring', a response we might typically associate with compulsory school texts. As mentioned earlier, many interviewees recall *Roma città aperta* in response to the question about cinema as a form of education. In her interview Ninetta (b. 1936, Naples) talks about the shift from *The Red Shoes* (Powell and Pressburger, UK, 1948) to *Roma città aperta* as something she learned to recognize when she was encouraged to see the latter by her teachers in the context of a debate about the war. One gets the impression, therefore, that this shift in taste from one form to the other was not entirely spontaneous. Another of our interviewees, Marta (b. 1939, Milan), within the context of an observation about the disregard for popular Italian cinema such as that of Totò at the time, says that viewings of films such as *Roma città aperta* and *Ladri di biciclette* were 'driven by adults who told us that those films were important'.

That these two films are so often grouped together speaks to a standard canonization that may have been perceived by some as externally imposed. Michele (b. 1930, Milan) acknowledges these films 'that made history as the best of Italian cinema' but at that age, they were a bit much – he conveys this through a gesture indicating a heavy weight and laughter rather than words, as if not quite daring to say the word 'heavy' (Figure 5.2). Michele reflects many respondents in our survey who use their age as an excuse for their not originally liking or understanding neorealism, repeating the expression 'at that age'. He hastens to add that 'obviously once he was forty, things changed', but the hand gesture he uses to convey the 'bitter taste such films left for him and his friends' conveys a different idea. Dario (b. 1937, Naples province) is more forthright. He also associates neorealism with education, and he followed Rossellini and De Sica a lot, but he got fed up with it, because he got fed up with the emphasis on poverty and difficulty – he'd been through that and felt they needed to move on. Neorealism showed the link between life and cinema. However, he felt that this vein of cinema got exhausted, and became too heavy for them as children, they were masterpieces, but they were a bit depressing, which he describes as 'a constant weeping to ourselves' while life went on. Of course, we might choose to link this narrative to the Andreotti law's political rejection of neorealism in 1949, with the notorious call to Italian cinema to show 'fewer rags and more

**Figure 5.2** Michele conveys the heaviness of neorealist cinema with a hand gesture (*Italian Cinema Audiences* dataset).

legs', attributed to politician Giulio Andreotti (cited in Wood 2006: 53), or a mainstream understanding of why neorealism did not last, but in the context of Dario's wide-ranging cinematic tastes, from Westerns to Disney, it comes across as something more spontaneous.

Reflecting a marked association of femininity with the private sphere and permission to share feelings, some female respondents personalize this response as a form of emotional weakness rather than situating it within this more collective rejection of neorealism. Graziella (b. 1932, Florence province) says she had a collection of videos of post-war films but later gave them away, partly because it is too painful for her to rewatch films about suffering and concentration camps. She cites *Roma città aperta* in connection with feeling great emotion, but then says that she does not want to rewatch it as there is too much suffering in it and she cannot stand to see that at her age, because she is 'sensitive'. This is an unusual example of older age, rather than younger age being used as a reason not to watch these films. Other forms of rejection, however, also relate to a kind of emotional overload that expresses itself powerfully in the video interview; Marcella (b. 1947, Florence province) remembers that sad scenes in *La ciociara* left an impression on her that was strong and left her shaken, which she describes with a firmly final horizontal hand gesture, and as for *Roma città aperta*, she cannot explain the effect it had on her, but she makes a gesture, a very particular kind of drawing back, hands held up as if to protect herself. Silvana (b. 1930, Palermo) describes Pina's death scene as a scene which she cannot bring herself to rewatch, even if the scene and the film itself are 'astonishing', because its emotional impact is 'intolerable'.

The testimony of Luciana (b. 1941, Sardinia) gives further insight into how it is that this film's affective power has not always enmeshed itself into the national psyche in an entirely positive way, partly thanks to the early exposure of a generation to some powerful scenes of torture. This testimony supports David Forgacs's suggestion that the unusual nature of these scenes, outside even adult viewers' horizon of expectations at the time of the film's release, made stronger by lighting and the inclusion of a suffering spectator in the priest, accounted for a neglected aspect of the film's contemporary impact (Forgacs 2018: 308). Luciana recounts the trauma that she carries from her particular memory of seeing *Roma città aperta*, aged 8, when 'the scenes of violence really upset her', describing the film as one that has marked her, leaving her unable to watch violence on screen.[12] Her nervous, fluttering hand gestures towards her ears underline her recalled confusion about how to stop the flow of this powerful affective response. Her traumatic memory of the torture scenes gains particular force in the context of Luciana's own tragic early childhood, which emerges in the telling of this tale: during the 1940s she lost her entire immediate family. However it also underlines a possible (and largely repressed) reason for negative responses to this film by many who were children at the time: fear. Returning to Annette Kuhn's work on memories of British cinemagoing in the 1930s, she notes how frequently her respondents remember films in detail because of fear:

> So uncommonly vivid and detailed are these stories that it sometimes seems as if, in the process of narrating them, informants are accessing the 'child's voice' within themselves and reliving the experience of being scared out of their wits.
> … Laughter is a common accompaniment to these stories. (Kuhn 2002: 67)

We can see all of this in Luciana's response, but while it may be acceptable to laugh about being frightened over *King Kong* (Merian C. Cooper and Ernest

---

[12] A comment reinforced by her contribution to our Facebook page: 'In 1949 I saw *Roma città aperta* which terrified me. I couldn't believe such cruelty. Since then I can't bring myself to watch scenes of violence and torture. I still close my eyes at some scenes. This was the film that struck terror into me as an 8 year-old girl', comment left 22 January 2014, on *Italian Cinema Audiences* Facebook page.

B. Schoedsack, United States, 1933), as in the case of many of Kuhn's respondents, perhaps it is a less commonly confessed response to this revered classic. Maria Grazia from the Rome pilot study (b. 1938, Rome) does describe how 'neo-realism showed things that could scare you', while Rosetta (b. 1940, Florence) reminds us that more protected children were spared this: she and her friends did not go to see those films with Anna Magnani, or *Ladri di biciclette*, because their parents said that they were a bit strong. The American films, with Esther Williams, with the swimming pools, they were what they liked at that age. They probably would not have appreciated those tragic films back then – although, she hastily adds, she can see their merit now.

Returning to the role of *Roma città aperta* in containing the messy matter of postmemory, it is no surprise though if we find so many responses that dismiss the film, and neorealism with it, as too heavy, or even too painful, when we consider all the confusion, violence, grief and mourning that the film contained, and often for vulnerable young people, as our interviews suggest.

## Conclusion: Reflections on the present

Our analysis in this chapter highlights how these memory narratives tell us more about the history woven around post-war Italian cinema by and for audiences than they do about the film's original reception in the 1940s and 1950s. The strong attachments to and rejections of neorealist films like *Roma città aperta* are both cause and effect of their barometer-like function for many Italians of the generations that we interviewed. It signals the national on multiple levels: the pride in Italy's cultural production ('our films') being acknowledged as a global leader, the suffering associated with the Second World War and the political hopes of post-war recovery. In our public presentations of this work, it often emerged that a present-day younger generation's ignorance about the films of this period was regarded as a measure of public and national amnesia and, in the more extreme accounts, a failure.

Sonia (b. 1945, Milan) describes how she still holds *Roma città aperta* in her heart with an emphatic hand gesture (Figure 5.3). If at least half of the generations we interviewed have learned to love these particular neorealist films passionately, primarily as a means of working through their own war-torn pasts, of empathizing with their parents, and finding a positive national identity, they sometimes regret that their grandchildren do not know them today. At the

**Figure 5.3** Sonia describes holding *Roma città aperta* in her heart (*Italian Cinema Audiences* dataset).

same time occasionally they themselves have also experienced a shift in attitude towards the film, which reflects the critical re-evaluation of *Roma città aperta* in particular as providing a 'glimpse of a future that was never to come' and for 'its unwitting elegy for a working-class life soon to be interred within the reconstruction and consumerist booms that were to follow the film's release' (Bayman, Gundle and Schoonover 2018: 299). In the words of one respondent (b. 1947, Palermo), he loved *Roma città aperta* because 'back then I believed in the nation (*la patria*) – I don't any more'. What is significant here is how the word 'belief' crops up more than once; in interview Mario (b. 1939, Rome) remembers adults talking about the film, when it seemed like the world was changing, but he rejects the spirit of that talk. He doesn't *believe* in men, he has suffered so many 'scams'. In both cases the beliefs here are clearly political, and we might relate these comments to the breakdown of grand narratives in a country in which has suffered dramatically the creation and the collapse of both Cold War and economic certainties. However, belief also has an emotional, affective register, so visible in our video interviewees' investments in *Roma città aperta*, and so we might also relate these disappointments and attachments to the location of cinema itself in the national imaginary, cinema as the frequently cited 'dream', but a dream that in the case of these films became synonymous with political dreams for the future, a future that turned out quite differently.

# Part Three

# Gender and cinemagoing

# 6

# A girl's-eye view of post-war Italian cinema

*Cinema influenced my way of being as a woman, it gave me a femininity.*
(Alma, b. 1943, Naples)

## Introduction

In the opening quotation, one of our interviewees, Alma, asserts the influence of the films she watched as a girl on her development as a woman, in a way that typifies the dominant, increasingly critiqued 'future-oriented' vision of the relationship between girlhood and womanhood (Driscoll 2002; Kearney 2009). The latter writes that 'although Simone de Beauvoir's most profound assertion – "One is not born, but rather becomes, a woman" – begins her exploration of how femininity is produced during childhood, an analysis of how one becomes *a girl* is not her objective' (Kearney 2009: 11). Italian girls of the early 1950s were rarely considered anything other than 'little women'; however, as Simonetta Piccone Stella (1993: 138) has written, later that decade young people were to be recognized as the first generation of teenagers. Understanding girlhood as a historically contingent notion (Dyhouse 2013), we here consider whether our cinema memories do still construct a pre-teen girlhood culture. We will demonstrate how these memories constitute a hitherto neglected, but essential narrative strand of Italian cinema history, and history more broadly.

While there has been some work on memories of women's childhood culture in the UK, by Annette Kuhn (2002, 2010a), and in the United States, by Rebecca Hains et al. (2011), as Kearney suggests, girlhood media studies still tend to be dominated by presentism. Nonetheless recent scholarly work on Italian film audiences has begun to pay attention to this young generation, from work that addresses the reception of girls on screen (Capussotti 2004), letters to women's magazines (Cassamagnaghi 2007), to fan mail (Buckley

2009), and diaries (Vitella 2015). Contributions from oral history are still relatively rare, but have also made some inroads (Colombo et al. 2012; Fanchi 2007; Forgacs and Gundle 2007; Grignaffini 1992). However, as mentioned above, while Anglophone culture has recently seen a 'significant movement away from studying girls as future women and toward analysing girls as members of a unique demographic group' (Kearney 2009: 18), in the context of thinking about historical Italian female youth audiences, the focus tends to be on young women in movement towards their future, as Enrica Capussotti confirms:

> Belonging to a generation provided young women with a point of identification and a space from which to develop expectations and desires that contradicted the destiny previously mapped out for women and ideas about being female. (Capussotti 2004: 152)

Chapter 7 of our book considers how young Italian women made their generational identity their own, and how they drew creatively upon the opportunities offered by cinema, and stardom in particular, to a teen identity still in formation, as Piccone Stella has pointed out: 'The [teen] generation of the 1950s did not produce its own collective identities, nor reflect on itself particularly ... As paradoxical as this may sound, these young women in the shadows developed a variety of new identities, personal and authentic solutions, without producing a precise model' (1993: 121). In this chapter, however, we will suggest that the same could perhaps be said of women's childhood and yet-to-be-invented 'tween' experiences of cinemagoing, fond memories of which also form a substantial part of our oral history narratives. Indeed, the oral history narrative, privileging the individual in a one-to-one context, brings to light the existence of girlhood memories about Italian cinema that have hitherto remained largely covered. We will begin by exploring in more depth how these memories can be uncovered by refining our understanding of Italian generational identities as gendered.

## Girlhood and generational identity

Recent work by Göran Bolin (2014) identifies the importance of the concept of generation in understanding the relationship between media landscapes and nostalgia over the life course. He sees this nostalgia produced by both 'objective' and 'subjective' media landscapes, the former based on shared material experiences of media availability (the mushrooming and popularity of local cinemas across post-war Italy, in our case) and the latter on individual experiences of and responses to media content. As discussed in the introduction to this book, the film *Nuovo Cinema Paradiso* is perhaps the narrative that resonates with and reflects official Italian memories of the 'objective' media landscape of the 1950s for the generations we interviewed. Yet the film also offers and crystallizes a particular 'subjective' nature of the media landscape of those generations, one that includes censorious parish priests, the appeal of the Western genre, the tears of the melodrama, the humour of popular comic star Totò and the seemingly indefatigable glamour of Hollywood. *Nuovo Cinema Paradiso* is now often taken to be an accurate account of that period (Colombo et al. 2012: 26). However, Bolin emphasizes that the subjective nature of any media landscape narrated in the context of social interaction can emerge quite differently according to the context and the type of social interaction (Bolin 2014: 117), and therefore since Tornatore's account, with its normative fixation on boyhood and the homosocial bond between the male child and the projectionist, appears definitively to exclude, marginalize and 'other' girlhood, it is not a watertight cultural narrative.[1]

As Carolyn Steedman has observed, our interpretation of the past is limited and sometimes in conflict with the grids or cultural devices we might use to articulate it: 'personal interpretations of past time – the stories that people tell themselves in order to explain how they got to the place they currently inhabit – are often in deep and ambiguous conflict with the official interpretative devices of a culture' (Steedman 1986: 6). This chapter aims to unpick the weave of that discourse and stitch back into the subjective media landscape memories of girlhood so that we might recompose a vision of that period to include a girl's-eye view of cinema history.

A further way in which Bolin's work is useful to this chapter is his identification of 'two kinds of formative years: one in childhood and one in youth'. He explains that

> nostalgic childhood memories also have a formative dimension, and are important for the self-construction of generation as actuality. And even if these memories are more subjective than the collective experiences in youth, they

---

[1] See Radstone (1995) on the subjective nature of the film.

> bring in the dimension of age and life situation to the generational experience in a qualitatively different way compared to the youth experience. (Bolin 2014: 128)

This finding is confirmed powerfully in the Italian context by Colombo et al., whose work on media and generations in Italian society leads them to describe 'childhood as a central resource in defining a generational identity'; furthermore, they suggest that the media represent a 'frame of reference through which knowledge of the world is constructed' (Colombo et al. 2012: 108, 118). Their work to date, however, makes relatively few references to the role of gender in this process. As discussed above, where there is work on girlhood in Italian cinema, this has tended to concentrate on the later formative years of youth, and indeed, as our next chapter on stardom suggests, this is unsurprising since women's memories of cinema tend to focus predominantly on stars as role models when girls are becoming adults, and therefore on the later teen years, particularly the key period between 16 and 25. It is also difficult on the basis of our interviews to define exactly which memories belong to 'girlhood', understood in this context as a child or a tween – the term *ragazza* (girl) is an increasingly elastic term that could define any moment between the ages of 8 and 25. However, certain experiences are identified with girlhood as an age defined by our own interviewees as roughly up to 15, where possible, with a focus on the more definite term in which girlhood and childhood coincide in Italian: *ragazzina* or *bambina* (little girl or girl child). Giuseppina (b. 1941, Palermo), for example, refers to herself as still having been a *bambina* at 15, contrasting her experience with the present day, in which 'at fifteen you're already an adult in all senses'. Often these experiences of girlhood remain 'covered over' or quickly dismissed,[2] but the breadth of our sample enables their recovery.

Thinking about the experience of girlhood in generational terms, it is important to consider the different generations actually present within our sample, and their formative experiences. For example, Italian commentators on this period recognize a generation born after the war, which is frequently associated with the radical break with systems of authority constituted by 1968.[3] However, feminist critics are more specific about this generation of women as

---

[2] Claudia Mitchell and Jacqueline Reid-Walsh associate this term with the idea of 'lost girlhoods', and women apologizing for or forgetting girlhood play (2008: xxix).

[3] See Colombo et al. (2012); also P. Aroldi and C. Ponte write that 'the Postwars tended to emphasize their radical difference from the past, taking credit for having addressed and changed the rules of collective behaviour "forever", making a real break from the traditional mechanisms of transmission "from generation to generation" still maintained by their parents' (2012).

a generation young enough to feel real consequences of second-wave feminism, who have often experienced a dramatic break with the maternal generation. In the words of Franca Bimbi (1993: 149), many of these women 'have broken explicitly with their primary socialization model and have legitimized a model of female social identity that is no longer exclusively oriented toward the family'. Looking at women of that post-war generation in the UK, Lynn Abrams (2014) labels them a 'transition' generation, who must devise diverse narrative strategies in order to negotiate a coherent narrative of the self in order to accommodate this break with their mother's generation.[4] At the same time, nearly half of our interviewees belong to a slightly earlier generation, born before the war, so it is important to consider whether differences emerge in terms of their negotiation of girlhood in narratives of the self. Working with the narratives of both groups, and drawing primarily on material from our video interviews, this chapter will consider how memories of girlhood emerge through narratives of cinemagoing, through memories of films, through discussions of romance and finally how they fit into the context of what we might describe as fragments of 'life narratives'.

## Girlhood cinemagoing and socialization

As Giovanna Grignaffini has written of this period, 'women experienced cinema as a form of socialization, they got out of the house collectively, and they acquired and shared a certain knowledge and social imaginary' (Grignaffini 1992: 122), but on closer inspection that experience of leaving the home and socialization would appear to be intimately linked to the experience of girlhood.[5] What both generations of women have in common is a memory of cinemagoing that suggests that cinema was precisely an experience of girlhood, one that got lost for many with the relatively early entry into motherhood. Memories of cinemagoing practices from the period are often delivered with the expanded pronoun *noi*

---

[4] She writes, 'Among this generation it is particularly important to be able to reconcile conflicts in the life story because their journey to autonomous selfhood often involved walking away from, and sometimes consciously rejecting, a model of womanhood represented by their mothers' generation' (2014: 20).
[5] An article by members of this research project has already shown how the memories of attending cinemas increasingly distant from the home can be mapped onto the experience of growing up for our respondents, looking at the case of one Roman woman's memories of her girlhood. See Ercole et al. (2017).

*ragazze* (we girls), demonstrating that the clear 'we-sense' of a generation that Colombo et al. associate with the post-war generation was gendered (Colombo et al. 2012: 110).[6] Prior to the common practice of going to the cinema with a boyfriend in later youth,[7] many respondents talk about going to the cinema together with female friends, and indeed for some this is the most important aspect of their cinemagoing memories. In the words of Danila (b. 1947, Turin), cinema was summed up as 'escape, peace, female friendship, a wonderful period'.

Both Jackie Stacey (1994) and Mariagrazia Fanchi (2017) have written about how we might read this emphasis on the social as a particularly female aspect of cinemagoing practice, structured around girls' and women's more relational identities.[8] Certainly, the memories of Lucia (b. 1936, Cagliari province) demonstrate a more spontaneous, and rebellious, embrace of female company. When her parents refused to accompany her, she snuck out to the cinema on her own, and a neighbouring girl who heard about her doing this eventually joined her. Anticipation of peer interaction undoubtedly informed decisions to go to the cinema too. Delia (b. 1936, Turin) saw *On the Waterfront* (Elia Kazan, United States, 1954) with her female cousin. She borrowed money (400 lire) from friends, because it was the film everyone was talking about at school. School itself had a role to play in encouraging the love of the cinema, since many mention going as part of school outings.[9] The influence of the female peer group was so great, in fact, that one older respondent (Maria, b. 1934, Bari) observes that it was the richer girls in her class, rather than the films themselves, that influenced her and her friends the most in terms of behaviour, a powerful reminder not to overestimate the role of the media alone in processes of gender identity formation.

---

[6] Their research, however, contradicts ours by finding this collective identity to be slightly less strong with women.

[7] While many respondents confess to using the cinema as a cover for physical contact, this is implied to be in their late teens and even twenties; Maddalena (b. 1935, Palermo province) is the only one to admit that she would hold hands with her boyfriend there as young as 13. It may well be that this was more common but the social rules associated with the period still hold sway over memory. It is interesting that she is the only one as her narrative is very fixated on the length of her relationship: sixty-seven years! So this may be a factor, wanting to emphasize duration.

[8] 'In every case, the value of sharing stands out as a distinctive feature of women's experience of cinema-going; it is different from the necessary sharing of the space and time of viewing in the cinema, but it is rather a socializing that is sought or and planned, an indispensable precondition of cinema-going' (Fanchi 2017); Stacey writes, 'The appeal of a utopian sense of community may be especially strong given the ways in which femininity is culturally constructed as generally more relational' (1994: 101).

[9] This pedagogical history has already been traced by Davide Boero (2013).

The cinematic space in Italy of the 1950s was a male-dominated one, as Fanchi (2007) has shown, but as we have discussed earlier in the volume the gendered picture of cinemagoing was complex. Many women mention being accompanied by male friends or relatives as a form of defence against a practice of molestation which our female interviewees narrate frequently, as discussed in Chapter 3. As a male space, the cinema is also remembered as a more positive point of connection with men for girls. The cinema provided both the opportunity and pleasure of seeing and being seen by boys, to which some girls responded with pleasure and others with anxiety, largely based on their sense of material readiness to be seen. At the same time, the opportunities for contact with men extended beyond the pleasures of peer company, providing girls with a source of contact with their father. That nearly one quarter of female respondents mention going regularly to the cinema with their father, often with great enthusiasm over shared tastes and experiences, suggests that the space provided an opportunity for father–daughter bonding and lessons forged in leisure that may not have found expression elsewhere. These memories allow women to revisit that bond with a pleasure expressed in words and also through body language. Piera (b. 1944, Turin) uses the word *allegria* (joy) twice and *felicità* (happiness) once to describe the experience of going to the cinema with her father, 'a cinema fanatic', who would bring sugared water along with him because there was no popcorn, and whose love of Westerns introduced her to questions relating to the law and race. This bonding opportunity takes on particular significance in the context of Piera's mother's limited movements – she would only go out to visit family. The memory of just going with father tallies in many ways with the findings that an older generation of women (the interviewees' mothers) did not go to the cinema as often as men in this period, and points to the difference that was already emerging between the post-war generation and their mothers. Sometimes these memories of the father–daughter bond express themselves in a particularly embodied way: Maria (b. 1943, Naples province) recounts how she used to go to the cinema with her father almost every day. She smiles and 'relives' this experience in an embodied way using direct speech and adopting a childlike tone as she says, 'Dad, take me to the cinema, take me to the cinema.' The opportunity provided by cinema to spend time with their father undoubtedly adds to the special quality of the memories of this aspect of life experience.

Sometimes, however, the presence of the father was a reminder that not everyone enjoyed the freedom to go with female friends, and regional differences suggest that in the more conservative south of Italy in particular this freedom was not always open. Nearly all our respondents agree that women who attended the cinema alone would risk negative labels or worse, a context that explains in part such parental reluctance. Sometimes parental control took the form of more overt expressions of power, such as the case of Giovanna (b. 1941, Naples province) who wanted to go to the cinema with her friends but whose father would not allow it. There are several memories of being in trouble for being late home, like Maria (b. 1932, Cagliari province), who had to take her shoes off in order to run home because she had missed a parental curfew. Self-censorship also reveals itself: Iole (b. 1942, Palermo) recounts that she and her female friends would sometimes actively avoid films that were 'too daring', influenced by the conservative attitudes of their parents ('you always tried not to transgress'). This finding is in keeping with the definition provided by Colombo et al. of this generation as aware of a social climate defined by 'social "rules" – experienced primarily in the family context – as a constant of daily life' (2012: 75). At the same time, the present-day positioning of these women, after 1968 and the feminist movement, leads some of them to reflect upon these rules as too much, such as Rita (b. 1935, Naples) whose parents kept her and her two sisters on a very tight rein since they were not allowed to go to the cinemas outside of their local area of Fuorigrotta. She stresses how they kept them 'under control' using a downward motion of a partially closed, tense hand here to indicate the sense of physical oppression (Figure 6.1), and describes this tendency to keep tabs on them as 'hell'.

The gendering of the cinematic space for girls, then, presents an ambivalent memory. It is remembered as a space in which girls (sometimes with boys!) might enjoy precious time together out of school, often away from adult supervision, but it was also a space in which they had to learn to negotiate, sometimes creatively, a society in which they were still regarded as highly rule-bound, potential sexual objects. It was also a space in which common interests with parents, and often with fathers, might be explored, opening up the doors of fantasy and learning in a radically new manner.

## Memories of girlhood viewing

Jackie Stacey, in her work with British women's memories of cinemagoing in the 1940s and 1950s, suggests that 'stars provide ideals of femininity for adolescent women in the audience who are preoccupied with attaining adult femininity' (1994: 158). While this is certainly true, as discussed in the following chapter,

**Figure 6.1** Rita describes parental control in her childhood (*Italian Cinema Audiences* dataset).

we would argue that sometimes our respondents also talk about characters, films and genres, about values and themes that were focused on the specificity of being and becoming *girls*, rather than adult women. In particular, therefore, in this section we will focus on those fleeting glimpses their memories offer of an engagement with girl characters, rather than the 'expectations for the future' described by Capussotti (2004: 153). Obviously, at times it is difficult to separate those two elements, as in the case of Rosa (b. 1935, Turin), who describes her love for the aptly titled *Little Women* (George Cukor, United States, 1933) and the role played by Katharine Hepburn: 'I liked it a lot for the character of Jo, who was a girl beginning to become independent, to think for herself'. The importance of the film text and the vocabulary here suggests that Rosa was engaging with Jo as a role model for her existence as a girl, and she also mentions the importance of her reading here too, as many female respondents do. However, elsewhere in her interview Rosa comments on how in US cinema 'you could find something that didn't yet exist in Italy … an independent woman, a thinking woman … as a woman you could recognize yourself in them'. Here *donna* (woman) and *ragazza* (girl) become interchangeable and the authoritative commentary here also reflects Rosa's subsequent professional status as a teacher. Her enthusiasm is echoed elsewhere, as in the exclamation of Pompea (b. 1938, Rome): 'Jo, what a marvel!'

Somewhat differently, but with an equally 'future-oriented' vision of girlhood, one of the female respondents to our questionnaire (b. 1941, Florence province) talks about how she also loved US stars: 'Betty Grable, Ginger Rogers, and Cyd Charisse: all these young talented artists represented freedom, because in the films there were never mothers or families involved, who might prevent them from going on a date, and this made me dream and go wild with joy for my future as a girl (who was going to be disappointed).' Here the respondent is already thinking about her future, using 'girl' in the context of the 'becoming woman' and looking, precisely as Stacey suggests, to adult stars to model behaviour that she could not find in everyday life.

Frequently, as Stacey found in her work on memories of stars, girls and women would look to cinema for distant lifestyles they might aspire to, such as the questionnaire respondent from Rome, b. 1938, who says her favourite film was *La dolce vita* (Fellini, Italy, 1960) 'because in this film there was everything that we girls couldn't have at that time, such as going to nightclubs, the clothes, etc.' These aspirations often led to copying and imitation practices, the importance of which will be explored in the following chapter. By contrast, however, there are instances when women remember looking to adult stars, less in the context of aspirations of consumption focused only on appearance typically associated with this period, but in relation to activities that they might pursue *as* girls.[10] One particularly striking example of this is the insistent reference to swimming star Esther Williams's film *Bathing Beauty* (George Sidney, United States, 1944). Stacey does mention one (dismissive) instance of her respondents' remembering this star, in the context of a swimming club, but attributes it to a more generic category of 'pretending' to be a star.[11] In the Italian context, however, while memories of this star do focus inevitably on Williams's beauty and her costumes, they also highlight her prowess as a performer,[12] and tally with Kirsten Pullen's

---

[10] See Capussotti, who identifies that 'fundamental elements in the construction of the self for young women were the centrality of the body for alternative representations, the importance of the mass reproduction of images, and the role of some places, such as the catwalks of the beauty contests and fashion, as a stimulus to seek out and imagine destinies that differed from those of the previous generation' (2004: 177).

[11] 'Esther Williams would fascinate me always. This was only vanity on my part. I was quite a good swimmer in those long ago days. I belonged to a swimming club and the young men there used to call me "Esther"' (Stacey 1994: 161).

[12] Women's memories from our questionnaires include: b. 1946, Bari: 'her way of dancing on the water, she was a mermaid'; b. 1934, Cagliari: '*Bathing Beauty*, with Esther Williams, I love synchronized swimming'; b. 1941, Cagliari: 'beautiful swimming choreography and dives in her films'; b. 1944, Naples: 'beauty, professionalism'.

recent reading of this swimming star as potentially empowering: 'representing the body as active at the same time as spectacular, Esther Williams demonstrates how the material body crafts cinematic performance, suggesting feminist possibilities within conservative texts' (Pullen 2010: 899).[13] One interviewee, Rosangela (b. 1943, Turin province), says, 'I don't remember the title of the film, but it was with Esther Williams and her swimming skills, and it taught us how to move, when we practised swimming in the River Po or the little lakes that there are here around us, so we would always try to follow these things.' As we have discussed elsewhere, in part, this kind of activity is more common in rural or provincial locations, where girls might have greater access to outdoor spaces (Hipkins et al. 2016).

We might also consider that in Italy, according to Forgacs and Gundle, 'the emphasis on the display of the female body in the post-war years was not the result only of commercial influences and the impact of American mass culture at a time of social and political flux. It was also shaped by the earlier development in Italy of sport and bathing ... Women, as well as men, were drawn into sporting activities' (Forgacs and Gundle 2007: 80). This engagement of women in sport arose as a result of the fascist regime's attempts at mass bodily discipline. From our own research the example of one of our oldest respondents, Eugenia (b. 1925, Cagliari), reinforces this: she appears to want to tell us more about her sporting prowess than her cinemagoing; such digression is a feature of the interview experience with women, to which we shall return.

In their research into girlhood memories in the United States from the 1940s and 1950s, Hains et al. also found that girls tend to remember more adult-centred media, despite claims that this era saw an explosion of girl-centred media. While that explosion of girl-oriented media was more diluted in Italy, it is also the case that our own respondents discuss more adult-centred media, as the examples above largely illustrate. However, children's films certainly do recur in our respondents' memories, from *The Wizard of Oz* (Victor Fleming and George Cukor, United States, 1939) to *Alice in Wonderland* (Clyde Geronimi, Wilfred Jackson and Hamilton Luske, United States, 1951) and *Bambi* (James Algar, Samuel Armstrong, United States, 1942). We might wonder about the extent to which a cinema addressing girls was influential for a generation of

---

[13] This reading is all the more striking since in *Bathing Beauty*, the only film with Williams our respondents ever named, but repeatedly, her swimming appearance only comes at the very end, admittedly in very glorious technicolour and as lavish spectacle.

young female cinema-goers. Liliana (b. 1940, Cagliari) remembers going to the cinema with her female friends to see films that she designates as 'well-known as girls' films'; Marta (b. 1938, Florence) talks about her father kindly taking her to see 'the genres I liked' with her girlfriends, films she associated with the United States, Elizabeth Taylor films like *National Velvet* (Clarence Brown, United States, 1944) and *Lassie Come Home* (Fred M. Wilcox, United States, 1943). Marta also remembers seeing Shirley Temple films, and notes that her father called her 'golden curls' after one of Temple's films, *Curly Top* (Irving Cummings, United States, 1935). Jackie Stacey mentions how in the British context she found one example of a woman who remembered Shirley Temple and 'begged' her mother to copy the diminutive star's hairstyle, concluding, 'These examples from childhood demonstrate the breadth of the impact of Hollywood stars on women in Britain during this period: it was not only regular cinema spectators with purchasing power who were addressed as consumers by Hollywood, but young girls, too, who relied on second-hand clothes for their star-like replications' (Stacey 1994: 205). Among our own interviewees the occurrence of Shirley Temple is less focused on consumption, and more tellingly on family memory, in particular on the father–daughter dyad, as Marta recalls her father taking her to her kinds of films.[14]

Shirley Temple is only mentioned once, however, and a more significant case of films well-received by girls seems to be that of the *Sissi* films, although the trilogy may not have been specifically intended for a female audience. The Austrian/German co-productions directed by Ernst Marischka, *Sissi* (Austria, 1955), *Sissi: Die junge Kaiserin* (*Sissi: The Young Empress*, Austria, 1956) and *Sissi: Schicksalsjahre einer Kaiserin* (*Sissi: The Fateful Years of an Empress*, Austria, 1957), recount the trajectory of a nineteenth-century Princess Elisabeth of Bavaria, from girlhood to marriage to the Austro-Hungarian emperor, and were very popular in Italy. Several respondents talk smilingly of dreaming of becoming princesses, in relation to the *Sissi* films themselves.[15] The fact that this series was a trilogy of great renown has helped to plant it in the memory of our respondents, although its continued frequent airing on Italian television is a factor that undoubtedly interferes with the 'purity' of these memories. Asked

---

[14] The father–daughter viewings of Temple's films are significant given her strong appeal to older males: see Kathryn Fuller-Seeley (2011) and Kristen Hatch (2015).

[15] The Sissi films also appear in the media word cloud that Colombo et al. form, based on their interviews with the post-war generation (Colombo et al. 2012: 85).

what memory of cinema from that period provokes particular emotion, Danila (b. 1947, Turin) pauses dramatically and smiles with pleasure, exclaiming, 'Oh, yes' twice, citing the *Sissi* cycle. She laughs about its perfect suitability 'for young girls of nine or ten', remembering dreaming with Sissi, or enjoying the romance between Sissi and Emperor Franz. Others also mention loving the detail of the costumes (a recurrent obsession among our female respondents as we shall discuss in the next chapter).

It is worth dwelling momentarily on these *Sissi* films, because they provide an interesting example of how this kind of film belongs to a girl culture in particular, and provide a bridge into the discussion in the following section of the role of romance in memories of girlhood. In the first film of the trilogy Sissi (Romy Schneider) is 16, and described in the film as 'still a little girl', incarnating the physical freedom of the tomboy associated with schoolgirl comedies of the fascist period discussed by Jacqueline Reich.[16] Like the tomboy protagonist of *Il birichino di papà* (*Daddy's Little Devil*, Raffaello Matarazzo, 1942), Sissi is a daddy's girl, aligned with the freedom of masculinity, enjoying fishing and hunting with great gusto (Figure 6.2), although maintaining a girlish sensitivity towards animals and not letting anyone shoot the deer she protects. We first meet her horse riding, her disregard for fine clothes juxtaposed with the decorum of her older sister, the intended bride for the emperor. Franz, however, falls for Sissi's free-spirited love of the outdoors instead, and her disapproving future mother-in-law tells her she will have to 'abandon [her] tomboy ways' before the first film ends in a wedding ceremony between Sissi and Franz with great pomp and circumstance.

In a more traditional interpretation of the film, we can read the promise of power through the status of marriage as the compensation for the relinquishment of girlish pleasures and freedom. As mentioned in Chapter 4, according to Jack Halberstam, 'tomboyism is tolerated as long as the child remains prepubescent; as soon as puberty begins, however, the full force of gender conformity descends on the girl' (1998: 6). In the *Sissi* films this period of grace is prolonged as fantasy into adolescence itself, and even beyond. What the text offers the viewer, however, is more than either/or, but both physical freedom *and* the handsome prince. There is a similarity, we would argue, between the popularity of Esther Williams and the first Princess Sissi film at least, for they both

---

[16] Jacqueline Reich (1995).

**Figure 6.2** Princess Sissi enjoys the outdoors and romance in *Sissi* (*Sissi*, Ernst Marischka, Austria, 1955).

promise the possibility of maintaining physical freedom, while still being physically appealing. Another aspect that Sissi offers is the possibility of rebellion – she does not succumb entirely to the demands of her future mother-in-law and for the most part of the film is comically disrespectful. We have already touched upon the tensions between rules and rebellion that emerge in our respondents' narratives, and Sissi's climbing out of palace windows with her fishing gear seems particularly pertinent here.

Children would be exposed to a wide range of films in this period, given the restricted choices available in local cinemas, and some responses point to the ways in which they would imagine themselves creatively into adult, even 'arthouse' films. Luciana (b. 1943, Turin) describes how Truffaut's *Les 400 coups* (*The 400 Blows*, France, 1959) really influenced her – she claims the little boy was her age at the time (although she was at least 16, so a little older than the 14-year-old protagonist of the film, Antoine Doinel), but many respondents describe a connection with the protagonist of *Ladri di biciclette* (*Bicycle Thieves*, Vittorio De Sica, Italy, 1948) along similar lines. It is clear that films featuring children, or child-like figures, offered a way (back) into childhood, and this might not always be through protagonists of the same gender. In particular the films *Marcelino, pan y vino* (*Miracle of Marcelino*, Ladislao Vajda, Spain/Italy, 1955), the most successful film of that year in Italy, and *The Yearling* (Clarence Brown, United States, 1946) are mentioned repeatedly and appeared to appeal mostly in terms of the vulnerability and charm of the male child protagonists. The insistence with which these films are mentioned, often in relation to the orphaned nature of the protagonists and missing family, suggests that the recent war had triggered a particular sensitivity to these issues, although depending on their age and inclination, female respondents also describe maternal and romantic feelings towards the beautiful Marcelino (apparently crossing gender boundaries himself, since he was dubbed into Italian by a girl, Ludovica Modugno).

There is no doubt that cinema was a powerful influence in Italy on young girls' value formations, particularly in the face of limited schooling and early work patterns.[17] In the words of Irma (b. 1935, Turin province), who started work young, 'What I've managed to become, I have learnt from cinema and books.' What, more precisely, do our respondents suggest they have learned as girls, and from which films? Although the models discussed above, of freedom, glamour and rebellion might suggest otherwise, the responses to the direct question are often quite conservative, in line with Colombo et al.'s interpretation of this generation as one subject to moral rhetoric (2012: 112) and with the elements of conformity discussed in Chapter 4. As the popularity of *Marcelino, pan y vino* suggests, the influence of parish cinemas and the Catholic Church made itself felt in the memory of films like this, as well as *The Song of Bernadette* (Henry King, United States, 1943) and *Il cielo sulla palude* (*Heaven over the Marshes*, Augusto Genina, Italy, 1949). More than one respondent talks about the importance of self-sacrifice in this context, although Daniela (b. 1945, Turin province) cites polar explorers and Anita Garibaldi as her more secular inspirations for such a model. Family values are also often mentioned in relation to the hugely popular series of Italian weepies starring Amedeo Nazzari and Yvonne Sanson, discussed in Chapter 4. However, while some respondents imply that cinema

---

[17] In Italy in 1951, 15.2 per cent of females were officially classified as illiterate, compared with 10.5 of males. In 1948–9, the proportion of girls in middle schools was 39.9 per cent, and 37.3 in secondary schools, although the number of girls in middle and secondary schools was to rise dramatically from the mid-1950s. In 1962, school reforms raised the school-leaving age from 11 to 14. See Perry Willson (2010: 117).

today does not teach such values, at least one other (Luciana, b. 1943, Turin) describes how her own acquisition of certain values shifted: if on the one hand the values about female purity 'have remained within me', she adds, 'then perhaps I deviated'. In the concluding section of this chapter, we will return to this apparently throwaway comment as typical of a tension visible in our respondents between a nostalgic, occasionally moralizing rhetoric and a new (post)feminist vision of the self.

## 'Little girls' stuff': Romance

When asked what cinema taught her, Iole (b. 1942, Palermo), like many other respondents, talks of behaviour, more specifically, 'a direction for our behaviour in life', learned from 'romantic films … those that gave us a sense of love'. In terms of sheer repetition, the category of film that deserves a particular focus in being formative for young girls was romance, showing a strong link to Annette Kuhn's work on the memories of female youth (2010a). While this might traditionally be associated with a slightly older stage of adolescence, however, we would like to use this opportunity to develop Naomi Wolf's suggestion that girls develop sexually in two ways: from what they perceive externally and what emerges internally.[18] This idea is clearly expressed by Maria (b. 1936, Bari province), who says that at 'aged 14, 15, 16, we had certain drives' and that at the cinema 'we saw them realized … cinema made these possibilities concrete'. Maria does not present this concretization simplistically, however, and talks about her generation as 'a generation that lived through its youth very romantically', going on to describe this experience as 'idealizing'. In the words of another interviewee (Liliana, b. 1940, Cagliari), this romance was 'the eternal illusion'.

Forgacs and Gundle, discussing their earlier batch of interviews with Italians (carried out in 1991), have pointed out that, for at least one of their respondents, Rosalia (b. 1913, Bari province), 'cinema helped nurture an idea of romantic love and personal choice that allowed the young woman some leverage in relation to custom' (Forgacs and Gundle 2007: 72).

---

[18] In discussing sexual maturity, Wolf argues that 'Girls "become women" as a result of two pressures: the external – what their culture tells them it means to be an adult sexual female – and the internal – the development of sexual desire itself' (1998: 8).

While Forgacs and Gundle's respondent is a generation older than most of our respondents, what many of our interviewees suggest is that cinema in Italy, particularly that which came from the United States, also influenced the development of their sentimental and sexual trajectories considerably. As one respondent suggests (Marina, b. 1950, Rome), 'the very daring films really woke young people up … for better or for worse … they showed many things … that helps as well, but it really wakes people up'. Marina is the youngest of our interviewees so is more likely talking more about films of the 1960s and implicates 1968 in her choice of vocabulary. This is confirmed when a more specific example of a film comes from our Rome pilot study, when Carmela (b. 1941, Rome) cites the film *Sedotta e abbandonata* (*Seduced and Abandoned*, Germi, Italy, 1965), as a film that had an important impact on perceptions of the outmoded practice of the *matrimonio riparatore* (marriage of repair).

The films of the 1950s were, however, as a rule heavily censored in matters of sexuality,[19] and in many instances provided a safe space (as long as the physical reality of wandering hands was kept at bay) for young boys and girls to explore feelings that were unlikely to be explained or articulated elsewhere. While both men and women talk about this element, men tend to do so more explicitly, while women often tend to have recourse in this context to the word 'dream' or 'dreaming', describing something perhaps less tangible. A good example is this Turin questionnaire participant's (female, b. 1950) comment about the Sissi film: 'the film about the Empress Sissi made me dream'. Interestingly, within the first Sissi film, the romantic relationship is presented in a similar way. After meeting Franz, Sissi lies back on her bed and says that she has 'been daydreaming'. We might reflect with Jackie Stacey on how 'the cinema space has been seen as a key site for heterosexual courtship and romance, reinforced by the Hollywood message that happiness for women lay in catching a man and keeping him' (Stacey 1994: 218). Although Stacey challenges this notion, there is no doubt that a considerable number of our respondents go on to express a revision of their responses and dreams in the light of experience, implying that at the time they did perhaps absorb them. In some instances, this may take the form of an ambiguous dismissal, such as 'little girl's stuff', which is an expression used by Rosangela (b. 1943, Turin province), after a rhapsodic description of her first sight of Elvis as a 'first falling in love'. Seeing and hearing him on film was

---

[19] As discussed by Treveri Gennari and Dibeltulo (2017).

an experience that helped her to recognize a new feeling, and that even now, if she sees or hears of him, she says, 'I am moved remembering the feeling I had', betraying a nostalgia about the experience of an emotion for the very first time.

In other cases the film narratives are actually challenged as mystifying from the perspective of the present, either through verbal commentary or body language. Often this challenge is good-humoured. When talking about her love of male stars, Alma (b. 1943, Naples) reflects ironically on how 'later I had to give up on my type', but she is confident about the process of bringing dream and reality together. Iole (b. 1942, Palermo) says that cinema allowed her to have certain expectations about romance and the idea of a 'happy ending', although this did not always transpire in reality, but she says, 'fortunately it let us dream, of things that didn't really exist', again presenting a more positive note about the function of dreams enjoyed as a girl. Carmen (b. 1936, Naples province), however, is more critical and describes the narratives of romance that they were given as 'protected'. In the final part of this chapter we will explore in more depth this tension between nostalgia and a dismissal or revision of experience in our female interviewees' memories of girlhood.

## Life narratives: Dreams, rules and nostalgia

It may appear paradoxical to mention 'life narratives', since, for reasons of breadth and focus, we do not follow the life narrative method in our interviews. One of our respondents, Lina (b. 1931, Cagliari province), suggests a hankering to engage in the life narrative: when the interviewer asks about the reason for her particular interest in films that attempt to resolve difficulty, such as *Ladri di biciclette*, she responds, 'it must be what I experienced as a little girl' (this included wartime bombing, evacuation from Cagliari, serious illness and work in her family shoe business from the age of 12), but, she adds, 'you'd have to know about it', alluding to the interviewer's lack of time to hear her narrate this fuller history.

Significantly, however, as we have seen, some of the concerns of life narratives still surface repeatedly in these interviews, bearing testimony to the way in which the media provides a strong frame of reference for this generation's experience, making cinema and life histories inextricable. One particular way in which this entanglement makes its presence felt is in the number of women who mention that they stopped going to the cinema when they became mothers, or because their husbands did not like going to the cinema, making these memories of girlhood cinema-going all the more precious.

While our interviewees are not held to the delivery of coherence required of a life narrative, there is still evidence of a struggle to bring together these traces of girlhood feeling and desire with the present self. Take, for example, the ambitions of Irene (b. 1945, Milan), which are rapidly dismissed as fantasy – an attitude that actually reflects the censorious attitudes of the time, and which continue today, towards girls' ambitions to perform. When disclosing her girlhood aspiration to be a dancer or a model, she becomes more animated saying, 'I'm not ashamed', an expression that implies that there might well be some shame attached to girlhood dreams, but she reinforces that they were just 'dreams', 'everyone dreamed'. Her body language, generally quite contained throughout, becomes more articulated. She looks upwards and waves her hand in the air underlining that these aspirations were fantasy. Looking back, she laughs: 'But as a little girl, those are the things that everyone thinks. Everyone dreams.' Caught between the desire to defend her girlhood dreams and a cultural dismissal of them she ends with that word: 'dream', one that seems to contain an awful lot of ideas not made explicit, but often associated with smiles of fondness and embarrassment.

We might also attribute this dismissal to an embarrassment about their childhood naivety. Returning to Giuseppina's assumption that 15-year-olds today are already adult, sometimes there is an embarrassment about how little girls knew back then. Looking back, Maria (b. 1935, Naples province) says that she and her peers were very 'naïve' and would be happy with whatever they were shown in the cinema. On occasion, the dismissal of girlhood is linked to the desire to display one's present self as more educated. We might relate this to taste cultures, for instance in the case of Carmen (b. 1936, Naples province) who dismisses *Bathing Beauty* and *Seven Brides for Seven Brothers* (Stanley Donen, United States, 1954) thus: 'I don't like them anymore now, obviously my tastes have evolved.'

As mentioned in the opening section, the rule-bound nature of these generations' upbringing is a matter many women mention. Sometimes, the sense of rupture with this tradition is alluded to quite vaguely, as in Luciana's 'then perhaps I deviated'. It is the women who mention 1968 or belonging to women's groups, who often seem clearest in their criticisms of the rule-bound past. Maria Concetta (b. 1936, Bari province), for example, talks about how she tried to obtain more freedom for her sisters, which relates to the small-scale rebellion of attending the cinema in secret discussed in the first section. This 'past' is not necessarily quite laid to rest, however, since Lizia (b. 1941, Bari province), from a similar regional background, discusses how a recently formed women's group with whom she goes to see films has helped to address what she describes, in the present tense, as the backward mentality of provincial Puglia.

There is nostalgia too, though: certainly nostalgia for female community, and Esther Williams and Sissi also emerge as examples of nostalgia for girlish/tomboyish physical freedoms. These examples also allow us to stretch our notion of what 'feminine cultural competence', as Stacey describes it, looked like for girls (Stacey 1994: 190). 'Tomboyish' practices have been bracketed out or 'covered over' in narratives of Italian cinemagoing and development more generally, as we also discussed in Chapter 4. Esther Williams is perhaps the acceptable face of yearning for this physicality, being both beautiful and active. A further insight into the nostalgia, associated perhaps with an insistence on early developments of feeling and love, is offered by one of our oldest respondents, Mariellina (b. 1921, Bari), who stresses that her age influences how she responds to cinema today: when you are young, she says, 'everything is different'. She does not experience the same intensity of emotion now: 'there is a disenchantment'. Although she still goes to the cinema, her enthusiasm has waned ('earlier I would want and want and want … now I just want'), so intensity is what is regretted. Above all, particularly among our older generation of respondents, the nostalgia is for a girlhood that was so very fleeting in the face of an early introduction to a hard-working life.

## Conclusion

Women's memories of cinemagoing as girls oscillate between narrative attempts at coherence in the face of dramatic social rupture, and dismissal or apology for a girlhood culture socially 'covered over', alongside varying levels of nostalgia for it. In all cases, a continued attachment to the 'moralising rhetoric' that Colombo et al. associate with this generation seems relatively weak. Most importantly, however, the women's narratives of girlhood are characterized by the half-sentences and silences that stretch between the cinema-focused interview and the life narrative. We are struck in particular by the case of Lina and the story she is not allowed to tell, with which I opened this section. Under our own single-minded instruction to focus on cinemagoing, our interviewer repeatedly brings her back to the topic of cinema, as she attempts to narrate the dramatic story of her girlhood, and she mutters her discontent. Memories of girlhood culture in Italy of this period, just some of which have begun to emerge through this project, have still to find more space, listeners and, most importantly, frameworks for their expression.

# 7

# Beyond 'belle e brave': Female stars and Italian cinema audiences

*Some film scholars have turned to ethnographic studies as a way of restoring complexity and contradiction in flesh-and-blood people in contrast to the abstract and often politically dismal pronouncements of apparatus theory.*

Judith Mayne (1993: 59)

Writing in the early 1990s, Judith Mayne commented that when it comes to studying cinema audiences, an ethnographic approach was 'more of a horizon of research in film studies than an actual practice' (Mayne 1993: 59). Over the course of the last two decades, this horizon of research has emerged as a creative, dynamic and rigorous discipline in the form of audience studies. Following on from the influential work of Jackie Stacey and Annette Kuhn, the aim of this chapter is to illustrate how the 'complexities and contradictions' of ordinary cinemagoers can lead to a greater understanding of stardom and the roles that individual stars played in Italian society in the post-war period.

Stacey's work on female cinemagoers in Britain in the 1940s and 1950s is particularly important when it comes to analysing the ways that audiences engaged with and responded to female stars, in that she set a precedent for a hybrid approach that combines the disciplines of audience studies and star studies. The analysis of audience identification presented here is indebted to Stacey's categorizations of identificatory practices.

The study of the ICA data put forward in this chapter highlights two key themes in relation to the question of female stardom: physical appearance and identification. In exploring these themes, we foreground how the memories of cinemagoers act as a springboard towards the examination of other historical sources. In particular, we use archival materials to contextualize the observations and assertions of respondents. As outlined in the introduction to this book, the methodologies that underpin the ICA project, including the triangulation of sources, allow for a more complete understanding of audiences and the various aspects of their cinemagoing experiences. In particular, this chapter examines the reception of stars among cinemagoers in the post-war period.

In the analysis of the aforementioned key themes, we first consider how the notion of beauty and the star's physical appearance are addressed by respondents in the questionnaires and video interviews. Given that much of the existing critical and popular discourse surrounding female stars focuses on the star's body and the meanings attached to it, it is important to assess precisely what it is that audiences are responding to when they refer to a star as *bella* (beautiful) or *bellissima* (very beautiful). Nevertheless, the aim of this chapter is to expand and diversify the discourses that traditionally frame female stars in the Italian context and, as such, less weight is given to the topic of beauty, which has traditionally dominated critical analyses of stars like Gina Lollobrigida and Sophia Loren (Gundle 2004; Masi and Lancia 1989). Instead, the second section of this chapter attempts to broaden the discourses of female stardom by providing a detailed examination of the various ways that respondents actively identified with Italian and Hollywood stars. In addition to those stars that emerged as being popular among our questionnaire respondents (see Introduction, Table 1.2), we also examine the prominence with which other stars, such as Audrey Hepburn, feature in memories of identification. By offering a contextualized overview of the ICA data when filtered through the lens of female stardom, we hope to illustrate how an audience studies approach can be productively employed alongside a study of stardom.

## Approaching narratives of cinemagoing through oral history

It is important to foreground the implications of using oral history testimonies in this study of the Italian audiences' reception of female stars. Alessandro Portelli's assertion that in 'doing' oral history, researchers are 'talking to people, not studying "sources"' is an astute caveat (Portelli 1991: x–xi), because in many ways analysing memories of stardom is as much about the processes of memory and remembering as it is about the content of the participant's memories. Although the triangulation of audience testimony with other 'official' sources can be used to substantiate, question or disprove certain claims made by respondents, the questionnaires and video interviews should not be seen as a fact-finding exercise. Rather, as Lynn Abrams notes, this kind of oral history work is instead about 'emotional responses' and 'the very subjectivity of human existence' (Abrams 2010: 22).

When dealing with video interviews, in particular, the question of subjectivity requires us to reflect on the way the interviewees position themselves in relation to individual stars, the interviewer and the audience they assume will later watch the interview. The complexity of these considerations can be seen in an interview with Sebastiana (b. 1927, Cagliari). When recalling how she used to imitate Alida Valli's hairstyle, Sebastiana uses gesture to convey 'the famous wave' that characterized Valli's hairstyle, but in her attempt to convey this embodied memory of her younger self she is aware of how her current physical self may be perceived by the interviewer/viewer. As she re-enacts her past self, she, somewhat self-consciously, acknowledges that she no longer looks like the girl of her memory: 'Now, I don't have hair anymore.' In a subsequent question about beauty contests, Sebastiana says that she followed them intermittently: 'I would take a look. During the period of Sophia Loren and Gina Lollobrigida, yes, I would follow them occasionally.' Reflecting on these 'great stars' she pauses momentarily and adds,

> Maybe I used to dream too. I would have had some dreams too, perhaps I used to look in the mirror and think, but I am … maybe I didn't realize at the time, because afterwards I was told that I was a beautiful girl, however … [shrugs shoulders and laughs]
>
> Interviewer: Well, you still are a beautiful woman, of course, absolutely! (*Italian Cinema Audiences* dataset)

The first point to note here is Sebastiana's language; her repeated use of 'maybe' and 'perhaps' suggests that this is speculation rather than pure memory. She appears to 'imagine' her younger self standing in front of a mirror (an archetypal image) as she surveys her appearance. Although she did not realize the extent of her beauty at the time, the words of others have allowed her to reappraise her image as a 'beautiful girl'. Sebastiana's memories of stars such as Valli, Loren and Lollobrigida serve as a catalyst that allows her to reclaim her sense of self. In narrating her memories of glamorous stars, it is important to Sebastiana that the interviewer (and the viewer) is aware of how she was seen by others at that time. This is reinforced by the anecdote she tells about how old friends and classmates would also remind her son of his mother's beauty:

> Now, many of my contemporaries are dead, poor things, but when they would meet my son – I had a son who worked in the bank – and when they went there and they recognised him as my son, they would say 'How is your mum? Ah, she was a beautiful girl your mum'. But serious, they always stressed that I was serious. (*Italian Cinema Audiences* dataset)

Sebastiana's final comment in this anecdote is particularly revealing in terms of how she constructs her subjectivity. Beauty notwithstanding, Sebastiana stresses that she was 'serious' and, most importantly, this was evident to others. Implicit here is the idea that beauty could also in some way be associated with loose morals, and although Sebastiana is now happy to reclaim or embrace her identity as a 'beautiful girl' she is careful to maintain her reputation as an upright young woman.

Sebastiana exemplifies how for some interviewees – particularly elderly interviewees (Abrams 2010: 142) – the interview process can become a performance in which the self is constructed and revealed through a series of performative strategies: her use of gesture, her verbal delivery and the use of direct speech in her telling of the anecdote. To date, analysis of the audience–star relation has typically focused on *what* audiences say about stars and how the *what* of their comments can be categorized in accordance with a typology of the audience–star relation which (as per the work of Andrew Tudor (2013) and Jackie Stacey (1994)) distinguishes various identificatory processes. In addition, Annette Kuhn's (2002) study of British audiences turns attention towards the need to address the significance of embodied responses. In this chapter, we build on the critical foundation laid by Tudor, Stacey and Kuhn by also considering the *how* of the audience–star relation: *how* do audiences express their identification with stars through embodied memories? What can modes of expression (a question which is also explored further in relation to male stars in Chapter 8) tell us about the ways individual stars were understood and are remembered today?

In using oral history to approach audience and star studies, we acknowledge the need to privilege the personal narrative while also looking for connections and patterns that feed into the discourses surrounding the broader cultural context. Even when memories of specific stars have faded, their influence and the tangible ways that they shaped culture and society at that time remain vivid. For instance, Maria Rosaria (b. 1953, Naples province) may not remember the name of the film that featured the actress with the short boyish haircut but she does remember the 'scandal' it caused when girls in her town began to copy this hairstyle. In other words, the audience–star relation is characterized by subjective experience in which – from a film scholar's point of view – seemingly pertinent details (such as a star's name) can occasionally be omitted, mistaken or forgotten. The challenge therefore in using oral history as a methodological tool with which to approach audience and star studies is how to make sense of the gaps, subjectivities and biases that characterize memory.

## A multiplicity of voices

In accordance with the guiding principle of oral history work, which seeks to 'give a voice to the voiceless' (Abrams 2010: 154), this chapter has been devised to foreground the individual voices of respondents and interviewees while simultaneously creating connections so that these individual voices form part of a larger tapestry. Rather than presenting the audience as a homogenous entity, we illustrate the multifarious nature of the audience by placing concordant and discordant or contrasting views side by side. For instance, Silvana Pampanini (a 1946 Miss Italy contestant and actress who starred in films such as *Bellezze in biciclette* (*Beauties on Bicycles*, Carlo Campogalliani, Italy, 1951) and *O.K Nerone* (*O.K. Nero*, Mario Soldati, Italy, 1951)) provides an interesting example of variations in the audience–star relation.

Thinking back to her girlhood, Pompea (b. 1938, Rome) identifies Pampanini as an aspirational figure whom she would 'often' see near the Orfeo cinema in via Agostino De Pretis, while shooting on location.[1] Pompea excitedly recalls the type of exchange that such sightings prompted among her and her friends: 'Look at those fishnet tights! Look, how marvellous! Look now, I'm going to buy them too.' As a fellow Roman, the possibility of seeing Pampanini in the flesh allowed for a sense of proximity between Pompea and the star. This is also reflected in Pompea's assertion that she 'knew her very well'. She does not mention having ever spoken to Pampanini, so the extent to which she really 'knew' her is debatable. However, Pampanini's regular appearances at Pompea's neighbourhood cinema undoubtedly engendered a degree of familiarity that diminished the sense of star as an 'unattainable' figure (Stacey 1994: 142–3).

---

[1] The Orfeo was a third-run cinema located in the Monti *rione* (district) between Termini Station and the Trevi Fountain.

By contrast, the notion of the star as distant other is described by a second interviewee, Antonina (b. 1937, Cagliari province). Although Antonina looked to Pampanini as a model for fashion trends, she acknowledges the impossibility of reproducing her 'elegant' look: 'Clearly we weren't able to follow the fashion in that way ... at that time Sardinia was very limited.' Notwithstanding the fact that Antonina's family owned a clothes shop – thereby allowing her greater access to the latest fashions than most – her comment again highlights the question of proximity. Cut off from the mainland or *il continente* (the continent) as some Sardinian interviewees refer to it, the perception of the gap between audience and star is greater in this instance. Like many of our participants from Rome, contact or encounters with the film industry were not unusual (Treveri Gennari 2015). As a young girl growing up in Rome, there is no apparent obstacle to Pompea's desire to emulate the star; indeed, the act of emulation can seemingly be achieved through a straightforward consumer transaction ('I'm going to buy them too'). But for the girl, now woman, in rural Sardinia there is the retrospective acknowledgement that they lagged behind the commodity culture that was more easily accessed by her compatriots in the capital. Viewed in light of Stephen Gundle's theorization of the concept of 'glamour', Pompea and Antonina's memories highlight how stardom was bound up with the 'seductive appeal of capitalism' in the 'early stages of mass consumption' (Gundle 2002: 95). On a general level, these examples illustrate how the commodification of the star image was similarly understood and verbalized by members of the audience. In both cases, the star (Pampanini) is associated with forms of consumerism, heralding what Gundle refers to as a 'transformation of the Italian imagination' whereby the act of consumption becomes a way to 'acquire' glamour (ibid.). While there is an evident commonality in the experiences of Pompea and Antonina in this regard, it is nevertheless important to attend to the regional differences, which set their experiences of identification and aspiration apart. It is the urban/rural, mainland/insular contrasts that alert us to the nuances of the audience–star relation, highlighting how the individual's engagement with any given star is governed by the broader social, cultural and geographical context.

## Physical appearance

It will come as little surprise that when referring to the physical appearance of stars, respondents cite beauty (*bellezza*) as one of the key factors that influence their preferences. The importance of beauty as a star quality has long been acknowledged, and as Edgar Morin puts it, 'Beauty is frequently not a secondary but an essential characteristic of the star' (Morin 1960: 41). Although the aesthetic appraisal of stars is largely a subjective exercise dictated by individual taste, the collective labelling of particular stars as *bellissimo/a* (very beautiful) is linked to the way audiences engaged with stars through imitation and aspiration. While it may be something of a generalization, responses to the star's beauty are typified by the female cinemagoer who sought to recreate the style and mannerisms of her on-screen idol, while the male cinemagoer admired the female stars as objects of (heterosexual) desire.

The star's ability to awaken this desire for beauty is exemplified by Sophia Loren who represents an unfulfilled aspiration for a number of questionnaire respondents. For one male respondent (b. 1937, Cagliari province) Loren was not only *bellissima* (very beautiful), but she was also 'the dream for us youngsters', while another (male, b. 1933, Rome) says that Loren encapsulated 'everything that a woman should have'. In the case of one female respondent (b. 1945, Cagliari province), Loren was 'kind of what I would have liked to have been'. In each of these responses, the unobtainable nature of the object of beauty is implicit. Loren's beauty comes to stand for something lacking, lost or unattainable for the respondents: the ephemeral nature of a childhood/adolescent dream and the ideal woman in the case of the first two examples, and the disappointment of an unrealized aspiration in the case of the third.

Among the generic descriptions of the star as beautiful, it is important to attend to the way language is used to describe different degrees of beauty. Respondents allude to the notion of beauty using various terms of reference,[2] which, in line with Roger Scruton's observations, 'offer less of a concrete description and more ... of a response' on the audience's part (Scruton 2011: 54). This is particularly evident when respondents attribute the star's beauty to her national identity. For example, Loren is repeatedly referred to as a *bellezza italiana* (Italian beauty), *bellezza mediterranea* (Mediterranean beauty) and *bellezza 'nostrana'* (home-grown beauty). This specification of Loren's beauty as distinctly Italian and as something that the respondents proudly claim as their own reinforces the view that audiences perceive Loren to be a national treasure (Gundle 2004: 77).

---

[2] See Appendix for table of most frequently occurring adjectives and nouns used by respondents when referring to physical appearance.

While Loren is described as 'a beauty that bewitches' (female, b. 1930, Cagliari), at the opposite end of this scale of perception are actresses such as Anna Magnani and Giulietta Masina who are viewed by some respondents as unconventional beauties. The tendency to highlight these actresses based on an absence of aesthetic beauty is typically coupled with praise for their acting talent. The view that Magnani 'wasn't beautiful like her fellow stars' is compensated by the acknowledgement that 'she was very good at acting' (female, b. 1934, Florence). Similarly, Masina's lack of conventional beauty does not diminish her acting prowess: 'She managed to convey different scenarios with realism and spontaneity even though she wasn't blessed with a beautiful appearance' (female, b. 1935, Milan Province). Appreciation for the beauty of the actress's craft rather than her physical appearance challenges Morin's idea that beauty is an *essential* characteristic of the star. Indeed, where the attraction to the star is driven primarily by physical beauty, her talent can be negated or at the very least sidelined so that the star as performer is denied any serious analysis. The danger of this is that the star is reduced to a series of clichéd ideas about spontaneity, naturalness and instinct.

In addition to responses that directly highlight the star's appearance, it is also important to consider the responses that link the star's attractiveness to an aspect of her star persona. For one respondent, Silvana Mangano's allure lies in her 'unbridled beauty' which is 'veiled by a vein of melancholy' (female, b. 1941, Turin province). This blurring of the star as person and star as persona highlights the reciprocity of the star/character relation. Morin (1960: 37) refers to this as the way 'the characters of her films infect the star'. On the one hand, the description of Mangano as a well-endowed beauty with an air of sadness could be read in terms of the kind of characters that she played, particularly later in her career,[3] while on the other it alludes to her public image as a star who tended to shy away from fame and whose private life was touched by personal tragedy.[4] The impossibility of separating the star from her characters is also reflected in the observation that Anna Magnani 'wasn't artificial, but natural' (female, b. 1944, Milan). The intended meaning here can be read in light of Magnani's physical

---

[3] Through her roles in films such as *Teorema* (Pier Paolo Pasolini, Italy, 1968), *Morte a Venezia* (*Death in Venice*, Luchino Visconti, Italy, 1971) and *Oci ciornie* (*Dark Eyes*, Nikita Michalkov, Italy/Russia, 1987), Mangano's star image came to be associated with the figure of the impassive upper-class wife/mother.

[4] Mangano's star image is often framed in terms of personal tragedy owing to a series of sad events that befell the star, including the death of her son Federico De Laurentiis who lost his life in a plane crash in 1981. See 'Sorriso Amaro: Silvana Mangano', *La storia siamo noi* (Rai Educational, 2009).

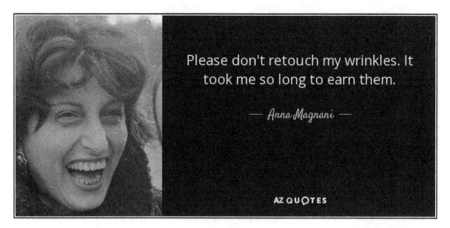

**Figure 7.1** An English language version of Anna Magnani's infamous quote (AZ Quotes website, https://www.azquotes.com/author/9287-Anna_Magnani).

appearance, her on-screen performances and her off-screen persona. The first point about Magnani's physical appearance and the notion of her 'natural' look ties in with the mythology surrounding her star image, which suggested that she often refused the assistance of stylists and make-up artists, preferring to avoid any ostentation. Indeed, Lizia (b. 1941, Bari province) illustrates how this mythology has become part of popular discourse when she paraphrases the famous (apocryphal) quotation attributed to Magnani: 'Please don't retouch my wrinkles, it took me so long to earn them.' As seen in Figure 7.1, the circulation and reformulation of this quotation has entered internet meme culture.

## Identification

> I was completely enraptured by the images of actors and actresses; nothing existed outside of me and the story that was developing around me, stirring strong emotions within me.
> —Female, b. 1941, Florence province

In the questionnaires, 'identification' in the broadest sense of the term is repeatedly cited as one of the key pleasures of cinema (as per the example above). For many respondents the cinema was a place to escape, to dream and to fantasize about other worlds and alternative realities. As one female respondent recalls, going to the cinema was an opportunity to 'dream with my eyes open, while putting myself in the shoes of the protagonist' (female, b. 1948, Cagliari province). To describe the process of identification as 'dreaming with your eyes open' may suggest a certain passivity; however, as Stacey notes, the identificatory practices of spectators are complex and very often unrepresented by the schematic categorization that psychoanalytic film theory forces upon the (abstract) spectator (1994: 126–75). Referring to the work of feminist film scholars such as Laura Mulvey, Anne Freidberg and Jacqueline Rose, Stacey concisely illustrates the shortcomings of psychoanalytic readings of female audience identification, especially when that audience is drawn from actual cinemagoers. The model for analysing spectator-star identification put forward by Stacey offers a valuable alternative to the psychoanalytic theories arising from feminist film studies in which identification with female characters was seen as the female spectator's 'complicity with [her] oppression under patriarchy' (ibid.: 133). While it is impossible to overlook the influence of Mulvey's school of thought on the landscape of film theory, in the context of New Cinema History such an approach to audience identification risks writing the pleasures of popular cinema out of the narrative of film history. A link can also be drawn here with the fact that throughout the post-war period (and indeed beyond), scholarly film journals in Italy have habitually dismissed the views and tastes of popular audiences (Cosulich 1958; Noto 2018; Viazzi 1949). By applying Stacey's model to our analysis of audience responses, it is possible to reclaim and re-evaluate the neglected opinions of ordinary cinemagoers.

Stacey devises three main categories of identification: 'Transformations of the self', 'Cinematic' and 'Extra-cinematic'. In the case of the first two, the processes of identification generally take place within the cinematic context, that is, during the viewing of the film. Echoing Nichols's description of the cinematic experience as something that extends before and after the actual viewing of the film (see Chapter 3), for Stacey extra-cinematic identification refers to practices that 'extend beyond the cinema itself' (1994: 159), that is, imitating stars through mode of dress, mannerisms and so forth. Each of these categories is made up of different processes of identification. Within the 'Transformations of the self' category, identification can be defined as either 'Transcendence' or 'Aspiration and Inspiration'. Defined as 'the temporary loss of self', as the 'spectator's identity merges with the star … or character she is portraying' (ibid.: 146), transcendence aptly describes the most common form of identification found among respondents of the ICA questionnaires. The pleasure derived from temporarily immersing oneself in an alternative identity is succinctly captured by a male respondent who wrote, 'I liked putting myself in the shoes of the characters in the film, I wasn't me anymore' (male, b. 1923, Rome province). Taking on the identity of stars and the characters they portrayed could manifest itself in a form of active participation, whereby cinemagoers would comment on the events unfolding before them: 'Sometimes it was as if you were directly involved in the story, so much so you would comment out loud' (male, b. 1948, Naples province).

Another interesting aspect of memories that convey moments of transcendence is related to cinema's ability to trigger romantic and sexual fantasies (see also Chapter 8). Defining the cinema as a 'heterotopia of courtship', Kuhn has described how the physical space of the cinema and the mental spaces of fantasy and imagination converge, thereby facilitating the activation of 'sexual instincts' (Kuhn 2002: 141–7). One respondent demonstrates how on-screen love stories could in turn influence social practices attached to romance and courtship: 'I would identify with love stories and I liked to embark on the kind of dalliances I saw in films' (male, b. 1948, Naples province). Cinematic representations of love, romance and sex could prompt recognition of physical desire even from a young age, as in the case of a female respondent who imagined that she was Disney's *Cinderella* (Cylde Geronimi, Hamilton Luske and Wilfred Jackson, United States, 1950) 'at the moment of the kiss' (b. 1948, Bari Province).

On-screen tales of love could also transcend their original cultural context to resonate with ordinary Italian cinemagoers. A male respondent attributes his fondness for *The Quiet Man* (John Ford, United States, 1952) to the fact that the story of Mary Kate Danaher (Maureen O'Hara) and Sean Thornton (John Wayne) mirrored 'mine and my wife's story' (b. 1947, Florence province). Using *The Quiet Man* as a cinematic shorthand for a personal narrative of romance gives the respondent's love story an epic and timeless quality.

Projecting oneself onto the characters of a film is expressed as a form of ownership, in that the film is typically described as 'our film'. The intensity of this kind of identification can take on greater significance in later life, particularly following the death of a spouse. For Elena, a female respondent from Bologna, *Love Is a Many-Splendored Thing* (Henry King and Otto Lang, United States, 1955) and its soundtrack hold a myriad of complex memories, which illustrate how the spectator's identification can evolve over time. The film's release in 1955 coincided with the early stages of Elena's courtship with her future husband. The film's theme song, written by Sammy Fain, became 'our music' and is bound up in her memories of romantic evenings spent dancing together at parties. However, following the death of her husband, repeat viewings of the film have brought a new identification with Jennifer Jones's character to the fore: 'I recall when the actress walks quickly through the streets of the city towards the little hill where they meet and I know what she is feeling, I've known that feeling for nineteen years, it's as if it was yesterday' (Elena, b. 1934, Bologna).[5]

Recalling the film's final scene when Suyin (Jennifer Jones) learns of Mark's (William Holden) death, the respondent's own loss is vividly articulated and fused with that of Suyin. Her use of the present tense in retelling the scene lends an immediacy that almost places her in the scene alongside Jones. The respondent's revised response to the film underlines how her identification with the love story and its star have absorbed new and more poignant meanings over time.

## Active identification

They really woke up the youth, for better or worse, I don't know.
—Marina, b. 1950, Rome

Born in 1950, Marina recalls how she was influenced by Audrey Hepburn and Catherine Spaak as a young girl. A representative of the baby boomers who came of age in the 1960s, Marina is one of the youngest interviewees. Her reflection on how stars 'woke up the youth' of that era 'for better or for worse' offers a retrospective take on the way her generation was shaped by their on-screen idols. This 'awakening' can also be seen in light of the rise of consumer culture, which, as David Forgacs and Stephen Gundle (2007: 63) note, was 'closely related to changing social uses of the body'. The imitation of stars is inextricably linked with those other industries that benefit from cinema: fashion, beauty, publishing, music and so on. As Stacey (1994: 169) puts it, stars are 'identified with particular commodities which are part of the reproduction of [masculine and] feminine identities'.

---

[5] Although Bologna was not one of the main eight cities included in this study, Elena contributed to the project through the project's Facebook page. This use of social media allowed us to extend the geographical reach of the project in a less systematic way. Response taken from Italian Cinema Audiences Facebook Group. https://www.facebook.com/groups/713853268637347/ (accessed 9 August 2019).

As previously highlighted in the discussion of Pompea and Sebastiana's imitation of Silvana Pampanini, the access which audiences had to the commodities that would allow them to successfully emulate their favourite star's style was influenced by location and the varying availability of consumer goods in urban and rural areas. In addition to the interviewee's location, Attilio from Naples (b. 1937) explains how their ability to imitate star fashion was subject to financial constraints: 'We were young kids, therefore imitation was a bit difficult when you needed to buy [to do it].' Nevertheless, donations of second-hand clothes sent from America could be found in Naples after the war, making it possible for youngsters to appropriate the latest Hollywood look.[6] Although both male and female interviewees speak of their memories of imitating stars, as previously noted, this form of identification typically follows a traditional gender binary (a pattern which is also noted in Chapter 4 in relation to genre preference). Therefore, it is unsurprising that the following discussion of audiences in relation to active identification with female stars focuses almost exclusively on female interviewees; however, the role of cinema in the consolidation of male gender identity is discussed in detail in Chapter 8.

> Within her model of identificatory practices, Stacey distinguishes between *imitation* and *copying* as forms of identification. She describes *imitation* as a 'form of play-acting or pretending' (1994: 163), while *copying* involves 'an intersection of self and other' by means of physical transformation (ibid.: 167). Memories of copying stars are the more dominant form of identification among interviewees.

## Copying

In January 1948, *Hollywood* magazine published an article entitled 'Be beautiful like the divas'. Translated from the original English, the piece was penned by B-list actress and model Anita Colby whose career in Hollywood was revived in the mid-1940s when David O. Selznick hired her as 'feminine director', a role which involved offering beauty and etiquette guidance to the female stars contracted to his studio. The article discloses some of the 'secrets' behind star beauty by providing readers with a six-step guide on how to replicate the beauty

---

[6] This is attested to by Attilio: 'After the war, American clothes arrived in Naples … they were second-hand clothes … the ones that you would see in the films, so we tried to dress the way we saw the actors dress.'

regimens of Maureen O'Hara, Rita Hayworth, Gail Russell and others. Read at a distance of more than seventy years, Colby's article invites easy ridicule, but it nevertheless offers a telling insight into the way paratexts were used to explicitly encourage the imitation of stars:

> Once upon a time there was a girl who said to herself: 'I want to be ugly.' Therefore every evening, she undressed and jumped straight into bed without even glancing at her night cream, hand lotion and hairbrush. And do you know what happened? Her wish came true: she became even uglier than fate had in store for her.
>
> But that girl is such a rarity that I wouldn't be surprised if they put her in a museum. The majority of women ask only this of fate: 'I beg you, grant that I am beautiful and attractive.'
>
> And you can have that, without the help of fate, if you just trouble yourself to read what I'm about to tell you.
>
> This is the story of what the beautiful divas of Hollywood do before they go to bed. They know that their success tomorrow depends on the care they dedicate to their beauty each evening. (Colby 1948: 6, our translation of article as it appeared in *Hollywood*)

Using a risible fairy-tale structure, the article positions the reader as a consumer and suggests that physical beauty is not an altogether elusive quality that one can only wish for, rather with the right products and dedication it can be obtained. This message is reinforced by the images and captions that accompany the text. A sequence of three glamour shots features Janet Blair (applying lipstick), Elizabeth Taylor (brushing her hair) and Virginia Field (applying face cream) – none of whom are actually mentioned in the article itself, and who are presented as models from whom readers can learn. The language used in the captions that accompany the images imply a teacher-student dynamic with the star occupying the role of expert, while the implicit reader is a novice. Readers are urged to 'imitate' Janet Blair who 'knows how to apply lipstick', while Elizabeth Taylor can 'teach' readers how to brush their hair. Similarly, Virginia Field can 'give a lesson' on how to apply face cream. This article serves as an example of the kind of press discourse that propagated new ideas of feminine identity and indicates the centrality of stars to the dissemination of these ideas (Capussotti 2004: 163–4). It is against this backdrop that interviewees' memories of copying stars can be seen.

## 'Everybody did it!'

Pompea recalls the practice of copying stars as a collective activity, which was almost a rite of passage ('everybody, everybody went through that phase'). Obviously, this view is informed by her own subjective experience and her assertion is contradicted by the experiences of many other interviewees who simply did not identify with stars in this way, have no recollection of doing so or will not admit to it. Nevertheless, most of those interviewees who recall copying stars remember it as something that they did collectively with their peers.

Rosa (b. 1935, Turin) recalls that Audrey Hepburn was 'a model for *all of* us', a sentiment that is echoed by Liliana (b. 1940, Cagliari) who refers to Hepburn as 'the celebrity of *our* group ... we used to cut our hair and wear ballet flats like her'. Reflecting on his observations of this kind of collective behaviour among his female peers, Renato (b. 1942, Turin) reinforces the comments of Rosa and Liliana when he says that 'all the girls' mimicked Hepburn in the trend of wearing a headscarf, which the star was seen wearing for her performance in *Charade* (Stanley Donen, United States, 1963) – although he misremembers this accessory as being from *Sabrina* (Billy Wilder, United States, 1954). These examples illustrate Maurice Halbwachs's (1992: 38) argument about the way that collective memory is born of a wider culture that unites us socially. More specifically with regard to the audience–star relation, this form of identification implies the importance of belonging and feeling connected to one's peers. Liliana's memory of how she and her friends would cut their hair to look like Hepburn or wear ballet flats in order to emulate their group role model is indicative of the importance of the collective formation of gender identity among young girls.

The figuring of Hepburn as a role model for young girls and the prominence with which she features in these memories of copying stars – indeed she is mentioned more than any other actress in this context – can be attributed to a number of possible factors. In stark contrast with 'shapely' stars like Sophia Loren and Gina Lollobrigida, Hepburn provided an alternative model of femininity, which was 'stylish, elegant ... the type of woman that ordinary Italian women could associate with and aspire to' (Buckley 2006: 328). Moreover, as Rachel Moseley notes in her study of Hepburn and British female cinemagoers in the 1950s and 1960s, the actress 'is never sexualised in relation to her body – the only erotic charge around her is an attraction engendered by beautiful clothes' (Moseley 2002: 76). For interviewees like Rosa and Liliana who would have been 17 and 13, respectively, when *Roman Holiday* (William Wyler, United

States) was released in 1953, Hepburn (who was 24 at the time) was associated with a narrative that foregrounded the transformation and formation of the self. This factor, coupled with Hepburn's 'gamine' appearance, goes some way to explaining her particular appeal to then-adolescent cinemagoers who were themselves negotiating the transition from girlhood to womanhood. Marina (b. 1950, Rome) illustrates this when, inspired by Hepburn, she began wearing 'blue jeans'. Her adoption of this new fashion is clearly linked with the discovery of her sense of self and a new level of maturity: 'She [Hepburn] used to wear blue jeans, so I also wore them when I was a little older.'

A second factor at play here for Italian audiences in particular was Hepburn's connection with Italy through her career and later her personal life, which undoubtedly raised her profile with the Italian public. Her association with Italy was first forged with her role in *Roman Holiday*. In the words of her son Luca Dotti, Hepburn became 'almost a second Colosseum: an icon of the city, an icon of a different, free-and-easy Roman spirit that was symbolised by a girl who travelled the world on a Vespa' (Dotti 2013). Hepburn also spent extended periods in the Italian capital, at Cinecittà during the filming of *War and Peace* (King Vidor, United States, 1956) and *The Nun's Story* (Fred Zinneman, United States, 1959). In addition to her professional associations with Italy, Hepburn's marriage to prominent Roman psychiatrist Andrea Dotti in 1969 made her a source of curiosity for Italian paparazzi who ensured that the star's image was never far from the public consciousness.

## Expressing individuality

In the examples of copying stars seen above, the emphasis on identification as a collective activity tends to privilege or idolize the star. Although the star becomes a model for the exploration of self-identity, the individual is somewhat subsumed by the star's shadow. As Rosa from Turin explains, their attempts to imitate Hepburn were always tempered by the recognition that they could never truly be what she represented: 'She was a model for all of us in her grace etc. But you were aware that you weren't like her, you didn't think that.' Nevertheless, this tendency to foreground the gap that separated audiences and stars contrasts with an opposing trend, whereby the star's identity is pushed to the side to allow for a foregrounding of the individual. In these cases, copying a star is characterized as a more creative endeavour that involves the interviewee embracing a fashion trend set by a star through the act of making or having clothes made by a dressmaker.

Maria (b. 1931, Bari province) gives a detailed description of the way the styles seen in American cinema inspired her and other girls in her town to buy fabric from the local factories, which they would then have made into the latest fashion item. The emergence of this practice in the early 1940s has been highlighted by Eugenia Paulicelli (2016: 106) who notes the impact that Joan Crawford's style had on the fashions worn by the Italian 'self-made girl'. Fashion magazines played an important role in the proliferation of this copying of star style. To quote Capussotti (2004: 177), these publications were 'important resources for those that had the ambition of following the trends of high fashion, but lacked adequate economic resources'.

Using the fashion magazine *Burda*,[7] Maria and her contemporaries took inspiration from the images of Italian and Hollywood stars and the pull-out sewing patterns, which they would show to the local dressmaker as a point of reference for the styles that they sought. Although this trend was practised by others of her generation, Maria repeatedly stresses her own individuality. Indeed, the identities of the stars she imitated are footnotes in her memory, and only one star is singled out as a direct influence. While she attributes her wearing of a 'zucchetto' ('headscarf') to a specific actress, the identity of said actress is unclear. Maria mistakenly identifies her as 'Lawrence Sanson', but based on her description of the headscarf and the gesture that accompanies it, it is likely that she is referring to the Hollywood actress Gloria Swanson.

On the surface, this confusion regarding the actress's name could easily be dismissed as an unremarkable example of faulty memory which occurs to some extent with the majority of interviewees. However, on closer consideration Maria's memory lapse is interesting for the way it contrasts starkly with her detailed memory of the outfits and accessories that she wore at that time. In particular, she recalls the year that long dresses and fitted overcoats (in a style reminiscent of the nineteenth century) were in vogue. Maria followed this trend, but in her own individual way by having the coat made from cyclamen-coloured fabric – much to her sister's embarrassment who refused to be seen in public with her dressed that way ('I was too visible'). Maria may have presented herself to the world wearing clothes inspired by the stars, but she unashamedly made

---

[7] Originating in Germany in 1950, *Burda Style* is an international magazine, which is still in circulation in over eighty countries. *Burda Style* distinguished itself in the fashion publishing industry by including sewing patterns in each monthly issue. Today *Burda Style* defines itself as 'the largest DIY fashion and sewing community' and has over half a million members. http://www.burdastyle.com/statics/about (accessed 16 August 2019).

these styles her own regardless of what others thought of her. In her telling of this anecdote she seeks to distinguish herself from the crowd. Unlike the other interviewees discussed above, who merge themselves with the collective, Maria repeatedly relates herself to the collective but without relinquishing her sense of self.

She begins by telling the interviewer that she was '*one* of those girls' who copied the stars' fashion. Her speech is punctuated with emphatic self-references: 'we – *I* – and many girls used to go to the factory', '*I* used to go around'. This emphasis on the self is further underscored by her body language in that her speech is often accompanied by gestures (pointing to self) that call attention to her desire to be seen as an individual. Maria triumphantly concludes her anecdote about her sister shunning her for her fashion choices with the following statement: '*I* went on my own ... *I* didn't care.' The gestures that accompany Maria's retelling of this event vividly illustrate how, to quote Jeff Friedman, 'embodied channels of communication are a significant part of the performance of the oral history interview' (Friedman 2014: 291). To overlook these elements of the interview is to neglect 'important cues for understanding a narrator's intentions' (ibid.). In Maria's case, it is a combination of her verbal delivery, gesture and facial expression that inform our understanding of the way she constructs herself as a modern and independent young woman. The image she conjures of herself walking defiantly through the centre of Putignano[8] (not an insignificant act given the conservative attitudes around the visibility of women alone in public spaces at the time) imbues her with a star quality of her own. In this way, fashion influenced by the stars can be seen to have played a perceptible role in the formation of female gender identity.

A further example of the self being fashioned as the 'star' or possessing starlike qualities is provided by Elena from Bologna (b. 1934) who, in an account shared via the ICA Facebook page, describes how she sent her dressmaker to the nearby cinema so that she could see a poster featuring Leslie Caron and the dress she was wearing:

> I remember that one year when attending the Navy Dance, which took place in Palazzo del Podestà in Bologna, I sent the dressmaker ... to look at the poster for a Leslie Caron film in which she was wearing a gorgeous dress. I had the

---

[8] Located in Bari province, Putignano had a population of nineteen thousand in 1951. 'Censimenti popolazione Putignano 1861–2011', *ISTAT*, https://www.tuttitalia.it/puglia/75-putignano/statistiche/censimenti-popolazione/ (accessed 19 November 2019).

dressmaker make me one just like (using different material) and it was a great success. I still have it, it's a bit worn out, but I can't bring myself to throw it out.

As with Maria, Elena's memory of copying star fashion is linked to performance and public display, in that she had the dress made specifically for a dance she was attending.

Through the memory discourse of Elena and Maria we are alerted to the way that star style, to quote Jane Gaines, 'is a direct and intimate link to the body and consciousness of the female spectator' (Gaines 1990: 16). In each of these cases, the star as real person is less important than the image she represents and the aspirations inspired by this image. We are also reminded of Richard Dyer's observation that 'fashion and notions of beauty were to be *shared* by star and fan' (Dyer and McDonald 1998: 35). By having clothes made to imitate the fashion of stars, Maria and Elena reconfigured the audience–star relation. Fashion, as a trapping of stardom and the glamorous lifestyle it implied, was no longer the exclusive preserve of famous actresses. In post-war Italy, before the economic miracle took hold extensively, the limited availability of new fashions led to a form of consumerism that was supported by small-scale or cottage industries. This is reflected in the testimony of these women, all of whom refer to going to 'la sarta' or 'dressmaker'. For these young women, managing the design and production of their own clothes was part of a *proactive* expression of self-identity.

## Conclusion

As this analysis of the questionnaires and video interviews has shown, identification is a complex and nuanced process. By definition, the audience suggests a collective entity, but as we have seen this entity is made up of many different individual and at times conflicting experiences. While it is possible to identify trends among these different experiences, the temptation to refer to the audience in completely homogeneous terms must be avoided. The identificatory processes described by questionnaire respondents and video interviewees highlight how the audience–star relation is an active process, which can be fixed in the memory of a past moment, as in the case of the women who copied Audrey Hepburn's look as young girls, or it can continue to evolve over time, as witnessed by Elena's identification with Jennifer Jones's performance in *Love Is a Many-Splendored Thing*. Approaching stardom in this way gives insight into the various ways that stars influenced gender identity and the self-image of cinemagoers in the post-war period.

As a research tool, the video-interview format reveals that for some interviewees it is the *act* of imitation that is prioritized while the identity of the star is of secondary importance as a source of inspiration. The video interview also creates space for those moments of blocked memory and faulty recall (Abrams 2010: 104). A perfect example of this, which was referenced in the introduction to this chapter, comes from Maria Rosaria (b. 1953, Naples province) who distinctly recalls how girls in her town began following a trend for short, boyish hair. Although she cannot recall the star that inspired this fashion,[9] her memory of this identificatory process – which she witnessed rather than participated in – has become fixed in her mind for the scandal it caused, thereby telling us something about the star's reception in a provincial community. We would argue that when investigating how audiences identified with stars, it is equally important to pay attention to the lapses, slips and absences in their narratives as it is in these blind spots that the permeation of the star's influence can also be found.

---

[9] It is possible that the trend Maria refers to was inspired by Ingrid Bergman or perhaps Audrey Hepburn. Indeed, the impact of the cropped hairstyle sported by Bergman for her role in *For Whom the Bell Tolls* (Sam Wood, USA, 1943) is noted by Claudio (b. 1931, Turin province): 'Ingrid Bergman … changed the hairstyles of all the women in Italy … including my future wife.'

8

# Narrative imaginings of masculinity through cinema*

Throughout the Italian Cinema Audiences (ICA) project our goal, as stated in the Introduction to this volume, was not to use the video interviews as mere supplementary sources providing further information on cinemagoing and films; rather, we have sought to use the audio-visual and other sources to offer a picture of how subjects construct themselves, and how they invoke a relationship to the remembered object (whether that object be the act of cinemagoing, the venue, the star, the film text or the past self). As Kuhn et al. (2017: 10) note, 'The aim of oral history research on cinema-going is not to objectively reconstruct the past based on subjective memories of respondents, … but to look at how memories of cinema-going are constructed.'

The desire to shed light on 'the role played by cinema – and cinema memory – in the complex and dynamic processes of identity formation' (ibid.: 9) is at the core of this chapter, which takes as its focus the ways in which, in the video interviews we gathered, cinema operates as a vector for the construction of particular male identities. We will here use Graham Dawson's concept of 'composure', which refers to the ways in which 'storytelling "composes" a subjective orientation of the self within the social relations of its world' (Dawson 1994: 22). The versions of the self that are 'composed' in the oral history interview by older men looking back at their young selves illustrate the power of cinema: this power refers both to the imagery and iconography of stardom that influenced them, but also to the cultural space of cinema in Italian society in the 1950s, and how it made available ways of imagining oneself as a man, offering shared cultural and gendered values within which men can and could locate themselves.

---

\* A part of this chapter was previously published in D. Treveri Gennari, S. Dibeltulo, D. Hipkins, C.O'Rawe, 'Analysing Memories Through Video-Interviews: A Case Study of Post-War Italian Cinema-going', in *The Routledge Companion to New Cinema History*, ed. D. Biltereyst, R. Maltby, P. Meers (Routledge, 2019), pp. 344–54. Reproduced by permission of Taylor and Francis, a division of Informa plc.

While there has been a fair amount of attention to the importance of oral history for women's history (see Bornat and Diamond 2007, and, in the Italian context, Passerini 1992), and as part of a broader process of challenging hegemonic accounts of public history, less attention has been paid to the 'narrative imaginings of masculinities' (Dawson 1994: 22) that oral history affords. Of course, these imaginings are fraught with silences and with gaps that respondents attempt to smooth over. The work of Dawson, and of Penny Summerfield, has been important in pointing to ways in which 'the construction of male identity within discourses of masculinity is ... fractured and insecure' (Summerfield 2004: 71). Thus in examining how the masculine self is constructed and performed in the oral history interview, we will first look at men's remembered relation to the male star image (focusing particularly on questions of imitation and anti-identification). We will then examine how cinephilia permitted a certain kind of politically inflected masculinity to be articulated, and finally at the gendered nature of the cinema space itself, and how gender relations were experienced, maintained and negotiated through the practice of cinemagoing.

## Stars

Analysing male spectators' responses to the star image makes for an intriguing counterpoint to Jackie Stacey's famous study of female respondents and their relationships to stars. Stacey argued that, for women, memories of stars were bound up in the idea of a 'representation of a fantasy self never realised' (1994: 65) due to the constraints of women's lives under patriarchy. This perspective resonates with Richard Dyer's observation of 'particularly intense star/audience relationships among adolescents and women', linked partially to the exclusions of these groups from 'the dominant articulacy of, respectively, adult, male, heterosexual culture' (Dyer and McDonald 1998: 32).

When thinking about older men's remembered relationship to the (male) star image, we want to think about how this is part of a nexus of 'imagined forms' of masculinity, 'made up of cultural activity and materialized in the social world' (Dawson 1994: 22). The oral history interview, with its necessary storytelling, its affective engagement with the past and expression of this in the present via body language and voice, can be, we argue, a key site for unpacking these imagined forms of masculinity and their function.

**Figure 8.1** Edoardo remembers the impact of Marlon Brando (*Italian Cinema Audiences* dataset).

Several of our male interviewees, or 'narrators',[1] invoked Marlon Brando and James Dean in the context of 'extra-cinematic identificatory practices' (Shingler 2012: 31). This is somewhat unsurprising, given the popularity of their films with young Italian audiences.[2] Yet in our ICA audience questionnaires, neither actor appeared in our top four male stars (who were Amedeo Nazzari, Marcello Mastroianni, Gregory Peck and Gary Cooper). However, Brando was named favourite male star by forty-two respondents, of whom two-thirds were male.

Brando's iconic image, as transmitted particularly in *The Wild One*, in which he wore a leather jacket and rode a motorcycle, represented, as Capussotti (2004: 126) notes, a 'rupture' with bourgeois values, and a new kind of virility. One of our respondents, Edoardo (b. 1938, Turin), explains how he and his classmates used to imitate Brando. His comment is noteworthy because he first explains how they, as schoolboys, wore a jacket and tie, something he emphasizes by repeating it and also tugging at his collar while laughing, to show how buttoned-up they were. He then segues into saying only Brando's name: 'Marlon Brando … eh … Marlon Brando!'

---

[1] This is the term suggested by Alexander Dhoest (2015: 67), as it highlights the extent to which oral history interviews clearly constitute narratives, revealing collective imaginations.

[2] See Capussotti (2004: 125–39) on the cultural influence of Brando's *The Wild One* (László Benedek, United States, 1953), released in Italy in 1954. She also discusses the importance of Dean's image for the youth generation in Italy in the 1950s (ibid.: 141–50).

This is pronounced in a particular tone of voice, a kind of pleasurable growl which indicates the power of Brando's persona for them, and is accompanied by an expressive hand movement (see Figure 8.1) and then a shake of the shoulders that denote a physical pleasure and immersion both in the imitative practices they engaged in and in the retelling of them.

This is a powerful example of what Frisch (2006: 107) terms 'aurality' in action in the oral history interview, that is, 'the actual voice (orality, in all its meanings), and embodied voices and contexts'. Interestingly, Edoardo does not specify a film or role, or even an aspect of Brando's persona they imitated, but the synecdochical action of the collar-touching complemented by the bodily movement is enough to tell us that Brando represented an important and liberating male role model for them. This resonates with what Capussotti (2004: 126) says of Brando's image and how it was received by the new teenage generation in Italy: 'Brando's "excessive" body was in tension with bourgeois values such as self-control, moderation, and respectability.'[3]

Renato (b. 1942, Turin) also invokes Brando's image from *The Wild One*, again without mentioning the film. He explains that they imitated Brando by buying Ray-Bans, clearly a reference to Brando's character wearing Ray-Ban Aviators in that film, which made them 'an essential accessory for non-conformists'.[4] He also comments that as well as imitating clothes, they imitated the behaviour of Brando and Dean, and would try to style themselves as a *bel tenebroso* (dark and brooding type) in order to make themselves more interesting to girls.[5] Meanwhile, Renzo (b. 1934, Milan province) alludes to the influence of a star like Brando on the cultural zeitgeist, where he says that even if you did not explicitly want to imitate him, a barber would inevitably cut your hair based on his hairstyle as it was the latest trend.

A more complex form of identification with a star is expressed by Giorgio (b. 1936, Turin). Giorgio, a particularly devoted and engaged cinemagoer, relives his reactions to the star performance of Marlon Brando in *A Streetcar Named*

---

[3] Our questionnaire responses about Brando emphasized his masculinity: there are references to him as *masculo* (masculine), *un duro* (a tough guy) and *un filibustiere* (a rogue). Piccone Stella (1994) discusses this Italian male generation's link to violence or aggression, which preoccupied the contemporary press: this is alluded to by Edoardo, when he says, 'You would act like a fake tough guy, but it ended there.'

[4] https://www.augustman.com/my/style/ray-ban-celebrates-80-years-eye-conoclasm/. See also Casetti and Fanchi (2002: 160) on the transgressive impact of Brando and Dean's fashions and hair on Italian men.

[5] See Kuhn's (2002: 172) distinction between imitation of stars and 'cinema effects', which include 'accounts of affective reactions and behavioural responses induced by the films'.

*Desire* (Elia Kazan, United States, 1951). It is a particular scene that he recalls, the one in which Brando's character smashes up the dining table in a fit of temper. Giorgio narrates the scene to the interviewer ('I remember him wearing just the vest ... I remember his outbursts of rage which frighten me, a simple spectator'), and as he narrates, he cowers in his seat as he recalls Vivien Leigh's character doing, adopts a frightened expression and brings his hands to his face, illustrating a powerful bodily response in remembering.[6] Giorgio's continuous narration in the present tense, which allows him to access the past as 'a kind of quasi-present' (Friedman 2014: 296), places him in the position of the female character/star and, beyond showing us a spectator with a nuanced appreciation for Brando's and Leigh's performances, seems to challenge the 'rigid distinction between either desire or identification' (Stacey 1987: 61), and allow for a complex play of erotic relation to the male star.

Giorgio also articulates a relationship to James Dean that is very interesting; when asked about his 'greatest emotion' at the cinema, he narrates or reimagines a scene he remembers from *East of Eden* (Elia Kazan, United States, 1955), in which Dean's character measures the height of the bean plants growing on his father's field (see Figure 8.2).[7]

For Giorgio, as he expresses it, this scene summarizes his memory of Dean. He again places himself in the position of the actor, imitating his gaze and head position in the scene, and smiles tenderly as he says 'this expression of James Dean' (see Figure 8.3).[8]

As Capussotti argues, Dean was an icon of sensitivity, as well as sexual ambiguity, and the Italian fan clubs which sprang up for him in the 1950s valorized this 'renegotiation' (2004: 150) of masculinity that he offered.[9] Although Giorgio does not go beyond defining himself as 'sensitive' and something of a loner, he does say that the films of Brando, Dean and Paul Newman offered him 'what I would like to find in my surroundings' in that period. For Giorgio, these

---

[6] Kuhn (2002: 147) describes the 'all-encompassing somatic, sensuous and affective involvement in the cinema experience' that often emerges in testimonies. In fact, Giorgio ends this narration of the scene by talking about how when he exited the cinema he was nearly run over by a tram, so strong had his sense of 'ecstasy' been. This affective spectatorial pleasure derived from a certain performance of masculinity links to Stacey's words (1994: 116) on 'the pleasure of losing oneself' and the desire for transcendence through cinema.

[7] This is also discussed in Treveri Gennari et al. (2019).

[8] Interestingly, this scene is difficult to locate when rewatching the film, since it lasts for only about thirty seconds. This seems an example of what Stacey (1994: 67) talks of as 'the frozen moment', or 'iconic memory', 'taken out of its temporal context and captured as "pure image"'.

[9] See McKinnon's (2009) similar findings among older Australian men. McKinnon cites Cohan (1997: 202) on Brando and Dean's 'deliberate contrast to the era's hegemonic masculinity'.

**Figure 8.2** James Dean in *East of Eden* (Elia Kazan, United States, 1955)

**Figure 8.3** Giorgio imitates James Dean in *East of Eden* (*Italian Cinema Audiences* dataset).

stars represent an aspiration to something new that cannot even be properly articulated, and they speak to him in a powerful and deeply personal way.

Several of our narrators also spoke of their imitation of Humphrey Bogart, an icon of more traditional Hollywood masculinity for an older generation of boys. Antonio M. (b. 1933, Naples) remembers 'Humphrey Bogart's cigarette … the smoke coming out … it made you want to smoke … his trench coat with the collar turned up'. Here Antonio's gesture is important, as he re-enacts the imitation of Bogart they engaged in as boys, lifting an imaginary cigarette to his lips with trembling hands, and turning up his imaginary collar. This gesture, as with Edoardo's, suggests an affective relationship with the star that cannot quite be described in language. The gestural language is part of the 'forces of encounter' that Seigworth and Gregg (2010: 2) define as affect. The male body, remembered, becomes a site of encounter with the star, with the star representing something more than what is accessible in daily life. Bodies are here defined 'not only by an outer skin-envelope or other surface boundary but by their potential to reciprocate or co-participate in the passages of affect' (ibid.).[10] The 'composure' of the individual's narrative of the self depends upon these instances of transmission of affect and moments of longing. Meanwhile Sergio M. (b. 1931, Rome) links the imitation of Bogart's smoking to a desire to have as many women as he did on screen, setting up an analogy between imitating the star and achieving their masculinity, which makes explicit what is implied in other accounts of star imitation.

Although there was a clear glamour associated with Hollywood stars, Italian stars were also objects of imitation. As mentioned previously, Amedeo Nazzari was our most popular male star, and the post-war weepies he starred in, directed by Raffaello Matarazzo, were invoked by many respondents. Antonio A. (b. 1927, Naples) alludes to a widespread imitation of Nazzari's hairstyle – which he terms the *spina di pesce* or 'fishbone' style, accompanied with a hand gesture; he emphasizes the communal (and homosocial) space of the barber where all the young men would imitate the same styles.[11]

---

[10] As Hillmer (1997) notes, 'We can slip into the role of Marlene, Humphrey, Audrey, James, speaking their language with our bodies. We are the copy, the variation, the improvisation, the parody' (quoted in Street 2001: 8).

[11] A younger respondent, Adolfo (b. 1940, Milan), talks of how they used to imitate the hairstyles of newer stars such as 1950s Italian icons Renato Salvatori and Maurizio Arena, as well as Mario Lanza, and he makes a hand gesture to illustrate Lanza's quiff or *boccolone*.

This allusion to a shared common sense ('We-sense') or generational culture (see Aroldi and Colombo 2007) is important because it speaks to a shared connection to cinema which was inscribed upon the body, and which also pointed to the 'available possibilities for a masculine self' (Dawson 1994: 23), bringing fantasy and 'real' masculinity into contact. The 'composure' of the past self and its orientation to a world of gender norms also inevitably occurs along a past-present axis veined with nostalgia. Edoardo, for example, agrees they imitated stars in dress but compares this unfavourably to a modern culture where everything is imitation. He has a strong sense of nostalgia and in fact towards the end of his interview he seems to weep when he declares himself *uno sconfitto* ('defeated by life'). Similarly, Antonio A., in mentioning imitation of Nazzari's hairstyle, compares the 'good' masculinity of Nazzari to the current male role models, footballers, felt to be a degraded version of the glamour of the stardom of the past.

The idea of a clear-cut identification and imitation of stars in the past is undermined, however, by Pietro (b. 1939, Florence province): Pietro (twelve years younger than Antonio A., and a child in the late 1940s and early 1950s when the Nazzari weepies were at their peak) explains how he and his friends used to mock Nazzari and his old-fashioned movies. He isolates Nazzari's dramatic voice as a key element of his (to them) absurd persona, and laughingly does an impersonation of his typical romantic declaration: 'Amore, ti amo!' ('My love, I love you!'). Pietro's love of American films, particularly adventure films and musicals, perhaps explains his antipathy to Nazzari, though it is also likely that his friend group, all of whom shared this antipathy, he insists, all resisted romantic films and saw Nazzari as a despised icon of romance and femininity, an issue already discussed in Chapter 4.

Another example of reluctance to be seen as an imitator or fan is that of Lorenzo (b. 1937, Milan), who comments that he once bought a leather jacket, but when he saw a Brando film he was embarrassed, thinking people would believe he was imitating the star, so he discarded the jacket. This anecdote about refusal of star imitation needs to be further contextualized in relation to Lorenzo's identity as a cinephile, attender of a cinema discussion club and staunch believer in the educational and cultural value of cinema. Lorenzo's statement echoes the repeated view by respondents that while other people around them may have imitated stars, they did not. This nexus of cinephilia and imitation emerges particularly strikingly in the example of Roberto (b. 1943, Turin), who worked in the Italian cinema industry as a dubber. Roberto shows off his cinephile knowledge, listing films and directors, and although he admits that they used to wear leather jackets in imitation of Brando and Dean, he proudly shows off the smart jacket he is wearing for the interview, and explains that it is just like the ones that director Luchino Visconti used to wear.

Roberto had met Visconti, and describes him as a 'great man', so the jacket functions as a material instantiation of the idea of auteur cinema as cultural capital.

## Gender and cinephilia

The 1950s, as Paolo Noto has shown, were a decade in which a nascent cinephilia was promoted and encouraged by left-wing film journals such as *Cinema Nuovo*, and this 'proto-cinephilia' (Noto 2018: 44) took various vernacular forms such as cinema clubs, some of which are discussed in our interviews. The male cinephiles in our sample construct their identities in various ways: as we have seen, engagement with the star image is one site of negotiation of desire and identification. A more pronounced factor is the way male cinephiles articulated a linkage between their experiences and a type of masculinity – left-wing, political, intellectually curious – that was supplied by certain films. These films included neorealism, but also auteur films, principally those of Fellini and Visconti, and these films are discussed by men as part of their political education, and as offering an element of cultural distinction they valued intensely. Piero (b. 1938, Bari province) saw cinema as part of his 'political formation', a term that is echoed by other respondents, and even proudly boasts about how he met Fellini twice while doing his military service in Rome and had drinks with him.

Another provincial southerner, Francesco (b. 1943, Bari province), has a very similar narrative: again, Fellini plays a strong role, and there is also a strong sense of exclusion from the cultural centre of Italy, with Puglia as a backwater, and cinema offering a political window onto Italy. Francesco attended the *cineforum* run by the Salesian priests, read film reviews and has amassed a collection of over two thousand DVDs, which he tells the interviewer to turn round and look at. Similarly, Antonio R. (b. 1941, Bari province) refers to cinema as particularly important 'in these Southern villages of ours', and self-consciously contrasts the 'cinema di paese' (village cinema) and 'cinema di città' (city cinema). Both men, to illustrate their commitment to seeing good films, explain that they would hitchhike or drive to neighbouring towns (Francesco explains that when a friend got a Fiat 500 they were able to go further afield to satisfy their desire to see and comment upon films, often watching two films in a row). As we saw in Chapter 2, male spectators often had more freedom to travel to distant cinemas than females.

Antonio R. – along with another interviewee, Riccardo (b. 1943, Naples) – engaged with an important site of male cinephilia by reading the magazine *Cinema Nuovo*. Founded in 1952 by leading Marxist critic Guido Aristarco, *Cinema Nuovo* was the most important left-wing film journal in Italy. Through a culture of debate and politicized engagement with highbrow film culture, it addressed (and aimed to produce) 'a supply of consumers psychologically trained to acquire all the accoutrements of a "modern" life' (*Cinema Nuovo* promotional flyer from 1958, cited in Noto 2019: 62). This modernity of the *Cinema Nuovo* reader singled him out from his provincial peers; despite (or perhaps because of) a circulation of only eighty thousand copies per issue, *Cinema Nuovo* was important in producing a faithful group of readers who felt themselves to be 'different' (Noto 2019: 63). This 'difference' was particularly felt in the south, where cinema clubs were rare, and where the distance from the metropolis was often felt more acutely.[12]

It is also significant that *Cinema Nuovo* deliberately constructed an address to a male reader by its policy of only featuring as cover stars beautiful actresses.[13] What Mandelli and Re (2017) call the 'internal ambivalence' of the magazine, caught between a highbrow critical discourse and an emphasis on female beauty, is actually constitutive of cinephilia itself, as Geneviève Sellier has argued.[14] Sellier's discussion of French post-war cinephilia resonates with the Italian

---

[12] See e.g. the letter to *Cinema Nuovo* from reader Francesco Castriotta, from the town of Manfredonia (Puglia), 1 May 1958, p. 257. Castriotta complains that lack of education and an enforced diet of westerns and comedies prevents most of his fellow spectators from understanding serious cinema, and compares their 'primitiveness' unfavourably to city audiences, who are more capable of appreciating highbrow films. Virgilio Tosi, in his study of cinema clubs, notes that they were by far more common in the north of Italy: at the first national conference of cinema clubs in 1947 in Liguria, there was no southern Italian club represented, and Tosi discusses the difficulties for southern groups of getting hold of films, but also the 'cultural revolution' that a cinema club or *cineforum* could represent in these villages and towns (Tosi 1999: 90, 93). See also Fanchi (2019: 391) on the uneven north-south distribution of cinemas in Italy in the 1950s, exacerbated by poor roads, transport and even electricity provision.

[13] Gremigni (2009: 125) counts, out of 338 readers' letters sent to *Cinema Nuovo* between 1956 and 1967, only 13 that were written by women.

[14] It also is consonant with the characteristics of the ideal Italian left-wing man in the post-war period, who should possess both 'virility' and 'moral rigour', should have a 'healthy heterosexual instinct' but also be 'serious' and 'sober' (Bellassai 2000: 294, 272).

context in many ways, not least in how the cinephile gaze is male, heterosexual and fetishistic, as we will see in the following section, and also often deliberately excludes women spectators (Sellier 2008: 29). This exclusion of women is particularly true of the various types of *cineforum* or cine-clubs that operated, where women, when they attended, tended to be silent.[15]

Two of our narrators, interestingly, both southern, mention Giuseppe Tornatore's nostalgic evocation of cinemagoing in the 1950s, *Nuovo Cinema Paradiso*, as a kind of model of their own experiences. Eugenio (b. 1942, Palermo) recounts that he cried when his childhood cinema (which he refers to as 'the real Cinema Paradiso') was demolished, and the fact that he went on to become a projectionist suggests a clear parallel with Tornatore's boy protagonist Totò.

Meanwhile, Antonio R. from rural Puglia, our *Cinema Nuovo* reader, also likened his experiences to *Cinema Paradiso*, suggesting the extent to which the film image can model an image of masculinity (the provincial southern boy who grows up to be a director, an image imbued with both eroticism and a strong sense of loss). For Sellier, this gendered dimension of cinephilia is central, and it is intrinsically linked to what she terms 'a form of masculine sociability' (2008: 28) which, as we will see, is imbricated in both an eroticized relation to the film image and to an idea of the cinema space itself as a theatre of gender relations, something already alluded to in Chapter 3.

## Masculinity sociability and gender relations

In the memories of our protagonists, both the cinema space and the remembered images become sites for the enactment and consolidation of gender roles, but ones which are also capable of revealing latent tensions. The key clusters we will address here are the cinema space as a site of (male heterosexual) sociability, the ways in which the film image itself is remembered as initiating or instructing boys into heterosexual desire, and how practices of molestation – with boys as both victims and perpetrators – point to tensions that undercut the compulsory heterosexuality that pervades the memory of the period.

---

[15] See also Giuseppe (b. 1943, Milan province) for whom reading left-wing film reviews in the Communist party paper *L'Unità* and attending the *Circolo del cinema* (cinema circle or club) of a Communist group was a core part of his life, but who admits that it was difficult to meet likeminded, intellectual girls ('if they weren't like us they got very bored').

As mentioned earlier, the cinema, from the late 1940s onwards, became a progressively masculine space.[16] As Mariagrazia Fanchi (2010) has noted, while in 1947, levels of male and female cinema attendance in Italy were roughly the same, by 1953 female attendance was in sharp decline, especially in rural areas and the south, while nearly 50 per cent of Italian men still attended the cinema at least once a week.[17] As mentioned in Chapters 2 and 3, the taboos on attending cinema alone for girls and the general norms around modesty and courtship saw the cinema become a strongly gendered space, and especially in the south of Italy, restrictions placed on girls' mobility.[18] Girls would generally attend the cinema in groups, but it was also a space, as Chapter 6 notes, where they learned to negotiate their status as sexual objects and engage in courtship rituals. Unspoken rules often governed the seating choices: several of our male respondents talk about how, for example, sitting in the gallery with a girl indicated that she was amenable to courting. This 'unwritten code', as Renato B. (b. 1942, Turin) describes it, shows a sophisticated knowledge of the semiotics of the cinema space itself.[19] Further, the choice of cinema itself might be strategic: Sergio M. (b. 1931, Rome) would choose to go with a girlfriend to the Cinema Delle Vittorie because it was small and had nooks and crannies which were desirable, as it was more important 'to fondle than to see the film'.[20]

The cinema as a space which reflected and enforced patriarchal gender norms can clearly be seen in many of our interviews, with many men unquestioningly repeating the dominant ideas of the time about women who attended the cinema alone. When asked whether it was acceptable for girls and women to go alone, Antonio M. from Naples laughed and responded, 'They would have immediately been made pregnant.' Marino (b. 1937, Milan) also gives a laughing reply

---

[16] See also on this phenomenon Gremigni (2009: 36–8); Casetti and Fanchi (2002).
[17] See also the report by Luzzatto Fegiz, based on DOXA surveys: he notes that by 1960, out of 48 million cinema tickets sold, two-thirds belonged to men, and a third to women (1966: 241).
[18] The important study carried out in 1959 by sociologist Lidia De Rita on the effect of television on a small rural community in the southern region of Basilicata offers more testimony on this. She found that girls faced 'heavy social penalties' if they dared to go to the cinema alone. See De Rita (1964: 47). But even in the north, women's attendance seemed markedly less frequent than men's: Malcolm MacLean, in discussing the ethnographic study of cinema-going in the province of Florence in 1958 he carried out with Luca Pinna, reports that their sample is 73 per cent male. This is attributed to women's lack of freedom of movement (MacLean 1958: 40).
[19] Fanchi (2001: 348) and Gremigni (2009: 31) confirm this.
[20] Enrico Biasin (2018) found, in his study of the memories of a sample of 1950s male cinemagoers in north-east Italy, that there was a strong sense of the cinema as 'the best opportunity for various types of sexual performance: conjugal, extra-marital, and furtive'.

that women who went to the cinema alone were 'puttane' (whores). This idea that women in the cinema were seen as 'easy' or as 'asking for it' is made very explicit in a disturbing anecdote by Antonio A. (b. 1927, Naples): he worked at the magistrate's court, and recounts that he was approached for advice by a man who claimed his daughter had been raped in a particular cinema. However, Antonio says cheerily, because that cinema had boxes, it was well known as a place where girls would do anything, so she clearly was not raped. He told the girl's father, 'Your daughter was up for it. There was no assault.' Antonio's matter-of-fact, even jovial, reproduction of the common sense of the time, that a girl who willingly chose to accompany a boy into a cinema box could not then be raped or sexually assaulted, speaks powerfully to the ways in which cinema as a part of social life reinforced contemporary patriarchal values.[21] As mentioned in Chapter 3, only a couple of our narrators, Antonio S. (b. 1936, Palermo province) and Alessandro (b. 1929, Rome province), admitted that they would touch up girls in the cinema, a confession that, in Antonio's case, is accompanied by some humour and a touch of embarrassment.

While girls were often circumscribed, regimented and judged in where they could safely sit in the cinema, the cinema space was one in which boys often roamed quite freely, pulling pranks and japes. Several male respondents talk of the tendency to shout inappropriate comments and wisecracks at the screen, exercising a vocal dominance of the space. They also would make fun of the ice-cream or sweet sellers, and Giancarlo (b. 1943, Cagliari province) recounts how one friend slapped the back of a man's bald head and how another always sneezed during the moments of suspense to frighten people watching thrillers. Pietro from Florence province remembers how the roof of the Cinema Garibaldi in his small town was covered in the debris of items they shot through pea-shooters during the films, and there is a clear sense of the connection between the cinema space, the adolescent friend group and the bonding rituals they engaged in. Male privilege was exercised over the space in different ways: Rodolfo (b. 1942, Naples) claims that young men would buy half a cigar and smoke it in the cinema in order to free up a space, so they could sit down (presumably other patrons would leave in disgust at the smell, despite the thick cigarette smoke that pervaded most cinemas).

---

[21] This perspective resonates with Gabriella Parca's famous designation of the Italian man in her 1965 ethnographic study, as 'having the tendencies of a sultan', for whom all women potentially belong to his harem (Parca 1965: 254).

The communal male experience is emphasized throughout: Sergio P. (b. 1924, Rome) emphasizes this collective experience through the use of the word *cricca* (friend group) which is remembered fondly via japes such as trying to steal the ticket books to get in free or persuading the ticket girl to let three of them in on one ticket. Vincenzo (b. 1928, Florence province) smiles fondly when he remembers the *bischerate* (foolishness) he and his pals got up to, but then talks of how at the end of adolescence, the *marachelle* or shenanigans had to end. This homosocial bonding could extend to mockery of girls' behaviour: Giancarlo (b. 1942, Cagliari province) laughingly reminisces about how they used to mock girls and women who cried over the romantic weepies starring Amedeo Nazzari, dismissively referring to them as *donnette* ('silly girls'). This communal experience could also move outside the cinema building: Pietro, for example, says that his friend group had a special whistle they would use to call each other, which was derived from a Gary Cooper film.

Although he is unable to recall the title, he whistles the tune: it is the famous refrain 'Do Not Forsake Me Oh My Darling' from *High Noon* (Fred Zinneman, United States, 1952). Cinema conditioned their 'boyhood cultures' (Dawson 1994: 234), as it did with those who imitated cowboys or adventure heroes.

However, as well as a space in which boys practised the rituals of courtship, the cinema venue was also a place where they learned about love and sex from on- screen images. The accounts are resolutely heteronormative: Vittoriano (b. 1941, Bari) mentions going to the cinema in order to see naked scenes (though in reality these were heavily censored). Vito (b. 1947, Palermo) talks of the attempt to find transgressive images in highly censored films as an adolescent. He frames this through a narrative of cultural decay: now teens know it all because they are watching porn, he argues, but back then daring images were enough – the image of a woman in a bikini or a low-cut top was enough to excite them.

For some boys, cinema offered constitutive images of femininity that inducted them into heterosexuality: Antonio M. from Naples describes seeing American swimming star Esther Williams in *Bathing Beauty* (George Sidney, United States, 1944) (which was released in Italy in 1948) as 'the discovery of something new and traumatic'. The interviewer does not press Antonio on what this trauma was, but we can imagine it as profoundly connected to the vision of her exposed body, in colour. For Enea (b. 1935, Milan), cinema also offered an initiation into heterosexual desire. He recounts that his first 'erotic' memory was seeing Rita Hayworth ('a splendid creature') in *Gilda* (Charles Vidor, United States, 1946) when he was 11 or 12 years old. Specifically, he remembers the glove scene, when Hayworth as Gilda begins to perform a striptease, removing her long black silk gloves seductively. Renato (b. 1942, Turin) had an even earlier experience: at age 6 or 7 he says he forced his grandmother to take him several times to see a film he insists was called *La schiava di Babilonia* (*The Slave of Babylon*) starring American actress Rhonda Fleming ('an amazing redhead') as he was in love with her and wanted to marry her. He recounts this with laughter as a 'crazy love'.[22]

Antonio R. from Bari province gives an example, which, although much later, illustrates how cinema was a resource for learning how to be a certain type of man. He cites a line from *Body Heat* (Lawrence Kasdan, United States, 1981) which he used to pick up women, successfully, he adds proudly. Meanwhile, Attilio (b. 1937, Naples) offers a slightly more complex view of how cinema educated them into heterosexuality: he talks of how they were in some ways educated as boys by their first 'film passionali', that is, those weepies starring Amedeo Nazzari and Yvonne Sanson, and until then they had no knowledge of emotions such as passion or jealousy. Cinema, he insists, was 'the only window onto the world outside' for them, not like now, when everything is known; through this past/present dichotomy he makes clear the importance of cinema as a pedagogical resource, in a period marked by restrictions and limitations of knowledge.

Of course, as we have seen throughout the book, the cinema space hosted not just films but also other kinds of spectacles. Variety performances were also singled out as significant by men for representing an illicit glimpse of female sexual display.

Giuseppe (b. 1946, Florence province) recalls that in his town on Fridays they were not allowed to go to the cinema as it would be preceded by a variety show (*avanspettacolo*) featuring 'the notorious dancers: it was only for over-18s'. Some boys did try to get in, and it was regarded as a great triumph if you did, but it rarely happened as everyone knew you in the town, he confides. Similarly, Roberto (b. 1943, Turin) reminisces about the dancers and 'girls in low-cut dresses' at the variety shows. There is a sense of the exciting proximity of these women in strait-laced times, and their vernacular glamour contrasts with that

---

[22] The film mentioned actually appears to be the Italian epic *La cortigiana di Babilonia* (*The Slave Woman*, Carlo Ludovico Bragaglia, Italy, 1954) so Renato would have been twelve, not seven, making his story more typical of a prepubescent boy, than the extremely naïve and innocent experience he conjures up. Fleming appears scantily clad in many scenes of the film.

of the film stars, but is not less enticing, although Marino describes the variety show unflatteringly as normally featuring dancers who were 'plain' and 'a bit fat'.

The cinema venue was thus a space where gender relations were learned, negotiated and performed, where sexuality was developed and where heteronormativity was learned. As Francesco Casetti (2000: 62) has described it, it was the 'site of the first transgressions': kisses, bunking off school, the first cigarettes, and represented both a place where social norms could be infringed and where more mature behaviour could be attempted. The homosocial dimension of cinemagoing was powerful, as we saw in relation to the collective japes and 'strong affective we- connection' displayed (Hanich 2010). If further evidence were needed of the way the space was experienced as a compulsorily heterosexual one, alongside the many accounts of post-cinema rituals such as going for pizza, or taking a walk, one man, Gianfranco (b. 1929, Florence), lists visiting *case chiuse*, or state-run brothels.

However, there is an undercurrent to the homosocial and compulsorily heterosexual nature of the cinema space which emerges quite notably in our interviewees' testimonies. That is the question of homosexual desire: this is always framed, significantly, in the context of molestation by older men. In Chapters 3 and 6, we discussed the strategies that girls engaged in to defend themselves against 'la mano morta' (the wandering hand), accepted as part of the cinemagoing experience. But we can understand from our interviews with men that this was also a significant factor in their own cinemagoing. It is often framed as something that happened to other boys, but nevertheless, as a common practice. Giorgio says that when a man sat down beside you and tried it on you just got up and moved, but there was no point complaining to the usherette as it was 'a tolerated thing'. Paolo (b. 1936, Florence) agrees that it was well known that if you went on your own you were a potential victim. Meanwhile, Giovanni (b. 1944, Florence) aligns himself unwittingly with the experience of many of the women in our sample, when he says he preferred to go to the cinema with a group of friends, as protection against molesters. There is one anecdote of a boy defending himself, though told by his sister: Maria Giovanna (b. 1936, Milan) says that her brother was targeted by men, and 'always' carried a pocketknife to defend himself. She recalls an occasion when he struck the hand of a man who tried to molest him. When the molester cried out, the house lights went up, but 'as usual' her brother did not let on what had happened.[23]

---

[23] Interestingly, Stefano Benni's comic description of the Cinema Sagittario in his *Bar Sport* (set in an undefined 1950s/1960s) includes, amidst the homosocial chaos of shouting and fighting, a mention

Interestingly, one of our respondents, Attilio (b. 1937, Naples), claims that some boys would accept advances from men in exchange for 'a few lire' because in Naples at the time everyone was 'in dire straits'. Again, he distances himself from this practice, but there is a sense in which the reference to the economic challenges of post-war Naples would legitimize and explain what surely was a fairly widespread behaviour. This kind of local common sense is evident when Antonio A. from Naples says that it was well known that there were 'notorious cinemas' where homosexuals looked for boys to approach. Antonio S. from Palermo province dismisses attempts by homosexual men to pick up boys as merely the 'other side' of a pleasurable phenomenon, which was boys trying to touch up girls.

Of course, these men are mainly expressing memories from when they were boys and adolescents: but what is importantly elided here is mutual homosexual desire. As Andrea Pini (2011) has discussed, in the post-war period cinemas were very common cruising locations, although this was rarely publicly discussed. Mauro Giori (2017a: 25) uses his account of homosexual cinemagoing in the same period to challenge the heterosexual bias of books like Gian Piero Brunetta's *Buio in sala* (1997) and to uncover a hidden history of repressed behaviours.[24] Brunetta, probably Italy's leading film historian, significantly prefaces his compilation of testimonies of cinemagoing by mainly male writers and intellectuals with a story of a man, courting with his girlfriend, ejaculating all over the other spectators in the cinema. Brunetta uses this story as a

> positive exemplum of a 'shared experience', of a connection and a physical contagion that affects an entire audience. It seems to me possible to interpret this powerful affirmation of vitality on the part of a young man, symbolically of course, as a wish that the younger generations might restore strength and life to the cinemas themselves, and produce in those spaces evocations of archaic divinities (the god Pan, for example) with whom today's world has lost all contact. (1997: xii)

---

of an old homosexual paedophile, something of a fixture in the cinema, and two younger ones, who 'smelt like a flower shop', testifying to how embedded this practice was in the cultural consciousness (Benni 1976: 87). Thanks to Paolo Noto for this reference.

[24] This silence around homosexuality is also discussed by Parca, who notes that of her 1965 sample of 1,018 men from all over Italy, 6 per cent state they have had homosexual experiences, while 41 per cent have had approaches from men, but none say they have ever made approaches to another man, and most judge homosexuality either an illness or a vice (1965: 246–8).

We have quoted this passage in its entirety to illustrate the pervasive connection between male heteronormative desire and the cinema space in the Italian cultural imaginary. As we have seen, although the homosocial can be articulated in official and unofficial accounts of the cinema space, through japes and collective behaviours including imitation, homosexuality is only speakable in terms of molestation, despite its widespread presence in cinemas.

## Conclusion

Despite the late 1950s and early 1960s in Italy being a period in which there was supposedly an 'erosion of the interdiction against queer sexualities' (Giori 2017b: 163), manifest through films such as *Comizi d'amore* (*Love Meetings*, Pier Paolo Pasolini, Italy, 1964), our narrators' recollections allow only a certain space for queer sexuality. It seems likely that going too far beyond heteronormative conceptions of the period would result in what Summerfield (2004: 135) terms 'discomposure', that is, a sense of psychic discomfort when the personal narrative is at odds with the broader discursive repertoire. What is clear, however, is that cinema could represent new possibilities for boys, in terms of models of the self and glimpses of different ways to be: there are parallels with what McKinnon (2009: 135) notes in the Australian sample he analyses, where 'male teens had experienced within the cinema moments of new possibilities ... in which their sexuality became a point of attractiveness; in which overt emotion and attention to style were aligned with toughness and strength; in which youth provided a context for difference and exploration'. This can certainly be represented by star preferences, for example, Marlon Brando versus Amedeo Nazzari; as Martin Shingler argues, star meanings can act as a touchstone for shifting cultural values: they 'have a tendency to reveal not so much what was happening socially and culturally at the time but, rather, what was coming into being or what was being left behind' (Shingler 2012: 151).

With Italian audiences becoming progressively 'masculinized' in the 1950s, the audience itself and its mode of occupying the space of the cinema are understood as gendered, in its relationships both to the opposite sex and to other men and boys. The parallel drawn with *Nuovo Cinema Paradiso* by some narrators also speaks both to a privileged identification with the male protagonist of Italian cinema history and ultimately to a kind of defeated masculinity, in which the best times are in the past. In remembering their youthful behaviour and desires, several of our male interviewees openly weep; Antonio M., who describes himself as 'very sensitive', says emotionally, 'I'm nostalgic, not for those films, but for that time.' As Stacey notes, 'Men may also feel a nostalgia for a time when attainment of desired identities still seemed a future possibility' (1994: 67). The nostalgia for this period also encompasses an ability to laugh openly at topics that social changes such as feminism have now deemed offensive, such as *la mano morta*. This can be related to Svetlana Boym's concept of 'restorative nostalgia' (2008: xviii): this type of nostalgia, unlike more critical or 'reflective' nostalgia, tries to preserve and reconstruct a lost 'home', seen as truth and tradition. In our interviews we have seen men often attempting, precariously, to restore this 'lost home', which is understood as broadly encompassing both the past and a particular idea of masculinity, one which is rooted in a gender regime which is now past. Film, and the (homo)social experience of cinemagoing offered Italian men both a training ground for masculinity and the possibility to question it.

# Conclusions

In 1948, director Dino Risi made a short film entitled *Buio in sala* (*Darkness in the Cinema*, Italy), which shows a depressed man going into a cinema in post-war Milan, sitting down to watch a Western surrounded by courting couples and shouting children, and, at the film's end, happily exiting the cinema and walking off through the rubble of the bombed city. While not all of the accounts of cinemagoing we gathered are so redemptive, we take our cue from this suggestion that cinema offered a powerful source of escapism for a country still emerging from the horrors and hardships of fascism and the Second World War. It also taught Italians about the world, about how to behave and how to love, especially those who, like many of our respondents, were very young in the post-war period. Throughout the book we have shown how a wide range of film genres, far beyond the neorealist films traditionally prized by critics, spoke to Italians on a deeply personal level, and how the communal and collective experience of cinemagoing lives on in their memories.

The Italian Cinema Audiences (ICA) project aimed to investigate audiences' memories of cinemagoing in post-war Italy in an effort to 'rethink the history of cinema *as* the history of the experience of cinema' (Allen 2011: 84, emphasis in original). With the bottom-up oral-historical focus at the heart of this project, Italian audiences' testimonies have offered a counter-narrative of the history of cinema (Fanchi 2019: 388) as well as shedding new light on the way in which cinema is remembered. Set in the context of daily experience and life cycles, our respondents' narratives have provided insights into the role of the cinema space, the significance of socialization in the cinemagoing experience, as well as the relevance of ancillary activities that occurred in conjunction with the act of film consumption, overlooked by Italian film history, as highlighted in Chapter 2.

Our participants have expressed great awareness of the multisensory dimensions of their cinemagoing practice inside the cinema venues. Moreover, our video interviews have highlighted the performative quality of cinemagoing in post-war Italy: this occurred through the performance of cinema rituals (such as dressing up or eating beforehand), and audiences' lively interactions with the film itself (discussed in Chapter 3). This aspect of cinemagoers' memories has allowed us to make sense of what took place in the cinemas at the time, and has allowed us to uncover the traces left by films on our participants once the audience exited the venues. On one hand, our research findings confirm the ephemeral nature of the film text in the memories of cinemagoers, as highlighted by previous scholarship (Harper 2019; Kuhn 2011; Kuhn cited in Biltereyst 2019: 36). On the other hand, they also suggest the deep ways in which certain films and stars can get intertwined in personal narratives. In particular, through video interviews we have gauged the embodied nature of memory and the affective charge of remembered films and stars, as revealed in our analysis of body language, voice and gestures of respondents. The affective qualities of the reminiscence process also reveal more clearly the close intertwining of memory and the plurality of emotions related to this process, from nostalgic modes to detached reconstructions of past events. These embodied cinema memories are at the heart of the book, and allow for the first time the tracing of an emotional history of cinemagoing, and its central role in post-war Italian culture and memory.

Within the context of post-war Italy, the project's findings have offered new perspectives on the role cinema played in relation to social change, gender and sexuality and regional identities. Moreover, our film audiences' memories have allowed us to re-evaluate film preferences, particularly as regards stars, and genres, revealing alternative histories of Italian cinema that do not rely on canonical narratives of great auteurs and the influential neorealist movement. At the same time, they make us more attentive to the diachronic relationship audiences might have developed with certain films, when they are visited and revisited as national treasures via television and rereleases, such as the case of *Roma città aperta* discussed in Chapter 5. Attention to the memory work and remediation processes, both at an individual and at a collective level, has also helped us explain the discrepancies between synchronic archival data on film popularity (specifically box-office performance and critical reception) and the generic preferences in the memories of our respondents.

Our focus on gender has allowed us to compare male and female modes of reminiscence, revealing somewhat different gendered forms of engagement with cinema, films and stars in the period in question. Female respondents revisit their girlhood with curiosity and pleasure (Piazza 2019: 43) sometimes regretting its all-too early loss and reviewing critically some of the myths about love and femininity presented to them at the time, as we discuss in Chapters 4 and 6. For male respondents, the intensity of nostalgic feelings may be more powerful, since the post-war promises of rebirth and renewal explicit in Italian cinema were directed towards them (see Chapter 5), while the models of virility offered by US cinema often proved transient or unattainable (see Chapter 8). Moreover, gender has been a key element in our reassessment of the relationship of post-war Italian audiences with stars. Specifically in the case of female participants, as discussed in Chapter 7, star preferences have shed light on the interconnection between gender identity formation and emerging mass consumerism in the period under scrutiny via different modes of identification.

From a methodological perspective, as films are experienced by audiences in very different ways according to variables such as geographical location, age, gender and social backgrounds, but also contexts of consumption, such as company and type of venue, our project had to engage with a variety of approaches able to capture the multifaceted and fragmented nature of audiencehood. Keeping the audience at the core of our project, we have attempted to reconcile the distinction between what Maltby (2006: 84) defines as the 'aesthetic history of textual relations among individuals or individual objects, and the sociocultural history of the economic institution of cinema'. We have achieved this in a twofold manner. First, we have aimed to reconstruct a history of cinema from below (ibid.: 85) by collecting testimonies directly from the real audiences who experienced cinema in the period under scrutiny. This bottom-up approach has been extended beyond the initial data collection phase, as we have engaged in further exchanges with our participants, as well as other older cinemagoers. This process – facilitated through the *Sharing Memories* events as well as through social media – has validated our findings, tested against participants' interpretations of their own memories of cinemagoing, and provided us with further insights into audiences practices, preferences and meanings of cinema.

Second, we have read the oral histories against other traces of cinema history through 'methodological integration, synergies and interdisciplinarity' (Biltereyst, Lotze and Meers 2012: 692), using archival research, digital humanities tools, geographical analysis, statistical investigations, film textual and film reception analysis. This holistic approach has uncovered points of contact and divergence between historical official discourses around cinema – as articulated by government, industry and the press – and cinemagoers' memories of post-war Italian film culture. It has also revealed the methodological and analytical challenges of employing and interpreting different types of data and sources, reminding us that 'our task – of the recovery and interpretation of audience response from the past – is an act of historical imagination' (Harper 2019: 688).

In bridging the divide mentioned above, as identified by Maltby, audiences' memories have also been employed in a process of reconstructing aspects of film culture unrecorded and unavailable in the archives: while box-office and programming data have given us a sense of what was available to audiences at the time, they fail to offer what Robert Allen (1990: 352) refers to as the 'immediate social, sensory, performative context of reception', which describes the surrounding context of consumption that attracted audiences, be that theatre location, level of comfort, noise, food or design. Moreover, audiences' testimonies have also been used to gauge the enduring significance of films and their place in cinema memory (Kuhn et al. 2017:10) both at an individual and collective level. Furthermore, it is important to note that our project – in an attempt to be representative in its analysis of all national territory – has also adopted a comparative approach. Juxtaposing local histories of cinemagoing across the country, we have become aware of the fact that these experiences were consumed and remembered in different ways by spectators in the north or the south of the country, and therefore our investigation was conducted both 'at a micro level (between cities, towns, and villages within a single region)' and at 'mid level (between different regions within a single country)' (ibid.: 11). In this sense, our project – despite the granular quality of oral history – shows the emergence of both a national and subnational dimension of the collective experience.

Like any form of research, the ICA project encountered challenges at different stages of the process. Being a collaborative endeavour that brought together a diverse team of academic researchers and partners from outside of academia, some methodological and interpretative obstacles were encountered along the way. In terms of methodology, careful consideration was given to the way the questionnaires and video interviews were designed and conducted. Echoing Harper's (2019: 688) warning to avoid any urge to *'give … a voice'* (our emphasis) to our interviewees, the aim of ICA has instead been 'to put that voice into an accessible form' (ibid.). As noted in the Introduction, the questionnaires provided the starting point for our ground-up approach to the study of the cinemagoing experience. Alongside this, the use of video interviews within our oral history approach has been a crucial part of the way we have sought to share the voices of ordinary cinemagoers.

Entrusting the data collection to external organizations was partly driven by practical limitations of time and cost. In order to ensure a consistent approach, this limitation was mitigated by giving the responsibility of all interviews to one researcher from Memoro, and providing training before the collection of the data. Moreover, it was agreed that the interviewer should avoid 'planting' information by suggesting the names of films or stars. Nevertheless, for some interviewees the inability to remember details such as the names of specific stars and films became a source of frustration (and occasionally distress) during the interview process. In hindsight, we have questioned the benefits of an overly rigid adherence to a guideline that sought to avoid any attempt to influence the interviewee by feeding information. An alternative, and possibly more fruitful, approach here could have been the careful use of ephemera (such as photos of stars) to act as triggers of memory in instances where the interviewee became blocked in their attempts to recall distant memories on the spot. We subsequently saw the benefit of this type of visual elicitation at our *Sharing Memories* events where participants commented positively on the way that the memories of their contemporaries and the clips of old films helped to 'refresh' their own memories that had been 'hidden in a drawer and forgotten' as one participant at our Turin event (2015) puts it.

The decision to have the video interviews conducted by a partner organization presented both benefits and limitations when it came to the analysis and interpretation of this data. By not interacting with the participants directly through the video-interview process, we were limited in our ability 'to look beyond the margins' (Harper 2019: 692–3) of each individual interview. On the one hand, this loss of the interviewer–interviewee exchanges before, during and after the interview – what Portelli (2018: 239–48) refers to as the 'personal encounter' – required us as researchers to depend solely on the content of the video interview. While this prompted us to speculate about some of the things that interviewees said or left unsaid, the advantage of our collaboration with Memoro is that it minimized the risk of introducing our own subjectivities and bias into the dialogue with participants. This 'distance' from our interviewees may constitute a limitation of our approach, but it has also allowed us to be more aware of our role as 'gamekeepers' (Harper 2019: 687) when interpreting the narratives of their memories.

In order to ensure the longevity of these memories, the decision to use video interviews as part of the project's methodological approach to oral history was also part of a strategy of capturing testimonies in a digital repository (https://www.cinericordi.it/). This is in line with the discipline's turn towards the internet as a conduit for the dissemination of research. The widespread use of video-sharing websites such as YouTube and Vimeo has made it possible for an ever-growing audience to instantly access high-quality video content from a range of personal devices. Reflecting on the impact of these new technologies on the discipline, Douglas A. Boyd and Mary Larson (2014: 4) write that 'the internet has blown the hinges from the doors of the archives and access has come to have a completely different meaning'. In order to safeguard the 'afterlife of cinema memory findings' (Kuhn et al. 2017: 11), we created a digital platform for our raw data so that this would be available to future and current researchers interested in cinema audiences. Moreover, for a research project that would fail to exist without the generous contributions of respondents and interviewees, the use of video interviews not only served to illustrate the value of this methodology, but it also ensured that these invaluable memories could be shared and enjoyed by a public that extends beyond the academic community, both during the project and after it ended.

In our Introduction, we quoted Gian Piero Brunetta's 1997 lament for an as-yet unwritten history of Italian cinema from the perspective of the cinemagoer. This monograph cannot hope to be a comprehensive study in that sense, or even an exhaustive analysis of the data collected during the three years of the project. We believe there are several avenues for further exploration and investigation: first of all, a more in-depth examination of the intersection between social background and the other variables discussed here (e.g. gender, and location) has the potential to offer further insights into the fragmented nature of film consumption. Moreover, future studies might adopt our methodologies as well as our data in a longitudinal study of the cinematic experience (especially after the arrival of television and other non-cinematic modes of film viewing). Another avenue of inquiry could be to further develop the relationship between exhibition structures and film consumption.

Further research in the *Archivio Centrale dello Stato* (the Central Archives of the State) in Rome could also assist in the historical reconstruction of the exhibition sector beyond the main cities analysed in our project. The collection relating to cinema venues across the country covering the period 1946–96 – although not fully catalogued – contains valuable information, including architects' plans for new commercial and parish cinemas, correspondence about the legalities of new building works and the practicalities of how many cinemas were legally allowed to operate in one area, as well as details of cinema ownership and attendance patterns. Funding for the full cataloguing of this valuable collection would enhance immeasurably our knowledge of cinemagoing and exhibition in the post-war period. Furthermore, expanding the ICA project beyond its national boundaries could help reconstruct a history of the experience of cinemagoing on a larger scale, comparing Italian practices with other countries. The European Cinema Audiences[1] research project has addressed this at a European level, but the ICA data has potential for further exploration beyond this geographical scope. Finally, we believe that integrating cinemagoing into broader research on leisure consumption, including other practices such as theatre attendance, music, dance and sporting activities, could widen our understanding of this field of inquiry. By making our data readily available to researchers on the CineRicordi website, it has been our intention to encourage further research in all these directions.

However, we want to emphasize that our research has already had a positive impact on communities of older people across the country. First of all, participants have commented on the pleasure of remembering, as Luciana (b. 1943, Turin) puts it: 'You're making me remember fragments of memory … which are amazing.' Overall, the ICA project and CineRicordi have enabled older people's participation in the creation of cultural heritage, while enhancing their well-being through reminiscence. Capturing memories of a pivotal moment in Italian film culture, the project has rescued and preserved intangible cultural heritage for current and future generations. By co-creating a digital archive, we have also ensured the sustainability of this legacy while enabling older people's digital inclusion (Dibeltulo et al. 2019). Moreover, the research has fostered intergenerational collaborations between older and younger audiences: younger people can be involved in the history of cinemagoing, by sharing cultural heritage in a creative online context.

The short film made by students at the Istituto Tecnico Casanova in Naples, which explored memories of the Mater Dei cinema, won the competition launched by ICA in collaboration with the Italian Ministry for Education, University and Research (MIUR) in 2018.[2] This film, about a cinema that has closed but that remains vivid in local memory, demonstrates a rich potential for Italy's cinema history to become part of its present and future. While many of our cinemagoers lamented the loss of their old haunts, now often turned into

---

[1] www.europeancinemaaudience.org.
[2] The film is online here: https://www.cinericordi.it/page/concorso/vincitori.

supermarkets and bingo halls, greater awareness both of this valuable cultural heritage and of the people who participated in it so deeply directs us to value above cinema as an affective communal space, in which social relations are made and remade, through 'the complex play between me, you, them, the film, the cinema building and the world outside' (Breakwell and Hammond 1990: 8).

# Appendix 1

# Questionnaire

The project, undertaken by a group of researchers from the Universities of Oxford, Bristol and Exeter, aims to carry out a systematic study of cinema audiences of the 1950s, analysing their film-going habits and tastes in order to reconstruct a crucial period in the history of Italian cinema. Ideally, the project will gather one thousand questionnaires filled in by people between the ages of 65 and 100, and in a second phase conduct video interviews with 250 people. By the end of the project (which will last three years) we intend to share the results of the research in the following ways:

1. Two books published in English
2. An exhibition of materials and the videos
3. Two conferences that will take place in Italy and England
4. A website displaying all the material gathered.

If you are interested in discussing your memories in a short video interview you are invited to contact Daniela Treveri Gennari – Oxford Brookes University (dtreveri-gennari@brookes.ac.uk) or simply add your details on the last page.

**1. Did you go to the cinema between 1950 and 1960?** Yes ☐ No ☐

**If not, please explain why:**
_____
_____

**2. In which years did you go most frequently?**

1950–3 ☐   1954–6 ☐   1957–60 ☐

**3. What did you like most about going to the cinema?**

_____
_____
_____

**4. On average how frequently did you go to the cinema?**

Less than once a month ☐  Between once and twice a month ☐
Once a week ☐  More than once a week ☐
Other _____ ☐

**5. What did you think about the cost of a ticket?**

Too expensive ☐  Cheap ☐
A fair price ☐  I don't know, I didn't pay ☐
Don't remember ☐  Other _____ ☐

**6. What else did you do in your spare time, apart from going to the cinema?**

**Select only the TWO main activities:**

Reading books ☐  Dancing ☐  Listening to the radio ☐
Reading magazines ☐  Theatre ☐  Going out with friends ☐
Political activity ☐  Sport ☐  Other _____ ☐

**7. With whom did you prefer to go to the cinema?**

Alone ☐  With family ☐
With friends ☐  With your boyfriend/girlfriend ☐
Other _____ ☐

**8. Which was your favourite day for going to the cinema?**

A weekday ☐  Saturday ☐
Sunday ☐  Any day of the week ☐

**9. What did the cinema mean for you?**

_____
_____
_____
_____

**10. What is your fondest memory related to the cinema?**

_____
_____
_____
_____

_____

**11. What kind of cinema did you go to?**

First run ☐   In your area ☐
Second run ☐   In another area ☐
Third run ☐   In the city centre ☐
Parish cinema ☐   In another village ☐
Cinema club ☐   Other _____
Open air ☐

**And why?**

_____
_____
_____

_____

**12. How would you describe the inside of your cinema?**

_____
_____
_____
_____

_____

**13. What made you choose a film?**

**Choose a maximum of THREE answers:**
**Film:** Actors ☐   Genre ☐   Nationality ☐
**Publicity:**
Posters on the street ☐   Publicity in the press ☐   Posters outside church ☐

**Other:**

Because someone recommended it ☐ I chose whatever was on at the cinema ☐ Other _____ ☐

14. **Could you describe in more detail the kinds of film you liked? Choose a maximum of THREE answers:**

    Adventure films ☐   Romantic films ☐
    War films ☐   Comedies ☐
    Melodramas ☐   Neorealist ☐
    Musicals ☐   Other _____

15. **Did you prefer Italian or US cinema?**

    _____
    _____

    **Why?**_____
    _____

16. **Can you give the name of a neorealist film?**

    _____

    **Did you like neorealist films?** Yes ☐   No ☐
    **Why?**_____
    _____
    _____

17. **Which film has remained most vividly in your memory?**

    _____
    _____
    _____
    _____
    **Why?**_____
    _____

18. **Which film made you cry?**

_____
_____
**Why?**_____
_____

19. **Who were your favourite male and female stars?**

    Male_____
    _____

    **What was it that you liked about him?** _____
    _____

    Female_____
    _____

    **What was it that you liked about her?** _____
    _____

20. **Have you ever:**

    – written to a film star?　　　　　Yes ☐　　　　No ☐
    – collected items linked to the cinema?
    (photos, papers, books, albums, articles)　Yes ☐　　No ☐
    If yes, can you tell us what and why?_____
    _____

21. **Did you ever read one of the following magazines during the period 1950–60?**

    **Choose ONE answer:**

    Star　☐　Gente　☐　Epoca　☐　Famiglia cristiana　☐
    Tempo　☐　L'europeo　☐　Oggi　☐　Hollywood　☐

22. **Did you read the reviews of films in these magazines?**

    Yes　☐　　No ☐

# Personal information

Name: _____
Date of birth: _____
Place of residence (today): _____
How many people were there in your family in the 1950s? _____
Where did you live between 1950 and 1960? _____
What job did your father do? _____
What job did you mother do? _____
Are you available for further interview?   Yes  ☐   No ☐
Telephone number: (**optional** – only supply if you are willing for us to contact you for further interview) _____

**What qualifications do you have?   How many times did you go to mass?**

| | | | |
|---|---|---|---|
| Primary school | ☐ | Less than once a month | ☐ |
| Middle school | ☐ | Once or twice a month | ☐ |
| A-level | ☐ | Once a week | ☐ |
| Degree | ☐ | More than twice a week | ☐ |
| Postgraduate qualification | ☐ | Never | ☐ |
| No certificate/diploma | ☐ | I don't remember | ☐ |

**What was your political leaning in the 1950s?**

| | | | | | |
|---|---|---|---|---|---|
| Left | ☐ | Centre | ☐ | Right | ☐ |
| No reply | ☐ | I was too young | ☐ | | |

Appendix 2

# Video interview questions

1. Photo of the interviewee in those years
2. Disclaimer
3. Photos of objects collected

## Topics to be discussed during the interview

1. **Personal details** (name, age, place of residence in the 1950s, did you move home in this period?)

2. **Stronger memories related to cinema** (childhood, adolescence, adulthood). What were your most memorable experiences of cinemagoing in those years? Discussion of the experience of cinemagoing in those years. What role did cinema play in your life? Compared to other aspects of your life?

3. **Relationship between cinema and other pastimes**
   If cinemagoing wasn't your only pastime, what did cinema mean in comparison with other pastimes? In what respect was it different? When you didn't go to the cinema, what did you do in your spare time? What made you choose between going to the cinema and another pastime?

4. **Meaning of cinema in social relationships**
   a. Was cinemagoing a usual thing or a special occasion? Was it something new? Would one dress up to go to the cinema (always or just in particular cinemas)? Was it something related to a specific social group (friends, partner, family)?

b. Was there a rituality of cinemagoing? Dressing, route taken, things done before and after, who chose? Multiple viewings of films? Taking part in film clubs?
　　c. How important was company in cinemagoing? Was watching the film or going out more important?
　　d. How much time in advance did you decide to go to the cinema or to watch a film in particular? How did you decide?
　　e. How have your cinema-going and film-watching habits changed?

5. **Cinema as education**

    Did cinema teach you anything? What?

6. **Films**

　　a. What do you remember the most about the films of those years (plot, actors, costume, sets, the logo of the production company, dates, etc.)?
　　b. Did you ever see any stars or films being made? Did you read any film magazines? What did you like about them? Did you collect photos of stars? Did you write to stars? If so, how did you get their address? Did you get a reply?
　　c. In what way were you influenced by films and your favourite actors? Did you copy the appearance of your favourite stars (fashion, hairstyles, behaviour, etc.)? Can you give an example? Did you follow beauty contests of that time? Do you remember the participation of anyone you knew? Or of anyone who then became a famous actress?
　　d. Were you active in choosing films (depending on stars, genre, reviews, etc.) or would you let others take you and watch any film? How would you choose to watch one film over another? Importance of film-makers in choosing films? Importance of newspapers publicity? Do you remember any stars doing advertising?
　　e. Did you have any preference in terms of nationality of the films and stars you watched? Besides Italian and American films, do you remember any other nationalities?
　　f. Was there a relationship between the films you watched and the reality you experienced in those years?
　　g. What film genre did you prefer? Can you give any examples of films of this genre? What stars did you associate with this genre in particular?

h. Did you cry for certain films or genres? What/what scenes/who in the film moved you?
   i. Were you ever aware of censorship?

7. **Cinemas**

   a. Were you faithful to one cinema in particular or would you go anywhere? Do you remember the route you took to go to the cinema?
   b. Do you remember the names of any cinemas you went to at that time?
   c. What are your stronger memories of cinema theatres (colours, smells, noises)?
   d. Was it common to see women going to the cinema on their own? Why?
   e. In choosing a cinema, was its distance from home important? Why? How far were you willing to travel to watch a film? How many cinemas were available to you nearby?
   f. Were the cinemas in your neighbourhood very different from the ones in the city centre? Were people different? What did going to the cinema in your own neighbourhood represent in comparison with going to the city centre? Did films arrive very late in second- and third-run cinemas?
   g. Do you remember any non-cinematic shows you attended at the cinema?
   h. Have you ever gone back to a cinema theatre you used to go to in the past? What reactions did you have? When you found out about the closure of a cinema theatre you frequented, how did you react?

# Appendix 3

# List of thematic areas

Chapter 2: Cinema runs, financial choice, programming choices, topographica memory

Chapter 3: Cinema as sharing emotions, as a reward, escapism, experience of the venue, rituals of cinema, collective experience, place memory

Chapter 4: Genre preference

Chapter 5: Personal affect; cinema as education and culture; cinema as reflection of contemporary reality; strong reaction to stars and characters: acting skills, roles played; memory: faulty memory, official memory, past/present, childhood memory, idiosyncratic film history; memory of films: plots, scenes, technical aspects, performance and characters

Chapter 6: Collective experience; first time in personal life; fantasy and dreaming; personal affect; cinema as education and culture; strong reaction to stars and characters; star identification; memory: childhood memory; memory of films: plots, scenes, performance and characters

Chapter 7: Collective experience; cinema as sharing emotion; personal affect; contact with film industry; cinema as form of aspiration; strong reaction to stars and characters; roles played; physical appearance; faulty memory; childhood memory; memory of films; performance and characters

Chapter 8: Experience of the venue; social experience of cinema; first time in personal life; first viewing; individual affect; escapism; fantasy and dreaming; cinema as education and culture; star identification; roles played: past/present; memory of scenes; memory of directors

# Bibliography

Abrams, L. (2010), *Oral History Theory*, London: Routledge.
Abrams, L. (2014), 'Liberating the Female Self: Epiphanies, Conflict and Coherence in the Life Stories of Post-War British Women', *Social History*, 39 (1): 14–35.
ACEC, *Sale parrocchiali*, private database, no place of publication or publisher (accessed 21 March 2015).
Acland, C. R. (2005), *Screen Traffic: Movies, Multiplexes, and Global Culture*, Durham, NC: Duke University Press.
Akbulut, H. (2017), 'Cinemagoing as a Heterogeneous and Multidimensional Strategy: Narratives of Woman Spectators', *Turkish Online Journal of Design, Art and Communication*, 7 (4): 530–41.
Allen, R. C. (1990), 'From Exhibition to Reception: Reflections on the Audience in Film History', *Screen*, 31 (4): 347–56.
Allen, R. C. (2011), 'Reimagining the History of the Experience of Cinema in Post-Moviegoing Age', *Media International Australia*, 139 (1): 80–7.
Altman, R. (1984), 'A Semantic/Syntactic Approach to Film Genre', *Cinema Journal*, 23 (3): 6–18.
Altman, R. (1999), *Film/Genre*, London: BFI.
Anderson, K., and S. Smith (2001), 'Editorial: Emotional Geographies', *Transactions of the Institute of British Geographers*, 26 (1): 7–10.
Antunes, L. R. (2016), *The Multisensory Film Experience: A Cognitive Model of Experiential Film Aesthetics*, Bristol: Intellect.
Aprà, A., and C. Carabba (1976), *Neorealismo d'appendice. Per un dibattito sul cinema popolare: il caso Matarazzo*, Rimini: Guaraldi.
Armbrust, W. (1998), 'When the Lights Go Down in Cairo: Cinema as Secular Ritual', *Visual Anthropology*, 10 (2–4): 413–42.
Aroldi, P., and C. Ponte (2012), 'Adolescents of the 1960s and 1970s: An Italian-Portuguese Comparison between Two Generations of Audiences', *Cyberpsychology: Journal of Psychosocial Research on Cyberspace*, 6 (2). Available online: https://cyberpsychology.eu/article/view/4268/3307 (accessed 6 December 2019).
Aroldi, P., and F. Colombo (2007), 'Generational Belonging and Mediascape in Europe', *Journal of Social Science Education*, 6 (1): 34–44.
Arrowsmith, C., and D. Verhoeven (2011), 'Visual Methods for Showing Cinema Circuits at Varying Temporal and Spatial Scales', in C. Arrowsmith, C. Bellman, W. Cartwright, S. Jones and M. Shortis (eds), *Proceedings of the Geospatial Science Research Symposium*, 1–15, Melbourne: RMIT University.

Ayers, E. L. (2010), 'Turning toward Place, Space, and Time', in D. J. Bodenhamer, J. Corrigan and T. M. Harris (eds), *The Spatial Humanities: GIS and the Future of the Humanities Scholarship*, 1–13, Bloomington: Indiana University Press.

B. (1950), 'Bollettino delle grane. Quando il portoghesismo esagera', *Bollettino dello Spettacolo*, no. 156, 31 March: 1.

'B'. (1952), 'Editoriale', *Cinema*, no. 85, 1 May: 228–9.

B. (1956), 'Il cinema regala ogni anno dieci miliardi per ingressi gratuiti', *Bollettino dello Spettacolo*, no. 312, 24 November: 1.

B. B. (1954), 'Per la tassa sui "portoghesi" ostacoli di ordine tecnico', *Bollettino dello Spettacolo*, no. 203, 30 June: 5.

Bagshaw, M. (2003), *Cinema Italia: Classic Italian Film Posters*, London: BFI.

Bailey, J., and I. Biggs (2012), '"Either Side of Delphy Bridge": A Deep Mapping Project Evoking and Engaging the Lives of Older Adults in Rural North Cornwall', *Journal of Rural Studies*, 28 (4): 318–28.

Baldelli, P. (1963), *Sociologia del cinema: pubblico e critica cinematografica*, Rome: Riuniti.

Barker, M. (1998), 'Audiences Я Us', in R. Dickinson, O. Linné and R. Harindranath (eds), *Approaches to Audiences: A Reader*, 184–91, London: Arnold.

Barker, M. (2003), 'The Newson Report: A Case Study in "Common-sense"', in W. Brooker and D. Jermyn (eds), *The Audience Studies Reader*, 74–90, London: Routledge.

Barker, M., and E. Mathijs (2008), *Watching the Lord of the Rings: Tolkien's World Audiences*, New York: Peter Lang.

Barthes, R. (1986), 'Leaving the Movie Theater', in R. Barthes (ed.), *The Rustle of Language*, trans. R. Howard, 345–9, New York: Hill and Wang.

Bayman, L. (2009), 'Melodrama as Realism in Italian Neorealism', in C. Mello and L. Nagib (eds), *Realism and the Audiovisual Media*, 47–62, Basingstoke: Palgrave Macmillan.

Bayman, L. (2014), *The Operatic and the Everyday in Post-War Italian Film Melodrama*, Edinburgh: Edinburgh University Press.

Bayman, L., S. Gundle and K. Schoonover (2018), '*Rome Open City*: Rupture and Return', *Journal of Italian Cinema & Media Studies*, 6 (3): 295–300.

Bellassai, S. (2000), 'Mascolinità e relazioni di genere nella cultura politica comunista (1947–1956)', in S. Bellassai and M. Malatesta (eds), *Genere e mascolinità: uno sguardo storico*, 265–301, Rome: Bulzoni.

Benjamin, W. (1969), 'The Work of Art in the Age of Mechanical Reproduction', in W. Benjamin and H. Arendt (eds), *Illuminations*, trans. H. Zohn, 1–26, New York: Schocken Books. Available online: https://web.mit.edu/allanmc/www/benjamin.pdf (accessed 6 December 2018).

Bennett, J. (2003), 'The Aesthetics of Sense-Memory: Theorising Trauma through the Visual Arts', in S. Radstone and K. Hodgkin (eds), *Memory Cultures: Memory, Subjectivity and Recognition*, 27–39, New Brunswick, NJ: Transaction.

Benni, S. (1976), *Bar Sport*, Milan: Mondadori.

Biasin, E. (2018), '"Se c'era Clark Gable, andavo a vederlo; se c'era John Wayne, andavo a vederlo". Formazioni di mascolinità nel pubblico cinematografico italiano del secondo dopoguerra', *Clionet*, 2. Available online: https://rivista.clionet.it/vol2/dossier/fotografia_storia_e_archivi/biasin-formazioni-di- mascolinita-nel-pubblico-cinematografico-italiano-del-secondo-dopoguerra (accessed 20 September 2019).

Biltereyst, D. (2019), 'Film History, Cultural Memory, and the Experience of Cinema: A Conversation with Annette Kuhn', in D. Biltereyst, R. Maltby and P. Meers (eds), *The Routledge Companion to New Cinema History*, 28–38, London: Routledge.

Biltereyst, D., K. Lotze and P. Meers (2012), 'Triangulation in Historical Audience Research: Reflections and Experiences from a Multi-Methodological Research Project on Cinema Audiences in Flanders', *Participations: Journal of Audience & Reception Studies*, 9 (2): 690–715.

Biltereyst, D., P. Meers, K. Lotze and L. Van de Vijver (2012), 'Negotiating Cinema's Modernity: Strategies of Control and Audience Experiences of Cinema in Belgium, 1930s–1960s', in D. Biltereyst, R. Maltby and P. Meers (eds), *Cinema, Audiences and Modernity: New Perspectives on European Cinema History*, 186–201, New York: Routledge.

Biltereyst, D., R. Maltby and P. Meers (2019), *The Routledge Companion to New Cinema History*, London: Routledge.

Bimbi, F. (1993), 'Three Generations of Women: Transformations of Female Identity Models in Italy', in M. Cicioni and N. Prunster (eds), *Visions and Revisions: Women in Italian Culture*, 149–66, Oxford: Berg.

Bizzarri, L., and L. Solaroli (1958), *L'industria cinematografica italiana*, Florence: Parenti.

Boero, D. (2013), *All'ombra del proiettore. Il cinema per ragazzi nell'Italia del dopoguerra*, Macerata: EUM.

Bolin, G. (2014), 'Media Generations: Objective and Subjective Media Landscapes and Nostalgia among Generations of Media Users', *Participations: Journal of Audience & Reception Studies*, 11 (2): 108–31.

Bornat, J., and H. Diamond (2007), 'Women's History and Oral History: Developments and Debates', *Women's History Review*, 16 (1): 19–39.

Bowles, K. (2009), 'Limit of Maps? Locality and Cinema-Going in Australia', *Media International Australia*, 131 (1): 83–94.

Bowles, K. (2013), 'Beyond the Boundary: Vernacular Mapping and the Sharing of Historical Authority', in J. Hallam and L. Roberts (eds), *Locating the Moving Image: New Approaches to Film and Place*, 221–44, Bloomington: Indiana University Press.

Boyd, D. A., and M. A. Larson (2014), 'Introduction', in D. A. Boyd and M. A. Larson (eds), *Oral History and Digital Humanities: Voice, Access, and Engagement*, 1–16, Basingstoke: Palgrave Macmillan.
Boym, S. (2008), *The Future of Nostalgia*, New York: Basic Books.
Breakwell, I., and P. Hammond (1990), *Seeing in the Dark: A Compendium of Cinemagoing*, London: Serpent's Tail.
Bru (1952), 'Bollettino delle grane. Tanti Tanti auguri', *Bollettino dello Spettacolo*, no. 160, 31 December: 5.
Brunetta, G. P. (1993), *Storia del cinema italiano, Vol 3: Dal neorealismo al miracolo economico 1945–1959*, Rome: Editori Riuniti.
Brunetta, G. P. (1997), *Buio in sala: Cent'anni di passioni dello spettatore cinematografico*, Venice: Marsilio.
Buckley, R. (2006), 'Elsa Martinelli: Italy's Audrey Hepburn', *Historical Journal of Film, Radio and Television*, 26 (3): 327–40.
Buckley, R. (2008), 'Glamour and the Italian Female Film Stars of the 1950s', *Historical Journal of Film, Radio and Television*, 28 (3): 267–89.
Buckley, R. (2009), 'The Emergence of Film Fandom in Postwar Italy: Reading Claudia Cardinale's Fan Mail', *Historical Journal of Film, Radio and Television*, 29 (4): 523–59.
Buckley, R. (2013), 'Dressing the Part: "Made in Italy" Goes to the Movies with Lucia Bosé in Chronicle of a Love Affair', in L. Bayman and S. Rigoletto (eds), *Popular Italian Cinema*, 163–82, London: Palgrave Macmillan.
Butler, J. (1999), *Gender Trouble: Feminism and the Subversion of Identity*, New York: Routledge.
Butsch, R. (2000), *The Making of American Audiences: From Stage to Television, 1750–1990*, Cambridge: Cambridge University Press.
Capussotti, E. (2004), *Gioventù perduta: Gli anni Cinquanta dei giovani e del cinema in Italia*, Florence: Giunti.
Caquard, S., and D. R. Fraser Taylor (2009), 'What Is Cinematic Cartography?', *Cartographic Journal*, 46 (1): 5–8.
Caquard, S., and W. Cartwright (2014), 'Narrative Cartography: From Mapping Stories to the Narrative of Maps and Mapping', *Cartographic Journal*, 51 (2): 101–6.
Casetti, F. (2000), *L'occhio dello spettatore*, Brescia: Quaderni DAMS.
Casetti, F. (2015), *The Lumière Galaxy: Seven Key Words for the Cinema to Come*, New York: Columbia University Press.
Casetti, F., and M. Fanchi (2002), 'Le funzioni sociali del cinema e dei media: dati statistici, ricerche sull'audience e storie di consumo', in M. Fanchi and E. Mosconi (eds), *Spettatori: forme di consumo e pubblici del cinema in Italia, 1930–1960*, 135–71, Venice: Marsilio.
Cassamagnaghi, S. (2007), *Immagini dall'America: Mass media e modelli femminili nell'Italia del secondo dopoguerra, 1945–1960*, Milan: Franco Angeli.

'Censimenti popolazione Putignano 1861–2011', ISTAT. Available online: https://www.tuttitalia.it/puglia/75-putignano/statistiche/censimenti-popolazione/ (accessed 19 November 2019).

Chapman, J. (2015), *Swashbucklers: The Costume Adventure Series*, Manchester: Manchester University Press.

CoDis Italiana (1961), *Il cinema e il suo pubblico. Indagine statistica e motivazionale sulla validità pubblicitaria del mezzo cinematografico*, no place of publication or publisher.

Cohan, S. (1997), *Masked Men: Masculinity and the Movies in the Fifties*, Bloomington: Indiana University Press.

Colby, A. (1948), 'Siate belle come le dive', *Hollywood*, 17 January: 6.

Colombo, F., G. Boccia Artieri, L. Del Grosso Destreri, F. Pasquali and M. Sorice (2012), *Media e generazioni nella società italiana*, Milan: Franco Angeli.

Comand, M., and A. Mariani (2018), 'Gli scrapbook di Tatiana Grauding: una spettatrice tra materialità e storia del cinema', *Cinema e storia*, 7 (1) (Special issue on 'Storia e storie delle audiences in era globale', eds M. Fanchi and D. Garofalo): 201–16.

'Comunicazioni della Presidenza' (1950), Bollettino di informazioni, Year VI, no. 103–4, 1–31 July: 1.

Corsi, B. (2001), *Per qualche dollaro in meno*, Rome: Riuniti.

Cosulich, C. (1957), 'La battaglia delle cifre', *Cinema Nuovo*, no. 98, 15 January: 19–21.

Cosulich, C. (1958), 'Le cifre della crisi', *Cinema Nuovo*, Year VII, no. 127, 15 March: 182–4.

Dawson, G. (1994), *Soldier Heroes: British Adventure, Empire and the Imagining of Masculinities*, London: Routledge.

Day, G., and B. Keegan (2009), *The Eighteenth-Century Literature Handbook*, London: Bloomsbury.

DeCuir-Gunby, J. T., P. L. Marshall and A. W. McCulloch (2011), 'Developing and Using a Codebook for the Analysis of Interview Data: An Example from a Professional Development Research Project', *Field Methods*, 23 (2): 136–55.

Del Casino, V. J., and S. P. Hanna (2006), 'Beyond the "Binaries": A Methodological Intervention for Interrogating Maps as Representational Practices', *ACME: An International E-Journal for Critical Geographies*, 4 (1): 34–56.

Deleuze, G. (2005), *Cinema 2: The Time-Image*, trans. H. Tomlinson and R. Galeta, London: Continuum.

De Luca, F. (1956), 'Guerra ad oltranza ai portoghesi del cinema', *Bollettino dello Spettacolo*, no. 294, 26 June: 3.

De Rita, L. (1964), *I contadini e la televisione. Studio sull'influenza degli spettacoli televisivi in un gruppo di contadini lucani*, Bologna: Il Mulino.

Dhoest, A. (2015), 'Audience Retrospection as a Source of Historiography: Oral History Interviews on Early Television Experiences', *European Journal of Communication*, 30 (1): 64–78.

Dibeltulo, S., S. Culhane and D. Treveri Gennari (2019), 'Bridging the Digital Divide: Older Adults' Engagement with Online Cinema Heritage', *Digital Scholarship in the Humanities*. Available online: https://academic.oup.com/dsh/advance-article-abstract/doi/10.1093/llc/fqz079/5637295?redirectedFrom=fulltext (accessed 1 December 2019).

Di Chiara, F. (2013), *Generi e industria cinematografica in Italia. Il caso Titanus (1949–1964)*, Turin: Lindau.

'Donne al cinema' (1953), *Rassegna del Film*, vol. II, no. 14, May: 6–9.

Dotti, L. (2013), 'My Fair Mother', *Vanity Fair*, 15 April. Available online: http://www.vanityfair.com/hollywood/2013/05/audrey-hepburn-life-in-rome (accessed 20 September 2019).

Dreyer, E., and E. McDowall (2012), 'Imagining the Flâneur as a Woman', *Communicatio*, 38 (1): 30–44.

Driscoll, C. (2002), *Girls: Feminine Adolescence in Popular Culture and Cultural Theory*, New York: Columbia University Press.

Dwyer, T., and S. Gaunson (2017), 'Introduction: Un/social Cinema – Audience Decorum Revisited', *Participations: Journal of Audience & Reception Studies*, 14 (2): 522–5.

Dyer, R. (1992), *Only Entertainment*, London: Routledge.

Dyer, R., and P. McDonald (1998), *Stars*, London: BFI.

Dyhouse, C. (2013), *Girl Trouble: Panic and Progress in the History of Young Women*, London: Zed Books.

Elkin, L. (2016), *Flâneuse: Women Walk the City in Paris, New York, Tokyo, Venice and London*, London: Chatto & Windus.

Elsaesser, T. (1981), 'Narrative Cinema and Audience-Oriented Aesthetics', in T. Bennett, S. Boyd-Bowman, C. Mercer and J. Woollacott (eds), *Popular Television and Film*, 270–82, London: BFI.

Ercole, P., C. O'Rawe, and D. Treveri Gennari (2017), 'Mapping Cinema Memories: Emotional Geographies of Cinema-Going in Rome in the 1950s', *Memory Studies*, 10 (1): 63–77.

Eugeni, R., and M. Fanchi (2015), 'Pubblici, consumi e trasformazioni culturali', in F. Colombo and R. Eugeni (eds), *Storia della comunicazione e dello spettacolo in Italia. Vol. II. I media alla sfida della democrazia (1945–1978)*, 291–305, Milan: Vita e Pensiero.

Fanchi, M. (1995), 'Tra storia e memoria: indagine intorno al *kolossal* attraverso le "storie di vita"', *Comunicazioni sociali*, 17 (2–3) (Special issue on 'Cinema e cultura popolare nell'Italia anni Cinquanta', ed. F. Villa): 296–311.

Fanchi, M. (2001), 'La trasformazione del consumo cinematografico', in G. De Vincenti (ed.), *Storia del cinema italiano: Volume X, 1960/64*, 344–57, Venice: Marsilio.

Fanchi, M. (2006), 'Non censurare ma educare! L'esercizio cinematografico cattolico e il suo progetto culturale e sociale', in R. Eugeni and D. E. Viganò (eds), *Attraverso lo schermo: Cinema e cultura cattolica in Italia*, vol. 2, p. 107, Rome: Ente dello Spettacolo.

Fanchi, M. (2007), 'Un genere di storia. Alcune considerazioni su storia di genere e storiografia del cinema', *La valle dell'Eden*, 19 (Special issue on 'Cinema e Gender Studies', eds G. Alonge and R. West): 183–93.

Fanchi, M. (2010), '"Tra donne sole": Cinema, Cultural Consumption, and the Female Condition in Post-War Italy', in I. Schenk, M. Tröhler and Y. Zimmermann (eds), *Film-Kino-Zuschauer: Filmrezeption = Film-Cinema-Spectator: Film Reception*, 305–18, Marburg (DE): Schüren.

Fanchi, M. (2016), 'Audience caleidoscopiche: le trasformazioni del pubblico e del consumo di cinema', *Cinema e storia*, 5 (1) (Special issue on 'Anni Cinquanta', ed. E. Dagrada): 227–38.

Fanchi, M. (2017), 'Mai da sole. Bambine, esperienza del cinema e processi di socializzazione', *Arabeschi*, 5.2. Available online: http://www.arabeschi.it/52-mai-da-sole-bambine-esperienza- del-cinema-e-processi-di-socializzazione/ (accessed 19 December 2017).

Fanchi, M. (2019), 'For Many but Not for All: Italian Film History and the Circumstantial Value of Audience Studies', in D. Biltereyst, R. Maltby and P. Meers (eds), *The Routledge Companion to New Cinema History*, 387–94, London: Routledge.

Ferraù, A. (1954), 'Come vanno le cose in casa nostra', *Cinespettacolo*, Year IX, no. 24–5, 24 July: 3–6.

Ferraù, A. (1956), 'Il "genere" prevalente', *Bollettino dello Spettacolo*, Year XII, no. 305, 28 September: 3.

Focardi, F. (2000), 'La memoria della guerra e il mito del "bravo italiano". Origine e affermazione di un autoritratto collettivo', *Italia contemporanea*, no. 220–1: 393–9.

Forgacs, D. (2000), *Rome Open City (Roma Città Aperta)*, London: BFI.

Forgacs, D. (2018), '*Rome, Open City*: Before and after Neorealism', *Journal of Italian Cinema & Media Studies*, 6 (3): 301–13.

Forgacs, D., and S. Gundle (2007), *Mass Culture and Italian Society from Fascism to the Cold War*, Bloomington: Indiana University Press.

Foucault, M. (1980), 'Questions in Geography', in C. Gordon (ed.), *Power/ Knowledge: Selected Interviews and Other Writings, 1972–1977*, 63–77, New York: Pantheon.

Fragola, A. (1954), 'Costruzione e apertura di nuove sale nelle decisioni del Consiglio di Stato', *Bollettino dello Spettacolo*, no. 213, 20 October: 3.

Friedman, J. (2014), 'Oral History, Hermeneutics, and Embodiment', *Oral History Review*, 41 (2): 290–300.
Frisch, M. (2006), 'Oral History and the Digital Revolution: Towards a Post-Documentary Sensibility', in R. Perks and A. Thomson (eds), *The Oral History Reader*, 102–14, London: Routledge.
Fuller-Seeley, K. (2011), 'Shirley Temple: Making Dreams Come True', in A. L. McLean (ed.), *Glamour in a Golden Age: Movie Stars of the 1930s*, 44–65, New Brunswick, NJ: Rutgers University Press.
Gaines, J. (1990), 'Introduction', in J. Gaines and C. Herzog (eds), *Fabrications: Costume and the Female Body*, 1–25, New York: Routledge.
Gaudio, V. S. (1997), *Manualetto della mano morta. Variazione sull'approccio tattile*, Valentano: Scipioni.
Gauntlett, D. (2006), 'Ten Things Wrong with the Media "Effects" Model', in K. C. Weaver and C. Carter (eds), *Critical Readings: Violence and the Media*, 54–66, Maidenhead: Open University Press.
Gerosa, G. (1954), 'Scene dalla nostra vita di provincia', *Rassegna del film*, Year III, no. 22, July, to Year III, no. 24, October.
Giori, M. (2017a), 'Cinema e omosessualità in Italia tra la seconda guerra mondiale e la nascita del FUORI. Appunti per una storia da (ri)scrivere', in U. Grassi, V. Lagioia and G. P. Romagnani (eds), *Tribadi, sodomiti, invertite e invertiti, pederasti, femminelle, ermafroditi ... per una storia dell'omosessualità, della bisessualità e delle trasgressioni di genere in Italia*, 11–28, Pisa: ETS.
Giori, M. (2017b), *Homosexuality and Italian Cinema: From the Fall of Fascism to the Years of Lead*, London: Palgrave Macmillan.
Giusti, M. A. (2007), 'Cinema Architecture in Italy: Dying Out Heritage?', in M. A. Giusti and S. Caccia (eds), *Cinema in Italia. Sguardo sull'Architettura del Novecento*, 13–15, Florence: Maschietto Editore.
Grant, B. K. (2007), *Film Genre: From Iconography to Ideology*, London: Wallflower.
Gray, J. (2010), *Show Sold Separately: Promos, Spoilers, and Other Media Paratexts*, New York: New York University Press.
Gremigni, E. (2009), *Pubblico e popolarità. Il ruolo del cinema nella società italiana (1956–1967)*, Florence: Le Lettere.
Grignaffini, G. (1992), 'Note in margine alla "Signora senza camelie"', in I. Ricci (ed.), *Senza camelie. Percorsi femminili nella storia*, 119–27, Ravenna: Longo Editore.
Gundle, S. (2002), 'Hollywood Glamour and Mass Consumption in Postwar Italy', *Journal of Cold War Studies*, 4 (3): 95–118.
Gundle, S. (2004), 'Sophia Loren: Italian Icon', in L. Fischer and M. Landy (eds), *Stars: The Film Reader*, 77–96, New York: Routledge.
Gyory, M., and G. Glas (1992), *Statistics of the Film Industry in Europe*, Brussels: European Centre for Research and Information on Film and Television (CERICA).

Hains, R. C., S. Thiel-Stern and S. R. Mazzarella (2011), '"We Didn't Have Any Hannah Montanas": Girlhood, Popular Culture, and Mass Media in the 1940s and 1950s', in M. C. Kearney (ed.), *Mediated Girlhoods: New Explorations of Girls' Media Culture*, 113–32, New York: Peter Lang.
Halberstam, J. (1998), *Female Masculinity*, Durham, NC: Duke University Press.
Halbwachs, M. (1992), *On Collective Memory*, trans. L. A. Coser, Chicago: University of Chicago Press.
Hallam, J., and L. Roberts (2011), 'Mapping, Memory and the City: Archives, Databases and Film Historiography', *European Journal of Cultural Studies*, 14 (3): 355–72.
Hanich, J. (2010), 'Collective Viewing: The Cinema and Affective Audience Interrelations', *Passions in Context. The Journal for the History and Theory of Emotions*, 1 (1). Available online: https://www.passionsincontext.de/index.php/?id=544&L=1 (accessed 30 September 2019).
Hanich, J. (2014), 'Watching a Film with Others: Towards a Theory of Collective Spectatorship', *Screen*, 55 (3): 338–59.
Harper, S. (2019), '"It Is Time We Went Out to Meet Them": Empathy and Historical Distance', *Participations: Journal of Audience & Reception Studies*, 16 (1): 687–97.
Harper, S., and V. Porter (1996), 'Moved to Tears: Weeping in the Cinema in Post-War Britain', *Screen*, 37 (2): 152–73.
Harry, B., K. M. Sturges and J. K. Klingner (2005), 'Mapping the Process: An Exemplar of Process and Challenge in Grounded Theory Analysis', *Educational Researcher*, 34 (2): 3–13.
Hart, R. (1979), *Children's Experience of Place*, New York: Irvington Publ.
Hatch, K. (2015), *Shirley Temple and the Performance of Girlhood*, New Brunswick, NJ: Rutgers University Press.
Hediger, V. (2015), 'The Existence of the Spectator', in A. Beltrame, G. Fidotta and A. Mariani (eds), *At the Borders of (Film) History, Temporality, Archaeology, Theories*, 315–24, Udine: Forum.
Hill, J. (2003), *Sport, Leisure and Culture in Twentieth-Century Britain*, Basingstoke: Palgrave Macmillan.
Hillmer, M. (1997), *Film und Mode: Mode im Film*, Munich: Prestel.
Hipkins, D., S. Culhane, S. Dibeltulo, D. Treveri Gennari and C. O'Rawe (2016), '"Un mondo che pensavo impossibile": al cinema in Italia negli anni Cinquanta', *Cinema e storia*, 5 (1) (Special issue on 'Anni Cinquanta', ed. E. Dagrada): 215–25.
Hipkins, D., S. Culhane, S. Dibeltulo, D. Treveri Gennari and C. O'Rawe (2018), 'Oral Memories of Cinema-Going in Rural Italy of the 1950s', in D. Treveri Gennari, D. Hipkins and C. O'Rawe (eds), *Rural Cinema Exhibition and Audiences in a Global Context*, 117–33, Basingstoke: Palgrave Macmillan.
Hirsch, M. (1997), *Family Frames: Photography, Narrative and Postmemory*, Cambridge, MA: Harvard University Press.

Hoffman, E. (2010), 'The Long Afterlife of Loss', in S. Radstone and B. Schwarz (eds), *Memory: Histories, Theories, Debates*, 406–15, New York: Fordham University Press.

Holohan, C. (2017), 'Introduction: Mapping the European Cinematic', *Studies in European Cinema*, 14 (1): 1–6.

Hubbard, P. (2003), 'A Good Night Out? Multiplex Cinemas as Sites of Embodied Leisure', *Leisure Studies*, 22 (3): 255–72.

'Il censimento di cinema e teatri nelle rilevazioni statistiche della SIAE' (1954), Bollettino dello Spettacolo, no. 206–7, 20 August: 5.

*Il Giornale dello Spettacolo* (1957), no. 31, 31 August: 2.

*Il Mattino* (1954), 28 January: n.p.

'Italiani ma distensivi: i film graditi agli esercenti' (1954), Rassegna del film, no. 21, June: 16–22.

Järviluoma, H. (2009), 'Soundscape and Social Memory in Skruv', in H. Järviluoma, B. Truax, M. Kyto and N. Vikman (eds), *Acoustic Environments in Change*, 138–53, Tampere: University of Joensuu.

Kearney, M. C. (2009), 'Coalescing: The Development of Girls' Studies', *NWSA Journal*, 21 (1): 1–28.

King, G. (2002), *Film Comedy*, London: Wallflower Press.

Kitchin, R., and M. Dodge (2007), 'Rethinking Maps', *Progress in Human Geography*, 31 (3): 331–44.

Klenotic, J. (2011), 'Putting Cinema History on the Map: Using GIS to Explore the Spatiality of Cinema', in D. Biltereyst, R. Maltby and P. Meers (eds), *Explorations in New Cinema History: Approaches and Case Studies*, 58–84, Chichester: Wiley-Blackwell.

Klinger, B. (1997), 'Film History Terminable and Interminable: Recovering the Past in Reception Studies', *Screen*, 38 (2): 107–28.

Klinger, B. (2006), *Beyond the Multiplex: Cinema, New Technologies, and the Home*, Berkeley: University of California Press.

Kuhn, A. (1984), 'Women's Genres', *Screen*, 25 (1): 18–29.

Kuhn, A. (1996), 'Cinema Culture and Femininity in 1930s Britain', in C. Gledhill and G. Swanson (eds), *Nationalising Femininity: Culture, Sexuality and British Cinema in the Second World War*, 177–92, Manchester: Manchester University Press.

Kuhn, A. (1999), '"That Day Did Last Me All My Life": Cinema Memory and Enduring Fandom', in M. Stokes and R. Maltby (eds), *Identifying Hollywood's Audiences: Cultural Identity and the Movies*, 135–46, London: BFI.

Kuhn, A. (2002), *An Everyday Magic: Cinema and Cultural Memory*, London: I.B. Tauris.

Kuhn, A. (2010a), '"I Wanted Life to be Romantic and I Wanted to be Thin": Girls Growing Up with Cinema in the 1930s', in V. Callahan (ed.), *Reclaiming the Archive: Feminism and Film History*, 58–73, Detroit, MI: Wayne State University Press.

Kuhn, A. (2010b), 'Memory Texts and Memory Work: Performances of Memory in and with Visual Media', *Memory Studies*, 3 (4): 298–313.

Kuhn, A. (2011), 'What to Do with Cinema Memory', in D. Biltereyst, R. Maltby and P. Meers (eds), *Explorations in New Cinema History: Approaches and Case Studies*, 85–97, Malden, MA: Wiley-Blackwell.

Kuhn, A., D. Biltereyst and P. Meers (2017), 'Memories of Cinemagoing and Film Experience: An Introduction', *Memory Studies*, 10 (1): 3–16.

*La Gazzetta del Mezzogiorno* (1953), 17 October: 4.

*La Nazione* (1954), 1 January: 4.

*La Stampa* (1956), 7 January: 4.

Landsberg, A. (2004), *Prosthetic Memory: The Transformation of American Remembrance in the Age of Mass Culture*, New York: Columbia University Press.

Landy, M. (2004), 'Diverting Clichés: Femininity, Masculinity, Melodrama, and Neorealism in *Open City*', in S. Gottlieb (ed.), *Roberto Rossellini's Rome Open City*, 85–105, Cambridge: Cambridge University Press.

Langford, B. (2005), *Film Genre: Hollywood and Beyond*, Edinburgh: Edinburgh University Press.

Larkin, B. (2008), *Signal and Noise: Media, Infrastructure, and Urban Culture in Nigeria*, Durham, NC: Duke University Press.

Leavitt IV, C. L. (2018), 'Notes on the End of *Rome, Open City*', *Journal of Italian Cinema & Media Studies*, 6 (3): 359–72.

'Lettere in Redazione. Sempre sui portoghesi' (1955), Bollettino dello Spettacolo, no. 315, 22 December: 5.

Lietti, R. (1995), 'Campioni d'incasso del cinema italiano degli anni Cinquanta', *Comunicazioni sociali*, 17 (2–3) (Special issue on 'Cinema e cultura popolare nell'Italia anni Cinquanta', ed. F. Villa): 315–29.

'L'italiano non paga' (1955), Bollettino dello Spettacolo, 12 May: 3.

Low, K. E. Y. (2013), 'Olfactive Frames of Remembering: Theorizing Self, Senses and Society', *Sociological Review*, 61 (4): 688–708.

*L'Unione Sarda* (1954), 20 January: 4.

*L'Unità* – Rome edition (1953), 20 December: 5.

*L'Unità* – Rome edition (1960), 10 October: 6.

Luzzatto Fegiz, P. (1956), *Il volto sconosciuto dell'Italia. Dieci anni di sondaggi DOXA*, Milan: Giuffrè.

Luzzatto Fegiz, P. (1966), *Il volto sconosciuto dell'Italia. Seconda serie – 1956–1965*, Milan: Giuffrè.

Macfarlane, R. (2007), *The Wild Places*, New York: Penguin Books.

MacLean, M. (1958), 'Preferenze cinematografiche a Scarperia', *Bianco e Nero*, 19 (2): 39–49.

Madgin, R., L. Bradley and A. Hastings (2016), 'Connecting Physical and Social Dimensions of Place Attachment: What Can We Learn from Attachment to Urban Recreational Spaces?', *Journal of Housing and the Built Environment*, 31 (4): 677–93.

Maltby, R. (2006), 'On the Prospect of Writing Cinema History from Below', *Tijdschrift voor Mediageschiedenis*, 9 (2): 74–96.

Maltby, R. (2007), *How Can Cinema History Matter More?* Available online: http://www.screeningthepast.com/2015/01/how-can-cinema-history-matter-more/ (accessed 24 April 2019).

Maltby, R. (2011), 'New Cinema Histories', in R. Maltby, D. Biltereyst and P. Meers (eds), *Explorations in New Cinema History: Approaches and Case Studies*, 3–40, Chichester: Wiley-Blackwell.

Mandelli, E., and V. Re (2017), '«Le donne in copertina "vanno"»: *Cinema Nuovo* e le attrici italiane (1952–1958)', *Arabeschi*, 3.3. Available online: http://www.arabeschi.it/33-le-donne-in-copertina-vanno-cinema-nuovoe-le-attrici-italiane-1952–1958/ (accessed 30 September 2019).

Manning, S. (2016), 'Post-War Cinema-Going and Working-Class Communities: A Case Study of the Holyland, Belfast, 1945–62', *Culture and Social History*, 13 (4): 539–55.

Marcus, M. (2004), '*Celluloide* and the Palimpsest of Cinematic Memory: Carlo Lizzani's Film of the Story behind *Open City*', in S. Gottlieb (ed.), *Roberto Rossellini's Rome Open City*, 67–84, Cambridge: Cambridge University Press.

Marks, L. U. (2000), *The Skin of the Film: Intercultural Cinema, Embodiment, and the Senses*, Durham, NC: Duke University Press.

Masi, S., and E. Lancia (1989), *Stelle d'Italia: piccole e grandi dive del cinema italiano*, Rome: Gremese Editore.

Mason, J., and C. Davies (2009), 'Coming to Our Senses? A Critical Approach to Sensory Methodology', *Qualitative Research*, 9 (5): 587–603.

Mayne, J. (1993), *Cinema and Spectatorship*, London: Routledge.

McKinnon, S. (2009), 'How to Be a Man: Masculinity in Australian Teen Culture and American Teen Movies', *Media International Australia*, 131 (1): 127–35.

Metz, C. (1974), *Film Language: A Semiotics of the Cinema*, trans. M. Taylor, New York: Oxford University Press.

Mitchell-Kernan, C., and J. Reid-Walsh (2008), *Girl Culture: An Encyclopedia*, Westport, CT: Greenwood Press.

Morandini, M., and M. Morandini Jr (2010), *I Morandini delle donne. 60 anni di cinema italiano al femminile*, Pavona di Albano Laziale: Iacobelli.

Morante, E. (1974), *La storia*, Turin: Einaudi.

Morin, E. (1960), *The Stars*, London: John Cadler.

Morin, E. (2005), *The Cinema, or, the Imaginary Man*, Minneapolis: University of Minnesota Press.

Morreale, E. (2011), *Così piangevano: il cinema melò nell'Italia degli anni Cinquanta*, Rome: Donzelli.

Mosconi, E. (1995), 'L'offerta, il consumo e la produzione di cinema nell'Italia anni cinquanta', *Comunicazioni sociali*, 18 (2-3): 330-43.

Mosconi, E. (2002), 'Il genere conteso: i film che parlano al vostro cuore', *Comunicazioni sociali*, 24 (2): 223-31.

Mosconi, E., and M. F. Piredda (2006), 'Oltre la sala: il cinema all'aperto', in F. Casetti and E. Mosconi (eds), *Spettatori italiani. Riti e ambienti del consumo cinematografico (1900-1950)*, 113-25, Rome: Carocci.

Moseley, R. (2002), *Growing up with Audrey Hepburn*, Manchester: Manchester University Press.

Neale, S. (1990), 'Questions of Genre', *Screen*, 31 (1): 45-66.

Nichols, E. N. (2017), 'Distracted Spectatorship, the Cinematic Experience and Franchise Films', PhD thesis, Lancaster University, Lancaster. Available online: https://eprints.lancs.ac.uk/id/eprint/88168/1/2017Nicholsphd.pdf (accessed 24 April 2019).

Nicoli, M. (2016), *The Rise and Fall of the Italian Film Industry*, London: Routledge.

Noto, P. (2011), *Dal bozzetto ai generi. Il cinema italiano dei primi anni Cinquanta*, Turin: Kaplan.

Noto, P. (2018), 'Immagini del pubblico nella stampa cinematografica italiana degli anni Cinquanta', *Cinema e storia*, 7 (1) (Special issue on 'Storia e storie delle audiences in era globale', eds M. Fanchi and D. Garofalo): 31-46.

Noto, P. (2019), 'Quale "mestiere del critico"? Un'intrusione nella corrispondenza di Guido Aristarco', *Cinergie*, 8 (15): 55-67. Available online: https://cinergie.unibo.it/article/view/9357 (accessed 13 May 2019).

O'Leary, A., and C. O'Rawe (2011), 'Against Realism: on a "Certain Tendency" in Italian Film Criticism', *Journal of Modern Italian Studies*, 16 (1): 107-28.

O'Rawe, C. (2008), '"I padri e i maestri": Genre, Auteurs and Absences in Italian Film Studies', *Italian Studies*, 63 (2): 173-94.

Ottaviano, M. (1952), 'Profilo dello spettatore di buona volontà', *Filmcritica*, no. 14, June: 169-71.

Parca, G. (1965), *I sultani: mentalità e comportamento del maschio italiano*, Milan: Rizzoli Editore.

Passerini, L. (1992), 'A Memory for Women's History: Problems of Method and Interpretation', *Social Science History*, 16 (4): 669-92.

Paulicelli, E. (2008), 'Framing the Self, Staging Identity: Clothing and Italian Style in the Films of Michelangelo Antonioni (1950-1964)', in E. Paulicelli and H. Clark (eds), *The Fabric of Cultures: Fashion, Identity, and Globalization*, 53-72, London: Routledge.

Paulicelli, E. (2016), *Italian Style: Fashion and Film from Early Cinema to the Digital Age*, London: Bloomsbury.

Peiretti, G. (1953), 'Gli spettatori si confessano', *Rassegna del film*, Year II, no. 15, June: 17.
'Per i portoghesi' (1950), Bollettino dello Spettacolo, no. 92, 31 January: 2.
Piazza, M. (2019), *La vita lunga delle donne*, Milan: Solferino.
Piccone Stella, S. (1993), *La prima generazione. Ragazze e ragazzi nel miracolo economico italiano*, Milan: Franco Angeli.
Piccone Stella, S. (1994), '"Rebels without a Cause": Male Youth in Italy around 1960', *History Workshop Journal*, 38 (1): 157–78.
Pini, A. (2011), *Quando eravamo froci. Gli omosessuali nell'Italia di una volta*, Milan: Il Saggiatore.
Pink, S. (2012), 'Advances in Visual Methodology: An Introduction', in S. Pink (ed.), *Advances in Visual Methodology*, 3–16, London: Sage.
Pinna, L., M. Guidacci and M. MacLean (1958), *Due anni col pubblico cinematografico*, Rome: Bianco e Nero Edizioni.
Pitassio, F. (2018), 'Popular Culture, Performance, Persona: Anna Magnani between *Rome, Open City* and *the Rose Tattoo*', *Journal of Italian Cinema & Media Studies*, 6 (3): 373–88.
Piturro, V. (2008), 'The Audience and the Film: A Reader-Response Analysis of Italian Neorealism', PhD thesis, Faculty of the Graduate School, University of Colorado, Denver. Available online: https://pqdtopen.proquest.com/doc/304620908.html?FMT=AI (accessed 21 May 2019).
Portelli, A. (1988), 'Uchronic Dreams: Working Class Memory and Possible Worlds', *Oral History*, 16 (2): 46–56.
Portelli, A. (1991a), *The Death of Luigi Trastulli and Other Stories: Form and Meaning in Oral History*, Albany: State University of New York Press.
Portelli, A. (1991b), 'What Makes Oral History Different?', in A. Portelli (ed.), *The Death of Luigi Trastulli and Other Stories: Form and Meaning in Oral History*, 45–58, Albany: State University of New York Press.
Portelli, A. (2018), 'Living Voices: The Oral History Interview as Dialogue and Experience', *Oral History Review*, 43 (2): 239–48.
Pullen, K. (2010), 'More Than a Mermaid: Esther Williams, Performance, and the Body', *Women's Studies*, 39 (8): 877–900.
Radstone, S. (1995), 'Cinema/Memory/History', *Screen*, 36 (1): 34–47.
Radstone, S. (2010), 'Cinema and Memory', in S. Radstone and B. Schwarz (eds), *Memory: Histories, Theories, Debates*, 325–42, New York: Fordham University Press.
Redi, R., and F. Rinaudo (1954), 'Piacciono in periferia', *Cinema*, no. 133, 15 May: 259–62.
Reich, J. (1995), 'Reading, Writing, and Rebellion: Collectivity, Specularity, and Sexuality in the Italian Schoolgirl Comedy, 1934–43', in R. Pickering-Iazzi (ed.), *Mothers of Invention: Women, Italian Fascism, and Culture*, 220–52, Minneapolis: University of Minnesota Press.

Renzi, R. (1956), 'Il tabù del pubblico', *Cinema Nuovo*, no. 87, 25 July: 33–4.

Rigney, A. (2005), 'Plenitude, Scarcity and the Circulation of Cultural Memory', *Journal of European Studies*, 35 (1): 11–28.

Rigney, A. (2016), 'Cultural Memory Studies: Mediation, Narrative, and the Aesthetic', in A. L. Tota and T. Hagen (eds), *Routledge International Handbook of Memory Studies*, 65–76, New York: Routledge.

Rosenwein, B. H. (2006), *Emotional Communities in the Early Middle Ages*, Ithaca, NY: Cornell University Press.

Rossetti, E. (1957), 'È cominciata per il cinema una lenta morte?', *Cinema Nuovo*, no. 110, 1 July: 6.

Ruffilli, W. (1950), 'Il cimitero delle Illusioni perdute', *Cinespettacolo*, Year V, March: 3–6.

Russell, N. (2006), 'Collective Memory before and after Halbwachs', *French Review*, 79 (4): 792–804.

S. (1956), 'Fuoriquadro', *Bollettino dello Spettacolo*, no. 310, 10 November: 1.

Scaglione, E. (1917), 'Il cinematografo in provincia', *L'Arte muta* (Napoli), no. 6–7, 15 December 1916–15 January 1917: 14–16.

Scarpellini, E. (2018), 'I consumi culturali in Italia nel lungo XX secolo', *Cinema e storia*, 7 (1) (Special issue on 'Storia e storie delle audiences in era globale', eds M. Fanchi and D. Garofalo): 21–9.

Schatz, T. (1981), *Hollywood Genres: Formulas, Filmmaking, and the Studio System*, New York: Random House.

Schatz, T. (1996), *The Genius of the System: Hollywood Filmmaking in the Studio Era*, New York: Holt.

Schoonover, K. (2012), *Brutal Vision: The Neorealist Body in Postwar Italian Cinema*, Minneapolis: University of Minnesota Press.

Scruton, R. (2011), *Beauty: A Very Short Introduction*, Oxford: Oxford University Press.

Sedgwick, J., P. Miskell and M. Nicoli (2019), 'The Market for Films in Postwar Italy: Evidence for Both National and Regional Patterns of Taste', *Enterprise and Society*, 20 (1): 199–228.

Seigworth, G. J., and M. Gregg (2010), 'An Inventory of Shimmers', in G. J. Seigworth and M. Gregg (eds), *The Affect Theory Reader*, 1–25, Durham, NC: Duke University Press.

Sellier, G. (2008), *Masculine Singular: French New Wave Cinema*, trans. K. Ross, Durham, NC: Duke University Press.

Shingler, M. (2012), *Star Studies: A Critical Guide*, London: BFI.

Shouse, E. (2005), 'Feeling, Emotion, Affect', *M/C Journal*, 8 (6). Available online: http://journal.media-culture.org.au/0512/03-shouse.php (accessed 24 April 2019).

SIAE (1957), *Cinema Italia*, private database, no place of publication or publisher (accessed 24 May 2014).

SIAE (1960), *Statistica Documentazione Annuario dello Spettacolo*.

Sobchack, V. (2004), *Carnal Thoughts*, Berkeley: University of California Press.

Spinazzola, V. (1957), 'Il termometro degli incassi', *Cinema Nuovo*, no. 106, 1 May: 284–5.

Spinazzola, V. (1975), *Cinema e pubblico: Lo spettacolo filmico in Italia 1945–1965*, Rome: Bulzoni.

Sprio, M. (2013), *Migrant Memories: Cultural History, Cinema and the Italian Post-War Diaspora in Britain*, Bern: Peter Lang.

Srinivas, L. (2016), *House Full: Indian Cinema and the Active Audience*, Chicago: University of Chicago Press.

Stacey, J. (1987), 'Desperately Seeking Difference', *Screen*, 28 (1): 48–61.

Stacey, J. (1994), *Star Gazing: Hollywood Cinema and Female Spectatorship*, London: Routledge.

Steedman, C. (1986), *Landscape for a Good Woman: A Story of Two Lives*, London: Virago.

Street, S. (2001), *Costume and Cinema: Dress Codes in Popular Film*, London: Wallflower.

Summerfield, P. (2004), 'Culture and Composure: Creating Narratives of the Gendered Self in Oral History Interviews', *Cultural and Social History*, 1 (1): 65–93.

Szczepaniak-Gillece, J. (2016), 'Revisiting the Apparatus: The Theatre Chair and Cinematic Spectatorship', *Screen*, 57 (3): 253–76.

Tosi, V. (1999), *Quando il cinema era un circolo. La stagione d'oro dei cineclub (1945–1956)*, Rome: Fondazione Scuola Nazionale del Cinema.

Treveri Gennari, D. (2009a), *Post-War Italian Cinema: American Intervention, Vatican Interests*, New York: Routledge.

Treveri Gennari, D. (2009b), 'A Regional Charm: Italian Comedy versus Hollywood', *October*, 128: 51–68.

Treveri Gennari, D. (2015), '"If You Have Seen It, You Cannot Forget!": Film Consumption and Memories of Cinema-Going in 1950s Rome', *Historical Journal of Film, Radio and Television*, 35 (1): 53–74.

Treveri Gennari, D. (2018), 'Understanding the Cinemagoing Experience in Cultural Life: The Role of Oral History and the Formation of "Memories of Pleasure"', *Tijdschrift voor Mediageschiedenis*, 21 (1): 39–53.

Treveri Gennari, D., C. O'Rawe and D. Hipkins (2011), 'In Search of Italian Cinema Audiences in the 1940s and 1950s: Gender, Genre and National Identity', *Participations: Journal of Audience & Reception Studies*, 8 (2): 539–53.

Treveri Gennari, D., and J. Sedgwick (2015), 'Memories in Context: The Social and Economic Function of Cinema in 1950s Rome', *Film History: An International Journal*, 27 (2): 76–104.

Treveri Gennari, D., and S. Culhane (2019), 'Crowdsourcing Memories and Artefacts to Reconstruct Italian Cinema history: Micro-Histories of Small-Town Exhibition in the 1950s', *Participations: Journal of Audience & Reception Studies*, 16 (1): 796–823.

Treveri Gennari, D., and S. Dibeltulo (2017), '"It Existed Indeed … It Was All Over the Papers": Memories of Film Censorship in 1950s Italy', *Participations: Journal of Audience & Reception Studies*, 14 (1): 235–48.

Treveri Gennari, D., S. Dibeltulo, D. Hipkins and C. O'Rawe (2019), 'Analysing Memories through Video-Interviews: A Case Study of Post-War Italian Cinema-Going', in D. Biltereyst, R. Maltby and P. Meers (eds), *The Routledge Companion to New Cinema History*, 344–54, London: Routledge.

Tribe, J. (2015), *The Economics of Recreation, Leisure and Tourism*, London: Routledge.

Tudor, A. (2013), *Image and Influence: Studies in the Sociology of Film*, London: Routledge.

Turroni, G. (1954), 'Alla scoperta del pubblico', *Rassegna del film*, Year III, no. 15, January–May to Year III, no. 24, October.

van Nes, A., and T. My Nguyen (2009), 'Gender Difference in the Urban Environment: The Flâneur and Flâneuse of the 21st Century', in D. Koch, L. Marcus and J. Steen (eds), *Proceedings of the 7th International Space Syntax Symposium Ref. 122*, 1–7, Stockholm: KTH, SSS7 Organising Committee.

Vasudevan, R. (2003), *Cinema in Urban Space*. Available online: https://www.india-seminar.com/2003/525/525%20ravi%20vasudevan.htm (accessed 24 April 2019).

Vélez-Serna, M. A., and J. Caughie (2015), 'Remote Locations: Early Scottish Scenic Films and Geo-Databases', *International Journal of Humanities and Arts Computing*, 9 (2): 164–79.

Viazzi, G. (1949), 'Il museo degli orrori', *Cinema*, no. 11, 31 March: 325.

Villa, F. (2002), 'Consumo cinematografico e identità italiana', in M. Fanchi and E. Mosconi (eds), *Spettatori: forme di consumo e pubblici del cinema in Italia, 1930–1960*, 189–203, Venice: Marsilio.

Vitella, F. (2015), 'Il diario intimo come fonte per la storia del fandom. Ritratto di una Bobby- soxer di provincia', *Bianco e Nero*, no. 582–3: 153–60.

Williams, B. R. (2012), 'Doing Video Oral History', in D. Ritchie (ed.), *The Oxford Handbook of Oral History*, 267–76, Oxford: Oxford University Press.

Williams, L. (1998), 'Melodrama Revised', in N. Browne (ed.), *Refiguring American Film Genres: History and Theory*, 42–88, Berkeley: University of California Press.

Willson, P. (2010), *Women in Twentieth-Century Italy*, Basingstoke: Palgrave Macmillan.

Wolf, N. (1998), *Promiscuities: A Secret History of Female Desire*, London: Vintage.

Wolff, J. (1985), 'The Invisible Flâneuse. Women and the Literature of Modernity', *Theory, Culture & Society*, 2 (3): 37–46.

Wood, D., J. Fels and J. Krygier (2010), *Rethinking the Power of Maps*, New York: Guilford Press.

Wood, M. (2006), 'From Bust to Boom: Women and Representations of Prosperity in Italian Cinema of the Late 1940s and 1950s', in P. Morris (ed.), *Women in Italy, 1945–1960: An Interdisciplinary Study*, 51–64, New York: Palgrave Macmillan.

Woolf, V. (1930), *Street Haunting: A London Adventure*, San Francisco, CA: Westgate Press. Available online: https://ebooks.adelaide.edu.au/w/woolf/virginia/w91d/chapter5.html (accessed 1 October 2019).

Zilioli, M. (2019), 'I lettori ci scrivono di cinema. La corrispondenza sui periodici comunisti *Vie Nuove*, *Il Calendario del Popolo* e *Rinascita* tra il 1945 e il 1960', *Cinergie*, no. 15. Available online: https://cinergie.unibo.it/article/view/9019/9438 (accessed 30 September 2019).

# Index

*20.000 Leagues under the Sea* (Richard Fleischer, 1954) 82

Abrams, Lynn 10, 13, 117, 137
ACEC xv, 17, 32
Acland, Charles R. 39, 68
affective narrative space 48
AGIS xv, 12, 17, 29, 78
*Alice in Wonderland* (Clyde Geronimi, Wilfred Jackson and Hamilton Luske, United States, 1951) 123
Allen, Robert C. xv, 27, 51, 175, 178
Altman, Rick 71, 76, 83
*An American Girl in Italy* (Ruth Orkin, 1951) 45
Anderson, Kay 43
Andreotti, Giulio 106–7
ANEC 17, 29
Antonioni, Michelangelo 31
Aprà, Adriano 8
*April in Paris* (David Butler, 1952) 78
archive xi, 17–18, 48–9, 178–81
*Archivio Centrale dello Stato* 15, 180
Aristarco, Guido 164
Aroldi, Piermarco 116 n.3, 162
Arrowsmith, Colin 43
*A Streetcar Named Desire* (Elia Kazan, 1951) 158
*At Sword's Point* (Lewis Allen, 1952) 82
audience research x, 17, 72, 72 n.1, 89
Ayers, Edward. L. 28

Bagshaw, Mel 101 n.8
Bailey, J. and I. Biggs 49
Baldelli, Pio 6
*Bambi* (James Algar, Samuel Armstrong, 1942) 57, 123
Bari 12, 16, 33–40, 53–7, 65–7, 86–7, 98–105, 118, 122 n.12, 128–32, 143–5, 151, 152 n.8, 163–9
Barker, Jennifer 55
Barker, Martin x–xv, 9, 16 n.22, 17, 72, 81
Barthes, Roland 2

*Bathing Beauty* (George Sidney, 1944) 122, 122 n.12, 123 n.13, 131, 168
Bayman, Louis 93–6, 105, 110
*Ben Hur* (William Wyler, 1959) 22, 77, 79, 81
Benjamin, Walter 53
Bennet, Jill 99
Benni, Stefano 170 n.23
Bergman, Ingrid 154 n.9
Biasin, Enrico 166 n.20
Biltereyst, Daniel 9, 17, 71–2, 75 n.3, 89, 176–7
Blair, Janet 148
BluMedia xiv, 12, 12 n.14
*Body Heat* (Lawrence Kasdan, 1981) 169
Boero, Davide 118 n.9
Bogart, Humphrey 161
Bolin, Göran 114–16
*Bollettino dello Spettacolo* 17, 17 n.24, 29, 32–4, 37, 79, 81–2
Bornat, Joanna 155
Bowles, Kate 27, 43
Boyd, Douglas A. 180
Brando, Marlon 156–9, 158 nn.3–4, 159 n.9, 162–3
Breakwell, Ian 182
Breslauer, Marianne 45
Brunetta, Gian Piero 2, 97, 171, 180
Buckley, Réka 58, 114, 149
*Buio in sala* (Dino Risi, 1948) 171, 175
*Burda* 151, 151 n.7
Butsch, Richard 51, 53, 62

Cagliari xv, 12, 30–9, 46, 53, 58–62, 78, 86, 97, 100 n.7, 105, 118–20, 122 n.12, 123–4, 128–30, 137, 140–4, 149, 167–8
Capussotti, Enrica 113–14, 121, 122 n.10, 148, 151, 157–9, 157 n.2
Caquard, Sebastien, xv, 48

Carabba, Claudio 8
cartographic dimension 9, 48, 49
Cartwright, William 48
Casetti, Francesco 4–6, 6 n.7, 55, 60, 158 n.4, 166 n.16, 170
Cassamagnaghi, Silvia 113
*Catene* (Raffaello Matarazzo, 1949) 1, 98
Caughie, John 27
CCINTB 10 n.11
Chapman, James 82 n.12
*Charade* (Stanley Donen, 1963) 141
Charisse, Cyd 122
*Chi è senza peccato* (Raffaello Matarazzo, 1952) 79
*Cinderella* (Geronimi, Clyde, Wilfred Jackson and Hamilton Luske, 1950) 66, 145
cinema as *aspiration* 122, 131, 139, 140–1, 144, 153, 161
    education and culture 13, 13 n.9, 88, 93, 105–6, 162–3, 164 n.12
    reflection of contemporary reality 92–3, 95, 98, 102–5
    reward 54
    sharing emotions 53, 56, 59, 63, 67, 86, 102, 107, 115–19, 118 n.8, 155, 162, 171
cinema exhibition processes 9, 16–17, 16 n.23, 19, 22, 27–42, 48–9, 180–1
*Cinema Nuovo* 8, 163–5, 164 n.12-13
cinema runs 3, 6. 16–17, 29–31, 37–40, 55
*CineRicordi* ix, 18, 48–9, 180–1
*Cinespettacolo* 76, 79, 81
Cohan, Steve, 159 n.9
Colby, Anita 147–8
collective experience 11, 47–53, 168, 175–8
Colombo, Fausto 11, 114–18, 116 n.3, 120, 124 n.15, 127, 132, 162
Comand, Mariapia 7 n.10
Comencini, Luigi 4, 103
*Comizi d'amore* (Pier Paolo Pasolini, 1964) 172
composure 155, 161–2, 172
Cooper, Gary 155, 168
Cosulich, Calisto 8
Crawford, Joan 151
Culhane, Sarah 65, 91 n.1
*Curly Top* (Irving Cummings, 1935) 124

Dawson, Graham 155–6, 162, 168
Dean, James 156, 159–60
De Beauvoir, Simone 113
DeCuir-Gunby, Jessica T. 15
De Laurentiis, Federico 142 n.4
Del Casino, Vincent J. 48
Deleuze, Gilles 96
De Rita, Lidia 166 n.18
De Sica, Vittorio 72, 105–6
Diamond, Hanna 155
Dibeltulo, Silvia ix, 61, 129 n.13, 181
Di Chiara, Francesco 30, 72
Dhoest, Alexander 156 n.1
Dodge, Martin 48
Dotti, Andrea 150
Douglas, Kirk 4
Driscoll, Catherine 113
*Duel in the Sun* (King Vidor, 1946) 82
Dyer, Richard 51, 52, 54, 65, 153, 156
Dyhouse, Carlo 23, 113

*East of Eden* (Elia Kazan, 1955) 159–60
Elkin, Lauren 45
Elsaesser, Thomas 53
Ercole, Pierluigi xv, 9, 42, 117 n.5
escapism xiii, 51, 54, 118, 143 175
Eugeni, Ruggero 57, 67
exhibitors 17, 22, 27, 30–3, 37, 40–2
experience of the venue 13, 32–3, 37, 57–8, 88, 155, 168–70, 175–7

Fabrizi, Aldo 101
Fain, Sammy 145
Fanchi, Mariagrazia xiv, 4–9, 6 n.7, 18–19, 29–30, 39–40, 46, 57, 67, 72 n.1, 88, 93, 114, 118–19, 118 n.8, 158 n.4, 164, n.12, 166, 166 n.16, n.19, 175
fantasy and dreaming 102–3, 105, 120, 125, 131, 143–5, 156, 162
Fascism xiii, 93, 105, 123–5, 175
Fellini, Federico 8, 72, 163
female attendance 5, 12, 18, 40–7, 65, 118
    restrictions 46, 55, 58, 90, 166
femininity 87–8, 107, 113, 118 n.8, 120, 149, 162, 168, 177
Ferraù, Alessandro 79, 81–2
Field, Virginia 148
*flâneuse/flaneur* 45–6

Fleming, Rhonda 169, 169 n.22
Florence 12, 33, 37, 55–8, 67, 100, 104–9, 122–4, 142–5, 162, 166 n.18, 167–8
Focardi, Filippo 94
Forgacs, David 94, 100, 104 n.11, 108, 114, 123, 128–9, 143, 146
*For Whom the Bell Tolls* (Sam Wood, 1943) 154 n.9
Fragola, Augusto 33
French realism 93
Freidberg, Anne 144
Friedman, Jeff 16, 152, 159
Frisch, Michael 158
Fuller-Seeley, Kathryn 124 n.14

Gaines, Jane 153
Gauntlett, David 81
gender xiii, 8, 11, 13, 19, 23–4, 43, 58, 99, 104, 125, 170
  gendered perspective 5, 12, 46–7, 85–8, 147, 152, 154–6, 163–6, 172–7
  girlhood/noi ragazze xiii, 113–20, 122–5, 130–3, 150
  tomboyism 87, 125, 132
generational identity 5, 11, 97, 114–16, 162
genre xi–xii, 4, 30, 71–9, 94–5, 115;
  genre and identification 85–90
  preferences 11, 21–3, 80–5, 121, 124, 175–6
*Gilda* (Charles Vidor, 1946) 168–9
Giori, Mauro 171
*Gli italiani si voltano* (Mario De Biasi, 1954) 45
*Gone with the Wind* (Victor Fleming, 1939) 67, 77–9, 82, 89, 92, 98
Grable, Betty 122
Grant, Berry Keith 71
Gremigni, Elena 3, 164 n.13, 166 n.16, n.19
Grignaffini, Giovanna 114, 117
Guidacci, Margherita 6
Gundle, Stephen 7, 29 n.1, 63 n.4, 84, 94, 105, 110, 114, 123, 128–9, 136, 140–1, 146

Halberstam, Jack 87, 125
Halbwachs, Maurice 54, 73
Hallam, Julia 28
Hains, Rebecca 113

Hammond, Paul 182
Hanich, Julian 53, 56, 59–60, 67, 170
Hanna, Stephen 48
Harper, Sue 86 n.14, 176–9
Harry, Beth 15
Hart, Roger 43, 47, 95
Hatch, Kristen 124 n.14
Hayworth, Rita 148, 168
Hepburn, Audrey 136, 146, 149–50, 153, 154 n.9
Hepburn, Katharine 121
*High Noon* (Fred Zinneman, 1952) 168
Hill, Jeffrey 53
Hipkins, Danielle ix, 9, 19, 19 n.28, 85, 123
Hirsch, Marianne 97
Hoffman, Eva 91, 98, 100
Holden, William 146
Holohan, Conn 42
'home based recreation' and 'away from home' 52, 66–8
Hubbard, Phil 54

idiosyncratic film history 91–2
*Il birichino di papà* (Raffaello Matarazzo, 1942) 125
*Il cielo sulla palude* (Augusto Genina, 1949) 127
*I pompieri di Viggiù* (Mario Mattoli, 1949) 1
Italian Cinema Audiences, ICA 1, 8, 12, 16–17, 27–8, 34, 42, 48, 52–67, 72–4, 82 n.11, 89 n.16, 91 n.2, 135–6, 144, 152, 155, 157, 175–81
*Italiani brava gente* (Giuseppe De Santis, 1964) 98 n.6
*Ivanhoe* (Richard Thorpe, 1952) 78

Jackson, Peter xiii
James, William 99
Järviluoma, Helmi 56
*Je suis un sentimental* (John Berry, 1955) 78
Jones, Jennifer 146, 153

*Kapò* (Gillo Pontecorvo, 1960) 98 n.6
Kearney, Mary Celeste 113–14
*King Kong* (Merian C. Cooper and Ernest B. Schoedsack, 1933) 108
Kitchin, Rob 48

Klenotic, Jeffrey xv, 43
Klinger, Barbara 51, 77, 89
Kuhn, Annette xiv, 10–11, 42, 57, 62, 67, 73, 75 n.3, 88, 102, 108–9, 113, 128, 135, 138, 145, 155, 158 n.5, 159 n.6, 176–80

*La ciociara* (Vittorio De Sica, 1960) 104–5, 107
*La cortigiana di Babilonia* (Carlo Ludovico Bragaglia, 1954) 169 n.22
*La dolce vita* (Federico Fellini, 1960) 122
*Ladri di Biciclette* (Vittorio De Sica, 1948) 80 n.8, 89, 92, 102, 106, 109, 126, 130
Lancia, Enrico 136
Landsberg, Alison 101
Landy, Marcia 94
Lang, Fritz 42
Langford, Barry 71
Larkin, Brian 56
Larson, Mary 180
*Lascia o raddoppia?* 3
*Lassie Come Home* (Fred M. Wilcox, 1943) 124
*La Storia siamo noi* (Rai Educational, 2009) 142 n.4
*La Terra Trema* (Luchino Visconti, 1948) 1
Leavitt, Charles 105–6
Leigh, Vivien 159
*Le quattro giornate di Napoli* (Nanni Loy, 1962) 103 n.10
*Les 400 coups* (Francois Truffaut, 1963) 126
*Little Women* (George Cukor, 1933) 121
Lollobrigida, Gina 136, 137, 149
Loren, Sophia 8, 136, 137, 141, 149
Lotze, Kathleen 17, 72, 177
*Love Is a Many-Splendored Thing* (Henry King and Otto Lang, 1955) 145, 153
Luzzatto Fegiz, Paolo 4–5, 166 n.17

McKinnon, Scott 159 n.9, 172
MacLean, Malcolm 6, 166 n.18
Madgin, Rebecca 27
Magnani, Anna 93, 95, 98, 99, 100 n.7, 101, 109, 142–3
Maltby, Richard 7, 8, 52, 71, 177–8
Mandelli, Elisa 164

Mangano, Silvana 4, 142, 142 nn.3–4
Manning, Sam 44
maps and mapping xv, 9, 27, 42, 43–4, 48
deep-mapping 49
*Marcelino, pan y vino* (Ladislao Vajda, 1955) 127
Mariani, Andrea 7 n.10
Marks, Laura U. 55
masculinity, imaginings of 87–8, 125, 155–63, 159 n.6, n.9, 165, 172–3
Masina, Giulietta 142
Masi, Stefano 136
Mastroianni, Marcello 157
Matarazzo, Raffaello 5, 8, 76, 79, 81, 88, 161
Mathijs, Ernest 9, 17, 72
Mattoli, Mario 1, 77 n.5
Mayne, Judith 135
'Media and Generations in Italian Society' project 11, 116
Meers, Philippe 9, 17, 71–2 177
melodrama, tearjerker, *film passionali* 1, 4, 30, 74–7, 77 n.5, 79–80, 79 n.7, 85–8, 93–5
Memoro xi, xiv, 13, 13 n.18, 179
memory 1–12, 44, 56–7, 108, 117, 119, 124–7, 165
children memory 5–6, 11, 43, 57, 62–3 96–8, 123, 126
cinema memory as cultural memory 73
faulty memory 105, 151, 154
of genre 75, 86–90
memory as performance 10, 55–68, 85, 138
memory of directors 31, 40
official memory 19, 78, 82, 93–4, 105, 115, 127 n.7, 136, 172, 177
postmemory 96–7, 105, 109
of scenes 96, 101–2, 108
memory studies x, xiv, 28
Metz, Christian 101
Milan 8, 12, 30–42, 54–63, 106, 161–70, 175
Millicent, Marcus 94
Miskell, Peter 8
Mitchell, Claudia 116 n.2
Modugno, Ludovica 127
Morandini, Morando 76
Morante, Elsa 96

Morin, Edgar 53, 141–2
Morreale, Emiliano 6, 76 n.4
*Morte a Venezia* (Luchino Visconti, 1971) 142 n.3
Mosconi, Elena 3, 32 n.5, 77 n.5
Moseley, Rachel 149
Mulvey, Laura 144
My Nguyen, Tra 46

Naples 8–9, 34–42, 53–66, 103–4, 147, 171, 181
national identity and memory xiii, 7, 74, 90, 91–2, 100–2, 104 n.11, 109–10, 141, 178, 181
*National Velvet* (Clarence Brown, 1944) 124
Nazzari, Amedeo 76, 79, 81, 127, 157, 161–2, 168–9, 172
Neale, Steve 71, 74–5
neorealism 4, 80, 91–109
*Neorealismo rosa* 4
New Cinema History, NCH 11, 6, 52, 71, 144
Newman, Paul 159
Nicoli, Marina 8, 28–30
Nichols, Elizabeth N. 67, 144
Noto, Paolo 5, 76, 163, 171 n.23
*Nuovo Cinema Paradiso* (Giuseppe Tornatore, 1988) 1, 115, 165, 172

*Oci ciornie* (Nikita Michalkov, 1987) 142 n.3
O'Hara, Maureen 145, 148
O'Leary, Alan 72
*On the Waterfront* (Elia Kazan, 1954) 118
open-air venues 27, 29, 32–3, 32 n.5, 56
oral history 9–11, 12, 18–19, 23–4, 27–8, 48–9, 72, 75–7, 82–3, 90, 114, 136–9, 155–8, 178–9
O'Rawe, Catherine 5, 72, 80
Orkin, Ruth 45

*Paisà* (Roberto Rossellini, 1946) 80 n.8, 97, 103
Palermo 12, 30–9, 62, 91, 104, 108–10, 165–71
Pampanini, Silvana 139–40, 147
*Pane, amore e fantasia* (Luigi Comencini, 1953) 39

*Pane, amore e gelosia* (Luigi Comencini, 1954) 4
Parca, Gabriella 167 n.21, 171 n.24
Pasolini, Pier Paolo 142 n.3, 172
Passerini, Luisa 155
past/present 169
Paulicelli, Eugenia 58, 151
Peck, Gregory 157
personal affect/narrative 94, 97, 102–3, 105–7, 115, 138, 145, 172, 175–80
Piccone Stella, Simonetta 113–14, 158 n.3
Pini, Andrea 171
Pink, Sarah 16
Pinna, Luca 6, 166 n.18
Piredda, Maria F. 32 n.5
Pitassio, Francesco 98, 100
Pitturro, Vincent 92
places and circumstances of watching xi, 42, 55, 122 n.10
place of memory 24
Ponte, Cristina 116 n.3
Portelli, Alessandro 10, 100 n.7, 136, 179
Porter, Vincent 86 n.14
*Portoghesismo* 32, 32 n.4
programming choices 8, 16–17, 22–3, 27, 29–31, 33–4, 37, 40, 48–9, 178
*Proibito rubare* (Luigi Comencini, 1948) 103
Pullen, Kirsten 122–3

questionnaires 9, 12–13, 15, 19, 52, 73–86, 92–3, 104, 122, 129, 136, 153, 183
qualitative 2, 9, 12, 15–16, 72, 83, 85, 90
quantitative 9, 12, 17–18, 78, 85
*Quo Vadis?* (Mervyn LeRoy, 1951) 78, 81

Radstone, Susannah 92, 95, 102–3, 115 n.2
*Rassegna del Film* 6, 30, 42 n.9, 67 n.8
Re, Valentina 164
Redi, Riccardo 6
Reich, Jacqueline 125, 125 n.16
Reid-Walsh, Jacqueline 116 n.2
Rigney, Ann 82, 87
Rinaudo, Fabio 6
*Riso Amaro* (Giuseppe De Santis, 1948) 104
rituals of cinema 13, 51, 54–5, 58, 66, 167–8, 170, 175
Roberts, Les 28

Rogers, Ginger 122
*Roma città aperta* (Roberto Rossellini, 1943) 23, 80 n.8, 89, 91–4, 96–110, 176
*Roman Holiday* (William Wyler, 1953) 149–50
*Romarcord* project 91 n.2, 96, 104
Rome 1, 4, 12, 30–46, 52–66, 94–110, 121–2, 129, 139–46, 163, 166–8
Rose, Jacqueline 144
Rosenwein, Barbara A. 55
Rossellini, Roberto 72, 100, 105–6
Rossetti, Enrico 8
Ruffilli, Weiss 76, 79–80
Russell, Gail 54, 148

*Salvatore Giuliano* (Fracesco Rosi, 1962) 104
Sanson, Yvonne 76. 79, 81, 127, 169
Scarpellini, Emanuela 52
Schatz, Thomas 74, 76
Schneider, Romy 125
Schoonover, Karl 94, 97, 105, 110
*Sciuscià* (Vittorio De Sica, 1946) 103
Sedgwick, John, xiv, 8, 17, 34, 34 n.7, 37–8, 40
*Sedotta e abbandonata* (Pietro Germi, 1965) 129
Sellier, Geneviève 164
Selznick, David O. 147
*Seven Brides for Seven Brothers* (Stanley Donen, 1954) 131
sharing memories 12 n.15, 13, 24, 40, 53, 56, 63, 105, 107, 115, 117–19, 118, n.8, 153–5, 162, 171, 177, 179–80
Shingler, Martin 156, 172
Shouse, Eric 54
SIAE 14, 2, 17, 19, 28, 29, 31, 31 n.3, 32, 34
*Sissi* 124–6, 124 n.15, 129, 132
*Sissi* (Ernst Marischka, 1955) 124, 126
*Sissi: Die junge Kaiserin* (Ernst Marischka, 1956) 124
*Sissi: Schicksalsjahre einer Kaiserin* (Ernst Marischka, 1957) 124
Smith, Susan J. 43
Sobchack, Vivian 55, 56
Spaak, Catherine 146

Sprio, Margherita 7 n.8
Spinazzola, Vittorio 8, 80 n.8, 88 n.15
Stacey, Jackie xiv, 11, 12, 88, 118, 118 n.8, 120, 122, 122 n.11, 124, 129, 132, 135, 138–9, 144, 146–7, 156, 159, 159 n.6, n.8, 173
*Stagecoach* (John Ford, 1939) 77
stardom 19, 23–4, 51, 76, 114, 116, 135–6, 140, 153, 155, 162
  female stars and beauty 122, 136–8, 140–2, 147–8, 153, 164
  stars' memories and identification 149–51, 153, 154, 159
Steedman, Carolyn 115
Street, Sarah 161 n.10
Summerfield, Penny 156, 172
Swanson, Gloria 151
Szczepaniak-Gillece, J. 57

Taylor, Elizabeth 124, 148
Taylor, D. R. Fraser 48
Temple, Shirley 124, 124 n.14
*Teorema* (Pier Paolo Pasolini, 1968) 142 n.3
*The Bitter Tea of General Yen* (Frank Capra, 1933) 77
*The Black Pirate* (Allen H. Miner, 1954) 77
*The Lord of the Rings* project xiii
*The Nun's Story* (Fred Zinneman, 1959) 150
*The Quiet Man* (John Ford, 1952) 67 n.8, 145
*The Red Shoes* (Michael Powell and Emeric Pressburger, 1948) 106
*The Robe* (Henry Koster, 1953) 81
*The Song of Bernadette* (Henry King, 1963) 127
*The Ten Commandments* (Cecil B. De Mille, 1956) 77–9, 81
*The Three Musketeers* (George Sidney, 1948) 77, 82
*The Wild One* (László Benedek, 1953) 157–8, 157 n.2
*The Wizard of Oz* (Victor Fleming and George Cukor, 1939) 123
*The Yearling* (Clarence Brown, 1946) 127
Titanus 30
topographical memory 27, 42–3
Tornatore, Giuseppe 1, 115, 165
Tosi, Virgilio 164 n.12

Totò, *Antonio De Curtis* 4, 8, 31, 75–6, 106, 115, 165
Treveri Gennari, Daniela 1, 8, 10, 13 n.17, 30, 37, 40, 54, 61, 65, 75, 82 n.11, 89 n.16, 91 n.2, 101, 129 n.19, 140, 159 n.7
triangulation xii, 9, 17, 23, 72, 77, 81–2, 89, 136
Tribe, John 52
Turin xv, 12, 34–42, 46, 63, 78, 104–5, 118–19, 121–9, 142, 149–50, 157–8, 179, 181

*Ulisse* (Mario Camerini, 1954) 4

Vajda, Ladislao 127
Van Nes, Akkelies 46
Vasudevan, Ravi 54
Vélez-Serna, Maria A. 27
Verhoeven, Deb 43
*Verismo* 93
Viazzi, Glauco 144

video interviews xvi, 2 n.2, 9–10, 12–13, 12 n.12, 13 n.17, 15–16, 19, 23–4, 43, 48, 63, 72, 83–6, 86 n.14, 92–3, 96, 107, 110, 117, 136–7, 153–5, 175–6, 178–80, 183, 189
Villa, Federica 3–4
Visconti, Luchino 163
Vitella, Federico 7 n.10, 114

*War and Peace* (King Vidor. 1956) 150
We Sense 118, 162
Williams, Brien R. 10
Williams, Esther 109, 122–3, 122 nn.11–12, 125, 132, 168
Willson, Perry 127 n.17
Wolff, Janet 46
Wolf, Naomi 128, 128 n.18
Wood, Denis et al. 48
Wood, Mary P. 107
Woolf, Virginia 45

Zilioli, Marco 7 n.10

CPSIA information can be obtained
at www.ICGtesting.com
Printed in the USA
LVHW051058301222
736212LV00009B/648